MW00334572

Archaeology as Political Action

CALIFORNIA SERIES IN PUBLIC ANTHROPOLOGY

Series Editor: Robert Borofsky (Hawaii Pacific University)

Contributing Editors: Philippe Bourgois (University of Pennsylvania), Paul Farmer (Partners in Health), Alex Hinton (Rutgers University), Carolyn Nordstrom (University of Notre Dame), and Nancy Scheper-Hughes (UC Berkeley)

University of California Press Editor: Naomi Schneider

Archaeology as Political Action

Randall H. McGuire

UNIVERSITY OF CALIFORNIA PRESS
Berkeley · *Los Angeles* · *London*

University of California Press, one of the most
distinguished university presses in the United States,
enriches lives around the world by advancing scholarship in the humanities, social sciences, and natural
sciences. Its activities are supported by the UC Press
Foundation and by philanthropic contributions from
individuals and institutions. For more information,
visit www.ucpress.edu.

Chapter 3 appeared in an earlier form as "Class
Confrontations in Archaeology," *Historical
Archaeology* 33, no. 1 (1999).

University of California Press
Berkeley and Los Angeles, California

University of California Press, Ltd.
London, England

© 2008 by The Regents of the University of California

Library of Congress Cataloging-in-Publication Data

McGuire, Randall H.
    Archaeology as political action / Randall H. McGuire.
        p.   cm. — (California series in public anthro-
pology ; 17)
    Includes bibliographical references and index.
    ISBN 978-0-520-25490-9 (cloth : alk. paper)
    ISBN 978-0-520-25491-6 (paper : alk. paper)
    1. Archaeology—Political aspects.   2. Archaeology—
Political aspects—Case studies.   3. Archaeologists—
Political activity.   4. Archaeology—Social aspects.
5. Archaeology—Philosophy.   6. Marxian archaeology
I. Title.

    CC175.M39   2008
    930.1—dc22   2007022786

Manufactured in the United States of America

17   16   15   14   13   12   11   10   09   08
10   9   8   7   6   5   4   3   2   1

This book is printed on New Leaf EcoBook 50, a 100%
recycled fiber of which 50% is de-inked post-consumer
waste, processed chlorine-free. EcoBook 50 is acid-free
and meets the minimum requirements of ANSI/ASTM
D5634-01 (*Permanence of Paper*).

For Ruth

Contents

Illustrations

Preface

Where does archaeology stand in relation to all this? Where
are its values? What is its purpose? In what direction should
the discipline develop? Is archaeology relevant or irrelevant to
the world? Is doing archaeology like playing the fiddle while
Rome burns? In short, why archaeology?

Christopher Tilley (1989)

Christopher Tilley (1989:105) challenged archaeologists to ask the question, Why archaeology? He answered it, saying that archaeology is a form of sociopolitical action in the present. Tilley accepted that archaeology cannot transform capitalism, or end war, or mitigate global inequality. He argued, however, that because archaeology is part of modern culture, changes in archaeology can filter through to affect various aspects of culture. Therefore, he contended that archaeology can be a source of, and a medium for, critiques of capitalist ideology. By the turn of the twenty-first century, many archaeologists had put down their fiddles and taken up Tilley's challenge to confront the sociopolitics of archaeology.

My reflections on these politics began with my book *A Marxist Archaeology* (McGuire 1992b, 2002b). In that work, I outlined an explicitly Marxist approach to archaeological praxis that sought to know the world, to critique the world, and to take action in the world. Since publishing that book I have worked to realize such praxis. *Archaeology as Political Action* offers a sustained discussion of my efforts to do so using three archaeological projects. First among these is an analysis of archaeology as a class-based endeavor that I undertook with Mark Walker. Second, is an exploration of the Trincheras Tradition Project in Sonora, México that evaluates the "double colonialism" that confronts U.S. archaeologists working on the international border. Finally, I synthesize the Colorado Coal Field War project with a focus on building a working class archaeology and community collaboration. The book discusses the dilemmas of praxis and critically appraises the outcomes of that praxis in each case.

In this work, I reflect upon how a theoretically informed and politically grounded archaeology might make a difference in peoples' lives and might contribute to a more humane world. The book begins with the premise that archaeology is always political. I argue that scholars should not try to deny this fact or obscure it behind a veil of false objectivity. Drawing on the history of archaeological theory and a Marxist dialectical theory I suggest that archaeologists may harness the sociopolitics of our discipline for emancipatory goals in the context of modern "fast capitalism."

The key to doing this lies in the craft of archaeology. Archaeologists can use their craft to evaluate interpretations of the real world, to construct meaningful histories for communities, to strive for real collaboration with communities and to challenge both the legacies of colonialism and the omnipresent class struggles of the modern world. Archaeologists can become more collaborative in their craft but this does not mean that we should give up our authority as good crafts persons. Speaking truth to power requires that we maintain the authority of our craft. For effective collaboration, however, we do need to enter into a dialogue with the communities that we work with and to surrender significant control over our research agenda.

When archaeologists put down their fiddles to engage the sociopolitics of our practice they enter into a dynamic, complex, and bewildering terrain. *Archaeology as Political Action* reflects my attempts to navigate this topography. My reflections do not result in a cookbook, or guidebook with step-by-step instructions on how to engage the sociopolitics of archaeology. Rather, I have written a journal of my travels that might aid others in their engagement. My journal confronts many core issues that face every archaeologist including the subjectivity/objectivity debate, heritage issues, working with communities, and the political, economic and cultural issues of the everyday practice of archaeology in the United States and abroad. I hope that my reflections will be of some use to all archaeologists but this book is primarily intended for those archaeologists who no longer wish to fiddle while fast capitalism burns.

The journey that brought me to *Archaeology as Political Action* took a decade and a half. I had many guides, *compañeros (-as)*, helpers, and mentors along the way. Some of these people assisted me in the formulation of my ideas and understandings. Others went beyond intellectual stimulation to actually aid me in the writing, revision, editing, and production of this book.

Binghamton University has provided a supportive and intellectual stimulating environment for my efforts. Interactions with all of my colleagues in anthropology have influenced my thinking, and my exchanges with Charles Cobb, Susan Pollock, Reinhard Bernbeck, Carmen Ferradis, Douglas Holmes, Dawnie Steadman, Deborah Elliston, and Thomas Wilson stand out. Very few of the Binghamton University faculty play the fiddle. I have benefited from discussions with scholars from many departments including Richard Lee, Immanuel Wallerstein, Kathryn Sklar, Thomas Dublin, Don Quataert, Jean Quataert, Herbert Bix, Dale Tomlich, and William Martin. My students at Binghamton University have been a constant source of inspiration and critique. I tried out most of my ideas and much of this text on them in the classroom, in the halls, and over beers. I would particularly like to thank Paul Reckner, Mark Walker, Michael Jacobson, Sarah Chicone, Felix Acuto, John McGregor, Amy Groleau, Robbie Mann, Genesis Snyder, Stacy Tchorzynski, Bridget Zavala, Rodrigo Navarrete, Claire Horn, Alex Button, Marie Hopwood and John Roby. One of the wonderful things about students is that the best ones never really leave you. Two of my first doctoral students, LouAnn Wurst and Maria O'Donovan, have become my colleagues and a constant source of support, critique, interaction, and insight. Thank you, LouAnn and Maria!

My interactions and collaborations with Spanish-speaking colleagues in Latin America and Spain have been critical and formative for my thought. I have twice taught at the Universitat Autònoma de Barcelona in Spain. I learned much from all of the faculty and students there but most especially Jordi Estévež, Assumpció Vila, Vicente Lull, María Encarna Sanahuja, Roberto Risch, Rafael Micó, Ermengol Gassiot, Beatriz Palomar, and Juan A. Barcelo. I have also benefited much from the counsel of the senior scholars of the Arqueología Social: Mario Sanjoa, Iraida Vargas-Arenas, Julio Montané, and Lucho Lumbreras. My own fieldwork in Sonora, México, has always been in collaboration with the Centro Sonora de INAH in Hermosillo and in cooperation with the Escuela Nacional de Antropología y Historia in México City. My thanks to Felipe Bate, Manuel Gándara, Ana María Alverez, Júpiter Martínez, Adrián López, and César Villalobos. In particular I must thank Elisa

Villalpando. We have worked together for twenty-five years, and she more than anyone has helped me see beyond my gringo blinders.

For the last decade, I have had the pleasure of being the part of the Ludlow Collective's archaeological study of the Colorado Coalfield War of 1913–1914. Dean Saitta, Phil Duke, and I began the project. The collective grew to include Mark Walker, Margaret Wood, Karin Larkin, Bonnie J. Clark, Amie Gray, Paul Reckner, Michael Jacobson, Sarah Chicone, Summer Moore, Clare Horn, Donna Bryant, and Jason Lapham. We did the project in collaboration with the United Mine Workers of America. I learned much from the working people of southern Colorado, especially from Michael and Yolando Romero and Carol Blatnick-Barros.

I have benefited greatly from my professional relationships and friendships among a group of archaeologists who collectively call themselves the "Closet Chickens." This group includes Native American and First Nations archaeologists and supporters. My thanks to Dorothy Lippert, Joe Watkins, Claire Smith, Sonya Atalay, George Nicolas, Julie Howell, Martin Wobst, Desiree Martinez, Deborah Nichols, T. J. Ferguson, and Larry Zimmerman.

Many of my colleagues gave me well-considered advice on earlier papers and chapters of this book. The list includes Mark Leone, Thomas Patterson, Julian Thomas, Adam Menzies, Ian Hodder, Becky Yamin, Theresa Kintz, Brian West, Steve Silliman, Margaret Conkey, Bruce Trigger, Robert Fitts, and Robert Paynter. In the end, I did not always take their advice, but the book is better for the comments that they gave me.

The birthing and production of a book requires much work and lots of help. Robin Barron and Heidi Kenyon of the Department of Anthropology at Binghamton University assisted me in too many ways to list. Ann Hull drafted the three maps included herein. I must also thank the Denver Public Library's photo department for permission to publish three of the figures in chapter 5.

It has been a pleasure to work with the University of California Press. My editor, Blake Edgar, held my hand and guided me through the process to make this a book. Robin Whitaker's copyediting helped me to improve my prose and the clarity of my arguments. I especially thank the University of California Press for respecting my wish that the production and manufacture of this book not be outsourced to India or Hong Kong. BookMatters of Berkeley, California, typeset the book, and the Maple-Vail Book Manufacturing Group of Binghamton, New York, printed and bound the book. Thank you to my union brothers and sisters of Graphics Communications International Union Local 898M of Binghamton, New York, for the craft that they put into manufacturing *Archaeology as Political Action*. Everyone involved in the writing, editing, and production of this book was paid a living wage, labored in a safe work place, worked reasonable hours, and is to be respected for their labor.

I wrote much of this book while a Research Associate at the Amerind Foundation in Dragoon, Arizona. John Ware has made the Amerind Foundation an intellectual oasis in the desert. I am never whole unless I am in the desert, and I have found the Amerind Foundation a haven where I can think, create, and thrive.

Most of all I must thank Ruth Van Dyke. Ruth has been with me every step of the way, from my first tentative pages through the trials of reviews to the final page proofs. She is my critic, my editor, and my colleague. My thought is clearer, my grammar better, my punctuation improved, my ideas sharper, my craft more masterful because of her.

Introduction

The philosophers have only interpreted the world differently;
the point is, to change it.

Karl Marx and Friedrich Engels (1947:199)

In July 1936, Fascist forces under the leadership of Francisco Franco swept through Spain to put down the legally elected government of the Second Republic. About half the country, including Andalusia, fell quickly to the rebels. Asturias and Vizcaya surrendered in October of the following year, while Madrid, Valencia, Murcia, and Catalunya continued the struggle until 1939. As the Fascists subjugated each area, they attempted to systematically wipe out Republican officials, intellectuals, officers, soldiers, and sympathizers. They also instituted a reign of terror, for example, executing 10 percent of the male population of Andalusia. What happened in the small Andalusian village of Santaella was typical. In 1936, Fascist troops, members of the Guardia Civil, and Falangist vigilantes entered the village on two occasions. Each time they rounded up town officials, schoolteachers, and others, twenty-two men in total, and took them on *paseitoes* (promenades) to the town cemetery, where they were shot to death. In haphazard acts of violence, Republican forces also executed civilians during the Civil War, but these atrocities did not match the systematic terror that the Fascists mobilized to pacify the areas they conquered.[1]

During Franco's forty-year reign, the dictatorship built monuments and put up markers to commemorate the victims of the Republic, but the graves of the victims of Fascism remained unmarked and obscured.[2] For almost thirty years after the fall of the dictatorship, these dead were officially forgotten. Today archaeologists are working to recover the memory of the victims of Spanish fascism. This is an overtly political act. Excavating mass graves uncovers the official amnesia about the Civil

War that the government used to establish the contemporary Spanish state following Franco's death in 1975 (Elkin 2006).

In June 2004, archaeologists, biological anthropologists, historians, and volunteers from the national organization Foro por la Recuperación de la Memoria Histórica (Forum for the Recuperation of Historic Memory) located and exhumed the mass grave of seventeen of the twenty-two individuals executed in Santaella. The excavations at Santaella revealed a macabre scene. The Fascists had laid the bodies across the width of a long trench. They made efficient use of the ditch, placing the bodies side by side, alternating head to foot to use the smallest amount of space possible. The skeletons bore the marks of the killings, including pelvises and vertebra shattered by bullets. Forensic analysis indicated that the victims had been placed standing against a wall, facing their assassins, and shot to death with submachine guns held at waist level. Uncovering the remains and identifying them will allow their descendants to claim and properly bury them. It also will recover the memory of Fascist atrocities and confront the fascism that remains in contemporary Spanish society and politics. In Spain, scholars have fashioned an emancipatory praxis of archaeology to confront fascism.

This is a book about the praxis of archaeology. It is my reflection on how to adapt the modern practice of archaeology to those who do archaeology, who want archaeology, and who are affected by archaeology. In *A Marxist Archaeology* (McGuire 1992b), I laid out a program for a humanistic, dialectical Marxism in this discipline. This book self-critically examines my attempts to make that program an archaeology of political action.

PRAXIS

My reflection begins with considerations of the broad theoretical, philosophical, and ethical issues that confront all modern Western archaeologists, including questions about social theory, the construction of archaeological knowledge, and the real-world consequences of our practice. These considerations continue a theoretical dialogue about archaeology that began in the mid-twentieth century (Trigger 2006). I enter this dialogue to elaborate a praxis that builds an archaeology of political action. At places like Santaella, Spain, some archaeologists have already begun such praxis.

Archaeologists have come to realize that people act as agents in social contexts only partly of their own making, in a dialectic between structure and agency (Silliman 2001:194). Agency becomes praxis only when people strive to alter that structure. Praxis refers to the distinctively human capacity to consciously and creatively construct and change both the world and ourselves. The minimal definition of praxis is "theoretically informed action." To engage in praxis, people must entertain concepts of possibility and change. Praxis becomes emancipatory when it advances the interests of the marginalized and the oppressed against the interests of the dominant. Praxis implies a process of gaining knowledge of the world, critiquing the world, and taking action to change the world. All archaeologists contribute to praxis, although only a minority of archaeologists ever complete the process and take action to change the world.

Virtually all archaeologists seek to gain knowledge of the world. We excavate sites, survey landscapes, count potsherds, reproduce lithic tools, sort modern trash, and do many other things to learn about the human condition. Within archaeology, scholars have extensively debated the best ways for us to gain knowledge of the world. These discussions have covered archaeological techniques, methods, and epistemologies (Johnson 1999; Gamble 2001; Wylie 2002; Trigger 2006). Since the 1980s, advocates of alternative archaeologies, including feminists, post-processualists, indigenous peoples, and Marxists, have engaged in critique, developing an extensive literature reflecting on archaeology and its place in the world (Johnson 1999; Watkins 2000; Gamble 2001; Thomas 2004; Conkey 2005a; Trigger 2006; Fernández 2006). Their critique has demonstrated that knowledge does not exist apart from its creation in a social context. It has led many archaeologists to realize that archaeology is a social and political practice and must be understood in those terms.

Most of the archaeologists who have criticized the discipline have done so with the goal of transforming archaeology. Focusing on the experience and practices of archaeology, they have sought to develop a self-critical archaeology (Shanks 1992), build self-reflexive methods (Hodder 1999), transform gender inequalities in the field and in our interpretations of the past (Gilchrist 1999), remake archaeological excavation (Lucas 2001), and rethink the language we use to do archaeology and interpret the past (Joyce 2002). Archaeologists have given far less attention to how our discipline has been and can be used as a means of political action to challenge society (Meskell and Pels 2005; Hamilakis and Duke 2007).

An emancipatory praxis is of no use to those archaeologists who wish to defend the status quo or to provide mythic charters for social groups. This is true whether that status quo is capitalist, communist, Hindu, fascist, or something else altogether. It is also of no use to those archaeologists who cannot see beyond their trench or their pile of potsherds. The theory that I present here is not a universal theory for archaeology or yet another theory to interpret the world differently. It is, rather, a theory for those archaeologists who want to engage in archaeology as political action.

A MORE HUMANE WORLD

Advocating an archaeology of political action raises the question, Action to what end? My answer to that question is, a more humane world in which there is less alienation and more emancipation. Alienation refers to the separation of aspects of the human condition that naturally belong together or to antagonism between aspects that are properly in harmony (Schmitt and Moody 1994; Schmitt 2002). For Marx (1959), capitalist workers who have to sell their labor power are alienated from both their labor and the products of their labor. They inevitably lose control of their lives by losing control over their work. Workers thus cease to be autonomous beings in any significant sense.

Marx dealt only with labor, but alienation may also spring from a wide range of social relations, including race, gender, sexuality, ethnicity, and religion (Schmitt and Moody 1994; Schmitt 2002). Alienated individuals may feel estranged from their milieu, other human beings, work, the products of work, sexuality, society, or self. Alienation may take on various aspects and dimensions, such as meaninglessness in the cultural dimension, powerlessness in the political dimension, and social exclusion in the social dimension. It is most often associated with minorities, women, the poor, the unemployed, gays, and other groups who have limited power to bring about changes in society. Alienation is usually understood as being incompatible with emancipation.

Emancipation frees people from alienation. Critical theories seek human emancipation by "liberating human beings from all circumstances that enslave them" (Horkheimer 1982:244). These theories aim to explain and transform *all* the circumstances that alienate human beings. Activists and scholars have developed critical theories that focus on each of these circumstances. The goal of transformation is a consensual form of social life in which each person can realize his or her full potential. Following Horkheimer, in such a society "all conditions of social life that are controllable by human beings depend on real consensus" (1982:249–250).

The Marxist perspective presented here is but one of several critical theories in archaeology; the others include feminism, post-processual archaeology, queer theory, and indigenous archaeology. Scholars can exploit the intersectionalities among these different approaches in pursuit of common goals and yet maintain their independence. Marxists confront class oppression. Feminists challenge gender oppression. Queer theorists contest the oppression of sexuality, and indigenous archaeology questions colonial and racial oppression. Each theory uses its object (class, gender, sexuality, race) as the starting point for the analysis of alienation and the struggle for emancipation. These different forms of oppression do not, however, exist independently of one another. They intersect in the lives of individuals. Thus, scholars should move beyond their own individual entry points to examine the intersectionalities of oppression (Hammond 1993; Conkey 2005b). My entry point is class, and the case studies in this book confront class and its intersectionalities with gender, race, and colonialism.

FAST CAPITALISM

Fast capitalism dominates the world that an emancipatory praxis of archaeology seeks to change (Agger 1989, 1997, 2004). We still live in a capitalist world where economic processes are based in the ownership of private property and wage labor. Modern capitalism, however, is an accelerated, hyped-up capitalism that holds a more profound sway over the peoples of the earth than it ever has before. The world is, in fact, more capitalist today than it was when Marx wrote in the middle of the nineteenth century. At that time, private property and wage labor dominated only in Europe. For most of its existence, capitalism has expanded by incorporating noncapitalist regions of the world. Today, virtually no corner of the world lies outside capitalism's control. Capitalism now expands by speeding up its processes and by penetrating all aspects of social life.

Many modern observers wish to believe that we live in a globalized, postcapitalist world. This is not the case. The globalization of the modern world is neither new nor unique. Private property and wage labor arose in early modern Europe as a result of a globalized economy (Wallerstein 2000; Lee, in press). English workers wove the cloth of Manchester from cotton grown in the southern United States and India. Capitalists sold the woven cloth in a global market. Tea from India sweetened with sugar raised by enslaved Africans in the Caribbean enabled the workers to stand at their looms longer (Mintz 1986).

We do not live in a postcapitalist world but rather in fast capitalism. The rapid expansion of information technologies (including computers, software, satellites, fiber optics, and the Internet) has transformed the global economic landscape (Foster et al. 2001), accelerating capitalism in terms of both its reach and its transactions. Advances in transportation, such as container ships, allow goods to be produced wherever wage rates are lowest in the world. The new information technologies allow technical, clerical, and even professional services also to seek the lowest wage. To make a profit, firms must cut wages and overhead. Workers who do not accept less lose their jobs when whole industries hop around the globe. The pressures to deliver all goods and services at the least possible cost create hypercompetitiveness. This process erodes workers' rights and benefits and proletarianizes professional occupations, including archaeology.

Fast capitalism expands by oozing into every nook and cranny of society to create new needs. Powerful capitalists in business, education, and government embrace hypercompetition to make market principles the dominant ethic for all social relations, evaluating all such relations in terms of costs and benefits and the bottom line. Their success corrodes socially derived moral frameworks and political programs (Holmes 2000). Fast capitalism attacks the values and social relations that have created and sustained archaeology. Hypercompetition leaves slight place for the life of the mind that does not produce profits (Siegel 2006). The camaraderie and shared purpose of fieldwork do not generate earnings. Fast capitalism undermines the relationships of apprenticeship and mastery and grinds down the community of scholars that have drawn most of us to the craft of archaeology. Capitalists' search for profit transforms archaeological knowledge and education into commodities to be produced at the lowest cost and to be sold in a competitive market (Tilley 1989:106–107). No wonder archaeologists feel confused and alienated.

BUILDING PRAXIS

In archaeology, processualists, post-processualists, classical Marxists, critical theorists, indigenous archaeologists, and feminists have sought to build a more humane world (Fernández 2006). Their critical theories provide a foundation and a dialogue that inform and enrich my efforts here. These efforts also point to the dangers of programs based in a categorical choice between objectivity and subjectivity. An emphasis on objectivity has too often led to a social engineering that assumes its designers can gain a true knowledge of the world that allows them to direct change. Subjectivity, on the other hand, can lead to a relativistic advocacy of multivocality that leaves scholars with no way to identify or reject those voices that are silly, delusional, or pernicious. The real question facing archaeological praxis is not whether archaeological knowledge should be objective or subjective but, rather, how scholars can connect the subjectivities of knowing and the realities of the world in our construction of archaeological knowledge.

A relational approach to the evaluation of knowledge involves a multifaceted dialectic between what I have termed the four Cs: coherence, correspondence, context, and consequences. *Coherence* refers to the logical and theoretical harmony of our interpretations. *Correspondence* considers how our interpretations fit the observations we can make of the world. *Context* reflects on the social, political, and cultural milieux of our interpretations. Finally, *consequences* involves a serious consideration of what interests our interpretations serve for the communities we work with. Thus, how we know the world is a complex mix of the world itself, the methods we use to study the world, and our social context as scholars in the world. Such complex knowledge provides a basis for making change in the world, which alters the world and necessitates new knowledge.

My theory of praxis begins with the idea of relational knowledge and draws on the intersectionalities among dialectical Marxist, feminist, and indigenous archaeologies (McGuire 1992b; Conkey 2005b; Lippert 2005). Feminism has been a significant source of praxis challenging the discipline of archaeology. Feminists confront and provide alternatives to the powerful andocentric bias in archaeology. The feminist idea of entry point (Wylie 1991) provides an effective method for considering race, ethnicity, gender, sexuality, and class in compatible analyses that do not reduce any of these phenomena to the other. Indigenous archaeologists have built a successful archaeological praxis to challenge the colonialism of archaeologies in which the descendants of the conquerors study the ancestors of conquered native peoples (Watkins 2000; Lippert 2005). Key to this success has been their collaboration with indigenous communities (Colwell-Chanthaphonh and Ferguson 2004, 2006; Smith and Wobst 2005; Zimmerman 2005). These efforts provide a model for building praxis with all communities.

Collaboration is key for praxis. Michael Shanks and I have argued that archaeology should be a craft that combats alienation by unifying hearts, hands, and minds (Shanks and McGuire 1996). As a craft, archaeology entails a practice that can be used to advance the interests of many communities through a range of endeavors from the technical to the interpretative, from the practical to the creative. Archaeologists have used four different, overlapping approaches to interact with communities: Opposition involves contesting and thwarting the interests of a community. Education entails imparting and acquiring knowledge while developing the powers of reasoning and acquiring self-awareness. Consultation is an instrumentalist process that involves a discussion between two or more parties to resolve a particular issue or question. Collaboration requires cooperating social groups to assimilate their goals, interests, and practices in a dialogue that advances the interests of all groups involved in the collaboration. Each of these approaches has a place in an emancipatory archaeology, but only collaboration will lead to praxis.

ENGAGING IN PRAXIS

Engaging in praxis is difficult. Social relations, political struggle, and ethics are never so clearly and distinctly defined in reality as they are in abstract discussions. They will always be complex, messy, ambiguous, and precarious. The four Cs provide a guide for action, but they do not resolve, remove, or reduce the intricacy and uncertainty of real life. Praxis has no relevance or meaning in the abstract. It is significant only in its application. The core of *Archaeology as Political Action* reflexively discusses three attempts at praxis in the real world.

Communities and their relationships result from historical processes of cooperation, struggle, and conflict. An emancipatory praxis serves the marginalized and challenges the dominant. The multifaceted and contradictory nature of social relations usually makes these two things hard to do. Rarely does a single, unequivocal "oppressor" clearly dominate other groups. When viewed from a universal perspective, power relations may seem clear, but when scholars focus on real communities embedded in larger sets of social relations, the seemingly straightforward relations of dominance frequently become perplexing and puzzling. Even subordinate groups may include oppressive internal relationships of power between genders and among age grades, ethnicities, or other factions or social parameters that subdivide them. An emancipatory scholarship cannot simply ignore such oppressive internal relationships in the struggle to advance the interests of the group in the larger society. Relations of power can also shift when groups that are subordinate in one context become dominant in a different context. Archaeologists enter communities as fully formed social beings with preestablished ethnic, racial, gender, sexual, and class identities. These identities usually have preexisting connotations to the communities that we work with, connotations that may be negative. Archaeologists can understand their relationship to the community only by knowing the histories that created the community as well as the community's present context.

The praxis of archaeology should first be self-critical and seek to transform social relationships within the discipline. Feminist scholars have extensively criticized patriarchy in both the ideologies of archaeology and the structure of our discipline. Indigenous archaeologists have criticized the colonialism inherent in archaeology in the Americas and other parts of the world, including Australia and New Zealand. In both cases, these scholars have offered alternatives to current practices and achieved some success in transforming the discipline, even though much remains to be done. Less attention, however, has been given to issues of class within archaeology.

Archaeology as a discipline serves class interests and, as a profession or occupation, has its own class structure. Archaeology has traditionally been a middle-class practice that has served middle-class needs. Reduced public funding for education and hypercompetition among contract firms undermines the craft of archaeology and replaces it with market principles of flexibility, competition, and profit. The corrosion of fast capitalism has reached into both the academy and cultural resource management. More and more, the discipline of archaeology depends on a proletariat of teaching assistants, adjuncts, and field technicians whom universities and contract firms increasingly exploit.

We practice archaeology in complex sociopolitical contexts. Elisa Villalpando and I created the Trincheras Tradition Project as a binational research effort on the international border between Arizona and Sonora, México. There we have threaded our way into the tangled skein of imperialism and colonialism. Our praxis attempts to confront and transform the relationships of imperialism and colonialism among four communities—U.S. archaeologists, Mexican archaeologists, Norteños, and the Tohono O'odham (the Papago). These communities have a long history of relations with one another. U.S. archaeologists have traditionally had an imperialistic relationship to both Mexican archaeology and the Norteños who live along the border. Mexican archaeologists engage in a nationalistic archaeology that, under fast capitalism, is being eroded by cultural tourism. The Tohono O'odham now primarily live in the

United States, but only because Mexican authorities drove most of those who lived south of the border north. Both México and the United States have subjugated and colonized the Tohono O'odham. Our praxis on the border is difficult, and we have met with failure as well as success in the pursuit of our goals.

In southern Colorado, the historical archaeology of the 1913–1914 Colorado Coalfield War offers a less complex stage for praxis, on which we study class warfare to participate in modern-day class struggle. In 1914, Colorado National Guard troops laid machine gun fire into a tent colony of striking coal miners at Ludlow, Colorado, killing twenty of the camp's inhabitants, including two women and twelve children. Enraged by these events, the strikers launched a ten-day class war, torching company towns, dynamiting mines, and killing National Guard troops and company men. On the basis of excavations at the site of the Ludlow Massacre and at the contemporary company town of Berwind, our project has built archaeological praxis in collaboration and solidarity with the United Mine Workers of America. Our efforts address a variety of communities that include archaeologists, educators, and the children and grandchildren of the strikers. We address these audiences to engage in the broader discourses and practices about labor and labor rights in the United States, but primarily we serve the interests of the descendant community—unionized workers in southern Colorado. Our collaboration has created a working-class archaeology that differs from the tradition of archaeology as a middle-class practice. Our archaeology joins working families in their struggle to hold back the erosion of their rights and dignity under fast capitalism.

For over a decade, I have presented talks about our research on the Colorado Coalfield War to both professional and popular audiences. When I have spoken outside the United States, in countries such as Spain, México, Brazil, England, Argentina, and Portugal, the audience has been enthusiastic about our project as a form of political action. In the United States and Canada, the reactions have been different. In the dozens of presentations that I have given in North America, someone has always asked me this question: "Why do you want to politicize archaeology?" And I have always answered, "I cannot politicize archaeology. Archaeology is inherently political, and we best deal with that fact by explicitly confronting the political nature of archaeology." These experiences have made it clear to me that many of my North American colleagues still believe what archaeologists do is apolitical, or at best they wish to ignore the troublesome fact that it is not. I argue that we ignore the political nature of archaeology at our own peril. For this reason, I begin this book by discussing how archaeology is political and how a dialectical Marxism provides one starting point for archaeology as political action.

NOTES

1. Contemporary historians have estimated that the Fascists executed at least a hundred thousand civilians and tens of thousands of prisoners of war, while the Republicans executed fewer than fifty thousand people (Juliá 1999). These approximations, based on government documents, almost certainly underestimate the number of people killed by the Fascists, because many executions were done in secret or were not documented. During and following the Civil War, the Fascists extensively documented Republican atrocities and often adulterated documents to make deaths look like executions when they had not been. For these reasons, the estimates of how many individuals the Republicans killed are, if anything, exaggerated.

2. The dictatorship continued to execute its Civil War enemies up until the 1970s. Conservative estimates of the number of individuals executed by the Fascists after the Civil War had ended run to around fifty thousand people (Juliá 1999).

CHAPTER I

Politics

Although it may seem to be a neutral act to study eighth
or thirteenth century Maya, such activity carries profound
political effects and implications. Some of these effects stem
directly from the ideological assumptions that undergird the
research paradigm and interpretive models, whereas others
derive from secondary manipulations by persons other than
the researcher. Once the archaeologist produces an interpretation of the past, that knowledge has a political life of its
own.

Quetzil E. Castañeda (1996:24)

Quetzil Castañeda's studies of Chichén Itzá (1996, 2005) reveal a contested space, a battleground for struggles over economic gain, heritage,
and identity. Under Mexican law, the ruins of Chichén Itzá are *patrimonio cultural* (a federally owned heritage site) and are controlled by the
Instituto Nacional de Antropología y Historia (INAH). INAH employees
at the site include archaeologists and the staff members who manage and
maintain the park. The Mexican government created Chichén Itzá as a
national park to reinforce a nationalist heritage of the Mexican state.
Increasingly, in a transition seen at similar sites around the world, the
park has been transformed into a market center for heritage tourism.

The growth of Cancún as a resort destination for U.S. and European
tourists in the last decades of the twentieth century greatly increased the
number of visitors to the site and the money to be made from sale of sou-
venirs and craft items. The state has given the employees of INAH a
monopoly on such sales, but Mayan Indians from the nearby community
of Pisté have challenged that monopoly in order to sell their own handi-
crafts in the park. Three times, during 1983–1987, 1993–1996, and
2003, artisans from Pisté invaded the park to sell their wares. This is

obviously an economic struggle, but it is also a struggle about heritage and identity. The state wishes to project a pleasing image of México and of the Maya to tourists so that these visitors will return and recommend their experience to others. The Mayan Indians contest this expropriation of their culture, heritage, and identity by invading the park.

The local Maya and the state are, however, not the only groups claiming the heritage of Chichén Itzá. The setting sun on the days of the vernal and autumnal equinoxes projects a shadow on the main pyramid that looks like a serpent. This phenomenon has attracted enormous international attention and interest. The INAH puts on a big show, with dancers, music, and theater to attract and entertain the tourists. In the spring of 1989, the equinox also attracted four other groups of people who laid claim to the spirituality of the monument—and indeed to the identity of the ancient Maya: a group of New Age neo-Aztecs, the Fraternidad Blanca de Quetzalcótal (White Brotherhood of Quetzalcótal), made up primarily of urban mestizos from México City; a tour group of North American New Agers led by a Mayan spiritualist; a group of Mexican followers of the Mexican American New Age prophet José Arguelles; and the Rainbow Family, a loose group of North American spiritualists who gather each year. When these spiritualists began celebrations and ceremonies that interfered with the official program, INAH officials and the police clashed with them. The real descendants of Chichén Itzá, the local Mayan villagers, saw (and continue to see) the whole event as nonsense.

In the Chichén Itzá arena of economic, ideological, political, and identity struggle, archaeology has played numerous roles. Mexican archaeologists have definite economic and political interests in the control of the monument and its interpretation through the INAH (see chapter 4). The interest of the international tourists originates from popular knowledge of the archaeological research done at the site, primarily by North American archaeologists. The North American and Mexican New Agers built their interpretations of spirituality in large part from the knowledge that archaeologists and anthropologists have produced of the ancient Maya. Throughout this tale, archaeologists have been intimately involved, politically interested, and broadly implicated in social relations and struggles.

Castañeda's analysis of Chichén Itzá demonstrates the complexity of the social contexts of archaeological practice. This complexity points to the importance of self-reflexivity on the part of archaeologists, that is, a self-critical examination of the political interests, ideology, and social positioning of archaeology in social contexts. Over the last two decades, substantial scholarship, public conflict, and legislation have made the political, social, and ideological nature of archaeological practice clear (Shanks and Tilley 1987; Tilley 1989; Conkey and Gero 1991; Hamilakis 1996; Castañeda 1996, 2005; Kehoe 1998; D. Thomas 2000; Meskell 2002a; Shanks 2004; Leone 2005; Meskell and Pels 2005; Hamilakis and Duke 2007). Many authors are concerned that archaeological interpretations take on a political life of their own. I seek to build a praxis of archaeology to exercise more control over the knowledge that archaeologists create, a praxis that guides our knowledge toward human emancipation rather than alienation. I find the theoretical basis for such a praxis in a dialectical Marxism.

ARCHAEOLOGY AS POLITICS BY OTHER MEANS

In a political sense, the discipline of archaeology is at once trivial and significant. Paradoxically, the significance of archaeology for political action springs from its triviality. Archaeology by and large does not directly engage in the key political struggles of the modern world. Archaeologists do not in any noteworthy way direct armies, shape economies, write laws, or imprison or free people from bondage. Nonetheless, a handful of archaeologists have become individuals of significant political importance. In 1917, the British government appointed the archaeologist Gertrude Bell as Oriental secretary to the British High Commission in Iraq. Bell helped draw the boundaries of Iraq, and she chose the first king of the new country (Wallach 1999). From 1949 to 1952, the archaeologist Yigael Yadin served as the second chief of staff for the Israeli Defense Forces (Silberman 1993). But, in no case has an individual risen to political prominence through or because of their his or her practice of archaeology.

Archaeology has been put to overt political use. In 1914, Leonard Woolley and T. E. Lawrence provided "innocent" archaeological camouflage for a British military survey of the Turkish-controlled Sinai Peninsula (Wilson 1989:137). During World War I, Sylvanus Morley used his investigations of Mayan sites in the Yucatán as a cover to negotiate with rebel Mayan leaders for their support of U.S. interests (Casteñeda 1996:118). These examples warrant mention primarily because they are exceptions in the history of our discipline. Even in these exceptional cases, however, archaeology primarily served as a stalking horse for political activities, rather than as a form of political action. It made an effective stalking horse because of its obvious triviality. Clearly archaeology is a weak instrument for overt political action, and in a sense, that should comfort archaeologists. We do not violate the civil rights of people if we wrongly reconstruct social hierarchy in the British Bronze Age. No one starves if we underestimate the productivity of Mayan-raised field agriculture. Nonetheless, the past is a locus of political struggle, and this struggle can have significant costs and consequences (Meskell 2002a, 2005; Leone 2005). It has manifested itself at many famous archaeological sites, such as Chichén Itzá and Stonehenge.

During the 1970s, the summer solstice ceremonies of the Ancient Druid Order at Stonehenge began to take on a new significance (Chippendale 1983:253–263). The ceremonies had for decades attracted rowdy onlookers. In 1974, a pirate radio station called for a festival of "love and awareness," and the Stonehenge Free Festival was formed. The festival grew over the next ten years and came to be a counterculture gathering for hippies, travelers, and the curious.[1] The conservative regime of Margaret Thatcher saw the travelers as a threat to social order (Chippendale 1986; Bender 1998). Eventually, government officials claimed that the festival was damaging archaeological sites around Stonehenge, and in 1985 they closed it on the solstice to all but the druids. They fortified the site with barbwire and dug a trench across the entrance road to stop travelers from driving into the site. In a conflict called the Battle of the Bean Field, the police attacked a large party of travelers trying to get to Stonehenge. In the struggle, the police destroyed or seriously damaged numerous vans, trucks, buses, and cars. Scores of people were injured. In the largest mass civil arrest in English history, the police detained five hundred people (Hetherington 2000). Conflicts between the police and travelers occurred again in 1988. All of this unrest resulted in the British courts awarding damages of twenty-three thousand (pounds) to twenty-four travelers in 1991 for assault and damage to their vehicles during the Battle of the Bean Field (Bender 1998:115). In 1994, the Tory government passed a criminal justice act that greatly restricted travelers' mobility and rights. In 2001, British Heritage reopened Stonehenge for solstice visitation under heavily controlled conditions.

In the battle over Stonehenge, which focused on who has rights to the past, British Heritage defeated the travelers' claim to Stonehenge as a site of counterheritage (Bender 1998). The struggle gave the Thatcher government a useful opportunity to regulate and disrupt the travelers, who live outside the tax-paying mainstream of British society. The government did not expel the Ancient Druid Order, whom they regarded as quaint eccentrics good for tourism.

Stonehenge was a locus of ideological struggle. Political struggles over the past are first and foremost ideological, especially when their political nature is hidden or obscured. The obvious triviality of archaeology for overt political action makes it a cloaked but significant weapon in struggles over the past. Jordi Estévež, a colleague of mine in archaeology at the Universitat Autònoma de Barcelona, once remarked to me that he works in an ideology factory. His point was that archaeological practice produces ideology. Therefore, the question becomes, What ideology should we manufacture? His metaphor is apt. We may direct our scholarship to produce knowledge that either reinforces or challenges the dominant ideologies of our times. As Christopher Tilley (1989) has pointed out, the products of the archaeological ideology factory have most commonly sustained, justified, and legitimated the dominant ideological values of capitalism. Archaeologists have done this by venerating stability and disparaging change, by equating social change with progress, by biologizing the social, and by rationalizing the economic.

Much of the discussion of archaeology and politics has focused on the ideological content of our interpretations of the past and archaeological practice. Scholars have deconstructed Cambridge lectures (Tilley 1989), living history museums (Leone 1981), communities (Potter 1994), gardens (Leone et al. 1987), histories (Patterson 1995b; Kehoe 1998; Estévež and Vila 1999, 2006), and cemeteries (McGuire 1988) to show how they are laden with politically significant ideologies. Too often, however, this process of deconstruction and critique provides no directions for alternative practices or, more important, no guide for a politically engaged praxis. We are left with the sure understanding that these things are political and ideological but with no clear sense of what to do about that fact. Many archaeologists, however, still wish to ignore or deny that archaeology is politics by other means.

POLITICAL DOUBTS

Overt discussions of archaeology and politics make many Anglo archaeologists uneasy and uncomfortable, especially in the United States (Ford 1973; Clark 1996). I concur with Lynn Meskell that "archaeologists have traditionally operated on the assumption that they are not implicated in the representation and struggles of living peoples and that all such political engagement is negatively charged" (2005:123). Alice Kehoe notes, "Archaeologists *chose* to disengage from politics, money-grubbing, socialite smoozing: out there in the desert or jungle or cornfield, they could epitomize the dedicated selfless seeker after objective knowledge" (1998:86). This unease and disengagement occur for both good and bad reasons, but denying the political nature of archaeology is not realistic. Furthermore, denying, ignoring, or discounting the political nature of archaeology presents real dangers. It leaves archaeologists with no say or role in the political life of the knowledge that we create.

In part, this disdain for politics in archaeology reflects a larger disdain for politics in U.S. culture. North Americans tend to spurn politics as a dirty business tainted by dishonesty, strong feelings, and self-interest. In popular discourse, politics is contrasted with dispassionate, objective science. The dominant ideology of the United States tends to view politics as a phenomenon separable from other aspects of society, such as economics and culture. Americans in general resist "making things political." This attitude contrasts strongly with the ideologies of European, Latin American, African, and Asian societies, which tend to see politics as an integral aspect of all social life, including archaeology (Hodder 1991; Schmidt and Patterson 1995; Politis and Alberti 1999; Fernández 2006).

Many archaeologists also resist any explicit discussions of politics, because such discussions can be emotional and acrimonious. Political positions necessarily involve moral and ethical attitudes about the world. These attitudes invoke powerful zeal in people. We are taught as young children to exclude politics from polite conversation, because politics creates tension and hostility among individuals. To engage in political discourse is to enter into an uneven and unstable terrain where you can make more enemies than friends. In the aftermath of theoretical tensions that occurred at the end of the twentieth century, many archaeologists just want to proclaim, "Why can't we all be friends?" and get back to sorting potsherds. They want to paper over differences to avoid confronting real political issues (McNiven and Russell 2005:223–231).

Politics is fundamentally about how groups advance their interests within society. If we accept that archaeology is political, then we must ask which interests we should support and which we should oppose. But what tools do we have to make these decisions? Archaeologists fear that others will use our knowledge or practice without our consent or cooperation to advance their interests. Even worse, we fear that we will be caught between conflicting interests. Nowhere is this fear more of a reality in the United States than in negotiations mandated by the Native American Graves Protection and Repatriation Act of 1990. In some contexts these negotiations have thrust archaeologists into the midst of conflicts among Indian nations. Fine-Dare (2002:131–132) discusses how anthropologists negotiating repatriation at Fort Lewis College, in Colorado, had to resist being drawn into disputes between the Navajo Nation and the Hopi Nation.[2] Even while Fort Lewis anthropologists attempted to remain neutral, both Native groups interpreted their actions as supporting or not supporting one or the other nation. In the United States, discussions of repatriation have shown archaeologists that we, too, have political interests, that our practice of science is not unsullied, dispassionate (D. Thomas 2000). Archaeologists must accept that our retreat to the desert, the jungle, or the cornfield has not removed us from the taint of politics.

Politics necessarily involves passions and interests because political practice has real consequences, and they are often pernicious. People lose their land or their jobs; they starve, die, or are imprisoned. As Trigger (1989a:381) points out, the political causes that archaeologists have will-ingly supported have been harmful to humanity as often as helpful. We have no better example of this than the use of archaeology in the Nazi Third Reich (Arnold 1990, 2004). German prehistorians elabo-rated Gustav Kossinna's notion that archaeological cultures equate with ethnic groups, and they turned this into a propaganda tool for German ideas of racial superiority. German archaeologists spread across eastern Europe looking for Germanic sites that would demonstrate Aryan racial superiority and justify the expansion of the Third Reich to include all of "ancient Germany." This archaeological practice did not wage war, bomb cities, or exterminate Jews, Gypsies, communists, homosexuals, and the disabled. It did, however, contribute to the legitimation of a genocidal regime. Unfortunately, we can call up many additional exam-ples of the use of archaeology in the service of totalitarian dictatorships (Galaty and Watkinson 2004).

In the discourse about archaeology, all totalitarian and racial con-cerns get neatly packed into the accusation of "political bias." A bias is a prejudice in a general or specific sense that gives a person a predilection to one particular point of view. A bias could lead a scholar to accept or reject the truth of a claim, not because of the strength of the claim itself, but because it does or does not correspond to the scholar's own precon-ceived ideas. When critics search Joseph Stalin's Soviet Union for exam-ples of the dangers of such biases, they easily find them (Shnirelman 1995). In archaeology, Nikolay Marr advanced a theory that languages change not as a result of historical processes but because of social evolu-tionary changes in the societies of the speakers. From this premise he argued that the prehistory of Europe was a history of a single people differentiated by their stages of evolutionary development. Under Stalin, Marr's views became official dogma, because they could be used to support Stalin's ideas of mechanistic unilineal evolution (Trigger 1989a:225; Klejn 1993:22). Soviet archaeologists could not challenge Marr's theory until Stalin finally decided to reject it in 1950.

To many archaeologists, it seems safer to remain aloof from politics and either ignore or deny the political nature of archaeology. Better yet, they advocate removal of "political bias" from our practice, thinking that this will make archaeology apolitical. They are mistaken about this strategy, however, because attacking political bias in archaeology is itself a political act. Just as the accusation of prejudice charges that the accused lacks objectivity, it implicitly claims that the accuser has objectivity. For the accuser to be unbiased, however, he or she would have to stand outside society and all its political interests and passions. This is not possible. Invocation of political bias silences the conversation that critique makes possible in praxis, a critical discussion of how knowledge is politically situated and how that situatedness affects what we can and cannot know about the social world. Unfortunately, ignoring or denying the political nature of archaeology does not make politics go away, just as accusing others of political bias does not make the accuser unbiased. More important, such self-deception can lead to the very consequences that the apolitical archaeologist fears.

A "politically unbiased" archaeology poses three dangers. These are triviality, complicity, and unexamined prejudice.

First is the danger of triviality. The most obvious form of triviality is a focus on the inconsequential details of the archaeological record. A good example of this can be seen in the development of West German archaeology after World War II. Before the war, German archaeologists had actively engaged in interpretations of prehistory, but after the war, in reaction to the insidious Nazi manipulation of prehistory, German archaeologists turned away from questions of theory and interpretation (Arnold 1990), focusing instead on the description and classification of archaeological minutiae. Entire dissertations were written on the classification and description of a style of brooch. Detailed description and classification of the archaeological record can be important and useful if it is done with specific interpretive and theoretical goals. But as the critique of science in archaeology has shown, such goals necessarily imply a political content. In the absence of such goals, archaeologists risk becoming like Chattus Calvensis II in Herman Hesse's novel *The Glass Bead Game* (1969:65). His life's work was a four-volume tome, *The Pronun-*

ciation of Latin in the Universities of Southern Italy toward the End of the Twelfth Century.

Second is the danger of complicity. Apolitical archaeologists risk involvement as accomplices in questionable acts or even crimes (Trigger 1989a:331). Archaeologists' complicity may spring from their false beliefs in objectivity combined with a failure to understand the political contexts in which they create knowledge. Susan Pollock (2003), Reinhard Bernbeck (2003b), and Yannis Hamilakis (2005) discuss how some archaeologists have become complicit in support of the current U.S. war in Iraq. Pollock (2003) notes that the April 2003 looting of the Iraq Museum in Baghdad attracted widespread media attention in the West, because Western news media has for over a hundred years treated finds in Mesopotamian archaeology as foundational to Western civilization. Archaeologists criticized the U.S. government and decried the destruction of the museum as a loss to Western civilization. The burning of the National Library, the National Archives, and the Koranic Library attracted far less attention and little or no comment from archaeologists. The books, manuscripts, and records in these collections pertain to the modern history of Iraq and its people. Even though many archaeologists were critical of the U.S. government, their comments reinforced popular Western perceptions of the Iraqi people as "others" by focusing on the destruction of ancient artifacts that the public associate with Western heritage and by ignoring the destruction of the libraries (not to mention the widespread looting of hospitals) (Bernbeck 2003b:115–116; Hamilakis 2005). By making the Iraqi people others, these archaeologists became complicit in the war, because the U.S. public will accept the destruction and slaughter of others, but not people like themselves. Pollock, Bernbeck, and Hamilakis suggest that archaeologists need to link their practice to larger social contexts in order to take a more nuanced and ethically responsible approach to the politics of the region and the media.

Third is the danger of unexamined prejudice in our knowledge creation. If archaeologists create knowledge without critically examining the political nature of that knowledge, we will naively reproduce ideologies. These ideologies may or may not be ones we agree with, and we may help or hinder human emancipation. Feminists have made this point very forcibly (Enloe 2004). As long as gender was unmarked (not explicitly considered) in social science research, women were invisible, because social agents were assumed to be male. Feminist scholars have shown how a failure to consider gender led archaeologists to attribute all major social transformations, from the origins of humanness to the rise of the state, to the actions of men; women were little more than passive bystanders (Gilchrist 1999; Sanahuja 2002). Feminists have gendered the study of such transformations, leading to new understandings of how women and men made the past (Nelson 2004). They achieved this knowledge production not by removing "bias" but, rather, by explicitly examining the gender politics of archaeological interpretation. They created new knowledge by applying gendered assumptions about the social world to the archaeological record.

Archaeologists have good reason to be wary of mixing politics with their discipline. One can easily find examples of archaeological knowledge that was fabricated to fulfill a political agenda or interpretations that were predetermined by the prejudice of the researcher. The idea, however, that we can straightforwardly eliminate political bias or just ignore the political content of our knowledge production is facile. Archaeologists make knowledge in social and political contexts, and our knowledge will always be in some part a product of that context (Tilley 1989; Conkey and Gero 1991; McGuire 1992b; Watkins 2000; Shanks 2004; Leone 2005; Fernández 2006). Once scholars recognize that the production of archaeological knowledge has political implications, some archaeologists need to develop an explicit, comprehensive praxis of knowledge creation, critique, and action to transform the world.

In an earlier book titled *A Marxist Archaeology,* I stated, "The notion that archaeology can change the world, that it can alter capitalism, or in any serious way challenge it is simply absurd" (McGuire 1992b:xv). I still believe this. Individuals who primarily seek a life on the barricades will not find it in archaeology. The vast majority of archaeological practice has been and should remain concerned with the acquisition and critique of archaeological knowledge. Archaeology is a weak weapon for political action, because it cannot be wielded directly in the struggles over land, life, liberty, and wealth that drive the political process. Archaeology, however, can be a powerful weapon in ideological struggles that have real consequences for people.

SECRET WRITING AND THE FOLLIES OF
UNBIASED ARCHAEOLOGY

The greatest danger of a politically unbiased archaeology lies in what Ben Agger (2004:49–55) has called the "secret writing" of fast capitalism. Secret writing flows from the pens of "objective" social scientists and culture industry pundits who produce texts, cultural artifacts, and meanings

that appear natural, given, and unalterable. These writings are secret in
the sense that their creators hide or obscure their authorship and agendas
and the politics with which they imbue the writings. By pretending objectivity, science becomes even more partisan, because the scholar denies the
political nature of research. The culture industry commodifies culture,
and thus culture is shaped by the people who stand to reap profits from it
(Agger 2004:55). Yet the presentation of culture is designed to deny the
authorship of these entrepreneurs. People consume culture as leisure and
entertainment. To be marketable, culture must be made comfortable,
unthreatening, and entertaining. Commodified culture sells a natural,
given, and unalterable reality. In both nationalism and heritage tourism,
secret writing creates mythic histories. In these uses of heritage, "unbiased" archaeology and "objective" science have, in fact, constituted political actions often dominating, alienating, and otherwise harming people.

Archaeology as the Secret Writing of Nationalism

The critique of archaeology as a political tool has often focused on how
nationalist movements have used and manipulated it to create nationalisms. When Trigger (1989a, 2006) and others (Ford 1973; Meskell and
Preucel 2004) bemoan the pernicious consequences of archaeology as
political action, they usually have nationalism in mind. Sian Jones
(1997:11) goes further, claiming that nationalist discourse permeates
archaeology at all levels of practice. The literature on archaeology and
nationalism is massive (Díaz-Andreu and Champion 1996; Kohl and
Fawcett 1995; Meskell, ed. 1998; Kane 2003; Galaty and Watkinson
2004). In their brief review of politics and archaeology, Lynn Meskell
and Robert Preucel (2004:318–319) cite over seventy works by archaeologists that discuss nationalism. Virtually all of these works criticize the
use of archaeology in nationalism. Most Western archaeologists would
probably agree with Yannis Hamilakis's observation that "a critical
archaeology should deconstruct and effectively oppose nationalist narratives of the past and the present, as hegemonic discourses" (1996:977). I
will not attempt a comprehensive review of this literature, but I will use
observations and examples from it to point out the folly and danger of
nationalism as political action through archaeology.

Despite an immense literature critiquing nationalist archaeologies, I
know of no how-to book for doing a nationalist archaeology. Such a
work could not exist, because it would expose the secret of the writing.
The power of archaeology in nationalist struggles springs from the fic-

tion that archaeology is an objective science and from the obfuscation of the political endeavor. Nationalists muster archaeology both to prove their myths dispassionately and to reveal and reconstruct an "authentic" objectified heritage.

Over the last hundred years, nationalism has been the source of great human suffering (Anderson 1983; Harris 1990; Smith 1991; Poole 1999; Grosby 2005; Kampschror 2007). Nationalism is a flawed project. The notion that every nation should have its own state or that every state should be a single nation does not have much value as either a normative or a realistic goal (Dunn 1994:3). Nationalists' projects use archaeology to reinforce and validate mythic histories. In the struggle of nationalistic movements, archaeology may be wielded to confront inequities, but with the success of such movements nationalist archaeologies inevitably become embedded in the status quo (Thomas 2004:108–116).

The ideology of the nation-state is grounded in an essentialist notion of a people (a nation) who share a common language and culture, heritage, and territory, which define the nation (Hamilakis 1996:977; Thomas 2004:109–110). Nationalism often rests on the idea of a golden age of ethnic and linguistic uniformity and promotes a culture that is supposedly still connected to that past. In reality, however, national identity is created, contested, and unstable (Poole 1999:67–82). Sharing a common history does not mean that people have shared a common experience of that history (McNiven and Russell 2005:211–231). The struggle over heritage among groups with different experiences of history both flows from and contributes to the instability and conflict of national identity (Kampschror 2007).

Nationalist movements pick and choose from the events of history to create a heritage (Lowenthal 1985:37). Poole (1999:17) notes that every nation has its own history of triumphs and tragedies, victories and defeats, but these events are never the sum total of all that the people of the nation have experienced. The chosen events are usually tied to the territory of the nation. National heritages typically favor those events that relate to how the people of the nation acquired their rightful territory or how they defended it from usurpers. National heritages also tend to glorify the death and suffering of the heroes of the nation; they favor martyrs rather than conquerors. Those who have suffered and sacrificed their lives for the nation demonstrate that the worth of the nation transcends other values.

In 1999, Catalán friends in Barcelona took me to the Gothic basilica of Santa María del Mar. Adjacent to the church is a memorial to the martyrs of the siege of Barcelona in 1714. During the War of the Spanish

Succession (1701–1714), Barcelona sided with the Austrians and English against the Spanish and French. Armies supporting the Bourbon Spanish king Felipe V attacked Barcelona in 1713. The city fell eighteen months later, after a horrific siege. Felipe ordered the construction of two fortresses to dominate the city, stripped the Catalán people of sovereignty, and outlawed the Catalán language. The Spanish took the leaders of the Catalán resistance to a plaza adjacent to the basilica and shot them dead. Over two hundred years later, at the end of the Spanish Civil War, Franco conquered Barcelona, executed his opponents against the walls of the city, and suppressed Catalán sovereignty, language, and identity. Barcelona regained partial sovereignty and cultural freedom following Franco's death in 1975. The Catalonian government then constructed the monument and inscribed it in Catalán to honor the martyrs of 1714.

On our way to Santa María del Mar, we walked past the main cathedral of the city. Here, on the west side of the cathedral, we passed a memorial erected in the nineteenth century to a different martyrdom. On a wall behind a fountain, tiles hand painted with Castilian text and drawings told the story of two residents of Barcelona who opposed the French during Napoleon's invasion of Spain (1808–1813). The French garroted the two, making them martyrs in the Spanish War of Independence. When I asked one of my Catalán friends about this memorial, he avowed no knowledge of the events, dismissing it with a wave of his hand as Spanish.

One problem that nationalist movements encounter in creating national histories and heritages is that the past is already taken (Bernbeck and Pollock 1996:140). One group's defeat is another's victory. As the two memorials in Barcelona show, the same territory includes events significant to different groups and nationalisms. In a discussion of U.S. nationalism and archaeology, Frank McManaman (2000) distinguishes between a civic nationalism available to all through citizenship and competing ethnic nationalisms claimed by specific groups such as Native Americans and African Americans but closed to others. In the end, he dismisses Native Americans' nationalist claims to an ancient U.S. past. He concludes, "There is no inherent barrier to modern Americans, no matter what their ethnic backgrounds, embracing ancient American history as their own" (McManaman 2000:133). Thus, a national heritage can have only one past and one history that define the essence of the nation. In picking and choosing between events, the silences, the events not chosen, are as significant as the ones trumpeted in the national history. These pasts remain outside the national heritage both as a challenge to it and as building blocks for conflicting ethnic nationalisms.

National heritages are built on mythical concepts of history in which little or no separation exists between the past and the present (Bernbeck and Pollock 1996:140). They move events, identities, and nation-states forward and backward in time in order to serve the interests of groups in the present. Only by ignoring this conflation of chronometric time with mythic time can secret writing remain undisclosed.

In Israel, the secular Zionists of the early twentieth century embraced the 74 C.E. Roman siege of Masada as a powerful symbol for their nationalist movement (Yadin 1966; Silberman 1993:271–273). Yigael Yadin (1966), archaeologist and retired chief of staff for the Israeli Defense Forces, mounted a massive excavation at Masada in 1963 to prove a nationalist myth of heroic resistance fighters choosing death rather than surrender (Ben-Yehuda 2002). The Zionists used the defense of Masada against ancient Romans to bolster the defense of the modern nation-state of Israel against Arabs and projected their nation-state back in time to connect it to the last semisovereign Jewish kingdom destroyed by the Romans in 74 C.E.

In May 1921, Great Britain ended the Irish-Anglo War by partitioning six of the nine counties of Ulster to form Northern Ireland. The rest of the island would become the Irish Republic (Bardon 1992). The partition boundary corresponded roughly to Black Pig's Dyke (Delle 1994). Built in the first century of the common era, Black Pig's Dyke is a discontinuous system of defensive linear earthworks and ditches that stretch from County Armagh to Donegal Bay. Similar linear earthworks with accompanying ditches exist throughout Ireland and probably represent Iron Age territorial boundaries. Unionists who wished for Northern Ireland to remain part of the United Kingdom projected the partition boundary of 1921 back in time onto Black Pig's Dyke. They claim that it was a formable barrier that had separated northern Ireland from the rest of the island and that, for this reason, the region had always been more closely connected by sea to Scotland than by land to the Irish Republic (Bardon 1992; Delle 1994).

National heritage is objectified in historic objects, structures, and places, such as Masada and Black Pig's Dyke. These things give the sense of reality to the past and become powerful, emotive symbols of nationalism. Their materiality creates an appearance of a known given past, even though their interpretation remains constantly malleable as secret writing. They offer the national history a tangible and material appearance of authenticity, because the history becomes confused with the thing. Archaeology's power in nationalism springs from the materiality of the historic objects, structures, and places that objectify nationalism. The archaeologist's ability to date events, reconstruct buildings, trade networks, production techniques, and activities seems to confirm an accurate national history. Archaeology's triviality in relation to practical political action diverts suspicion from the secret political nature of such findings. The pockmarked wall of the basilica Santa María del Mar verifies the execution of the Barcelona martyrs of 1714. The archaeologists' excavation of the Roman camps and works at Masada confirm the reality of the 74 C.E. siege. When archaeologists plot and map Black Pig's Dyke, its course parallel to the 1921 partition line becomes obvious. Scholars' ability to accurately locate these places and things adds credence to other aspects of the nationalist story and the struggle.

Struggles over heritage focus on the objects, structures, and places that symbolize it (Golden 2004). During the American Revolution, battalions of the Continental army invaded upstate New York to destroy the Iroquois Confederacy. The soldiers burned fields and villages and chopped down orchards to drive the Indians out. They also pulled down the wooden markers in the cemeteries and obliterated petroglyphs at Picture Rocks, Pennsylvania (Wilkinson 1992). Following the Greek War of Independence (1821–1831), the new Greek state cleansed the Athenian Acropolis of an Armenian cemetery, Muslim buildings, and medieval structures, just as the revolution had cleansed the Greek countryside of Muslims (Hamilakis 2003:64–69). In 1993, Croat forces shelled and destroyed the baroque Ottoman bridge in Mostar as part of their attempt to cleanse Bosnia and Herzegovina of Muslims (Yarwood 1999). All of these examples of nationalist archaeologies show that the symbolic is not something apart from real politics but, rather, is real politics expressed in powerful and consequential ways.

The most compelling example of such power lies in the conflicts over the Babri Mosque in Ajodhya, India (Bernbeck and Pollock 1996; Ratnagar 2004; Romey 2004). At the Babri Mosque, the ideological struggle has generated archaeological debates over the authenticity of materiality. Hindu nationalists have marshaled seemingly inconsequential debates over stratigraphy, column bases, and the context of artifacts to raise passions and inflame nationalistic sentiments (Mandal 1993; Romey 2004:50). Here the triviality of archaeology has become consequential in horrifying ways.

This conflict over heritage has directly resulted in the deaths of thousands of people. In December 1992, a mob led by members of a radical Hindu nationalist political party tore down fences surrounding the Babri

Mosque and razed the structure. They claimed that when the first Mogul emperor, Babur, built the mosque in 1528 he razed a temple marking the birthplace of the Hindu god Rama. They destroyed the mosque to rebuild the temple to Rama and to right a wrong done over four centuries ago. Rioting in India and Bangladesh followed, and over three thousand people died. In February 2002, Muslims in the city of Gujarat attacked a trainload of pilgrims returning from erecting a Hindu altar in the ruins of the mosque. Fifty-eight people died in the attack. In retaliation, Hindu mobs attacked Muslim neighborhoods in that city, and over nine hundred people died. On July 7, 2005, six armed Muslim men attacked the Hindu altar in the ruins of the old mosque, but police killed them in a gun battle. Violent reactions to these events continue to rage as I write these words.

These violent events were preceded and followed by archaeology. In 1990, B. B. Lal, the former director of the Archaeological Survey of India (ASI), published a report on his late 1970s excavations adjacent to the Babri Mosque in a Hindu nationalist publication (Romey 2004:50). He reported that he had found a series of brick pillar bases and that stone pillars in the mosque may have originated from a temple to Rama. Following the destruction of the mosque, D. Mandal (1993) published a book disputing Lal's claims. Mandal argued that the pillar bases were too insubstantial to support large stone columns and that they occurred in different stratigraphic layers and thus could not be from the same building. In 2002, in a civil suit over the mosque site, the Lucknow Bench of the Allahabad High Court ordered a ground-penetrating radar survey to look for remains of a Hindu temple. On the basis of the results of this survey, the court ordered archaeological excavations at the site starting in March 2003. The excavators worked under difficult and rushed conditions, producing a final report by August of that year. The court ordered the two-volume descriptive report of the excavations sealed, releasing only a summary final report. This report indicated the discovery of a large building under the mosque, and nationalists leaped on this finding as evidence for the temple of Rama. Other critics found the results far more ambiguous and argued that the large structure may be an earlier mosque. They also called into question the objectivity of the ASI and alleged that the organization had sold out to the nationalists.

Bernbeck and Pollock (1996) see the controversies over the Babri Mosque as a cautionary tale for a politically active archaeology. They warn that archaeologists cannot indiscriminately support the claims of subordinate groups. Instead, archaeologists must be critical of all identities and histories and should demonstrate the fluidity and dynamism of identities in the past. Bernbeck and Pollock want archaeologists to challenge the essentialism of nationalism and expose the secret writings.

Yet even as archaeologists are coming to grips with the discipline's involvement with nationalism, heritage and the uses of the past in a global economy are changing. The terrain of nationalism has become much more rugged. The disintegration of the Soviet Union and Yugoslavia has resulted in a plethora of nationalist archaeological projects in central Eurasia (Chernykh 1995; Kohl and Tsetskhladze 1995; Kampschror 2007). The reinvention of Europe as a confederation of states under the umbrella of the European Union has fanned the flames of suppressed nationalisms, such as Catalán. To establish its own ancient precedent, the European Union has allocated significant monies to the archaeological study of the Celts (Arnold 2004:208; Levy 2006:144–145). Thus, in contemporary Europe, archaeology serves four overlapping and often contradictory nationalist agendas: those of the existing nation-states, those of emerging nation-states, those of suppressed ethnic nationalisms, and those of a unifying Europe. Perhaps more important, the role of heritage and the past has shifted on the global stage. The commodification of the past in heritage tourism has converted patriotic shrines into theme parks (Silberman 1995:258–261) and has involved archaeologists in new secret writings.

Archaeology and the Secret Writing of the Culture Industry

Yorke Rowan and Uzi Baram argue that, "at the start of the twenty-first century, nationalism is not the only political force impinging on archaeology, and it may not be the most significant" (2004:3). They identify globalization and the marketing of the past for consumption as the new political forces impinging on archaeology. Following Marcuse (1955), Agger (2004:39) notes that because fast capitalism in core states has fulfilled people's basic needs, capitalists can increase profits only by creating fresh needs through the culture industry. Fast production and the movement of production overseas create leisure time, and leisure time creates a need for entertainment. People must spend their leisure time consuming (being entertained) to keep profits flowing. In this context, heritage remains the mobilization of the past in service of the present, but it takes on a new significance (Hall and Bombardella 2005:6). Globalized fast capitalism transforms the unique heritage of nations into a universal commodity for sale in heritage tourism (Rowan and Baram 2004:6).

Secret writing appears both in the marketing of this heritage and in the ways capitalists make heritage accessible and entertaining for tourists.

This commodification is obvious in theme parks and destination resorts. The quintessential theme park is Disneyland. The tourist comes into Disneyland through a portal on the past, Main Street. Main Street is an idealized reproduction of the heart of a turn-of-the-nineteenth-century, small, midwestern American town (Wallace 1996). Walt Disney had the street built at five-eighths of actual size. He "improved" the past by decreeing that everything on the street would remain fresh and new and that all its elements would function together in harmony and unison. Tourists enter a safe, gated space and experience a hyperreal past that is comfortable and unthreatening. The historian Mike Wallace (1996:136) noted, "It is like playing in a walk-in doll's house that is simultaneously a shopper's paradise, equipped with dozens of little old-time shops with corporate logos tastefully affixed."

The use of the past as nostalgia and exotica to lure the consumer to spend is not limited to theme parks like Disneyland. In Las Vegas, the gambling tourist can visit ancient Egypt, ancient Rome, medieval England, and Renaissance Venice. In South Africa, destination resorts with casinos have tried to enhance Africa as an exotic destination through new architecture and design (Hall and Bombardella 2005:10). The tourist can experience the grandeurs of the Dutch East India Company in Johannesburg and a full-scale Tuscan town on the highveld, all improved like Main Street (but without the dancing cartoon characters). These obviously commercial manipulations of heritage invoke authenticity, but they do not claim to be authentic. "The visitor is a knowing participant in the illusion" (Hall and Bombardella 2005:22).

The commercial commodification of the past is not new. Walt Disney built Main Street in 1954. But as the twentieth century drew to a close, objectified heritage became increasingly commodified, and patriotic parks became theme parks. In the current triumph of the logic of commodification, fast capitalist market forces apparently can convert almost every use value to exchange value. Archaeologists see this process in the marketing of heritage. Some, such as Mexican archaeologist José Luis Lorenzo (1998:157), have declared tourism a menace to the preservation of archaeological heritage. The use value of heritage is to define a group of people or a nation that shares a history. The rise of the heritage industry has converted that use value to an exchange value by transforming nostalgia for the past into a commodity to be sold (Shanks 2001). In Manchester, England, yuppies buy lofts built in restored historic industrial buildings, with a Starbucks on the first floor; thousands of miles away in Denver, Colorado, yuppies buy lofts in restored historic industrial buildings with a Starbucks on the first floor (Rowan and Baram 2004).

In the 1980s, Great Britain suffered an extreme economic decline as its industries collapsed under foreign competition, and ships carried South African coal to Newcastle. This period of economic decline saw the growth of a heritage industry in Great Britain (Hewison 1987). This industry created a past in which the British could find a refuge from the realities of economic decline and in which tourists, primarily from the United States, Canada, Australia, and New Zealand, could encounter a heritage. Consumers purchased nostalgia and roots along with their hotel rooms, meals, tours, and souvenir coffee mugs. The flagship of this industry has been the Jorvik Viking Center, in York, a commercial enterprise that uses information from archaeological excavations to construct a Disney-like ride under the city of York, into the Viking past (Merriman 1988). Here, authenticity matters, because tourists come to experience a trip into the past, not an illusion. Nonetheless, this authenticity has had to be packaged, refined, molded, and marketed in order to be consumed as experience in the ride and to be sold as trinkets in the shop at the end of the ride. It is not "improved" quite like Main Street, but the writing that has created the cultural object for sale has remained secret.

Global fast capitalism has created heritage tourism as a major industry of worldwide scope. The wealthy and even the well-off of North America, Europe, Japan, and Australia, all core capitalist societies, can travel to heritage sites anywhere in the world (Rowan and Baram 2004:6). They go to these places as themselves, demanding security, ease of travel, and comforts when they arrive. They seek the exotic, but they want a comfortable exotic that is not threatening or unpleasant. They are, after all, on vacation. Alejandro González Iñárritu's 2006 movie *Babel* effectively captures the contradictions inherent in a comfortable exotic. In the movie, Western tourists are enjoying a tour of Morocco. After a boy accidentally shoots an American woman on the tour, their bus is diverted from the tourist path into a local village, where the exotic quickly turns threatening, and the comforts of the West disappear. The tourists' experience becomes one of alienation and fear.

Many countries in the Third World have found it profitable to turn their patrimony, such as Chichén Itzá, into theme parks (Kohl 2004). To do so, however, they have to create a social, infrastructural, and economic bubble to protect the heritage tourists from the threatening and unpleasant realities of poverty, exploitation, violence, and rebellion that exist in and around the heritage sites. Such bubbles are expensive. Most often their creators are multinational resort companies that reap massive profits from the heritage industry (Meskell 2003:162). Most of these profits leave the country and go into the pockets of investors in the capitalist core. The local people, who may be the descendants of the site builders, reap little economic gain from their ancestors' monuments. Heritage sites thus become loci of political struggle that involves archaeologists and sometimes has pernicious consequences for the interest groups involved (Casteñada 1996, 2005; Joyce 2003, 2005; Ardren 2004; Meskell 2005).

In 1988, the National Geographic Society proposed the creation of the Ruta Maya (the Mayan Route) to a group of five Central American nations in order to define a tourist itinerary linking the major Mayan sites of the region (Joyce 2003:82). These five nations, México, Belize, Guatemala, El Salvador, and Honduras, formed a marketing confederation called the Mundo Maya (the Mayan World) to promote tourism along this route. To create the Ruta Maya, the National Geographic Society used an archaeological narrative, which treats the Maya as a phenomenon that transcends the borders of the five nations (Joyce 2003:82–85). It thus defines the Maya as an international cultural heritage not owned by any of the participant states that make up the Mundo Maya. These states apparently saw the increased income from tourism as more important than the nationalist narratives that made Mayan sites the objectified heritage of individual nations.

The secret writings of the Mundo Maya largely exclude the indigenous Maya of the region from the interpretation, management, and economic benefits of the Ruta Maya (Ardren 2004:107). Advertising for the route prominently displays indigenous Maya in native costume as timeless inhabitants of the ruins. The marketing equates the Maya with nature and includes images that highlight exotic, eroticized Mayan women posed among equally exotic ruins (Joyce 2003; Ardren 2004), recreating the Mayan monuments to satisfy the heritage tourist's desire for escapism and entertainment. Although the marketing of the Ruta Maya commodifies the indigenous Maya, these people receive little direct benefit from the tourism. The occupation of the site of Chichén Itzá by Mayan people is not an isolated example of contested space and indigenous struggles for economic gain, heritage, and identity along the Ruta Maya (Castañeda 1996, 2005). In 1998, two thousand to three thousand Chorti Maya occupied the archaeological park at Copán, in Honduras (Joyce 2003:92–93; 2005:260). For two weeks they brought tourism to a halt to advance their demands for land claims and indigenous rights. In both these cases, Mayan Indians contested the expropriation of their culture, heritage, and identity by reclaiming that heritage to try to advance their contemporary interests

Cultural heritage has been the focus of similar but even more violent political confrontations in Egypt (Meskell 2003, 2005). Western scholars in Egypt have a long history of seeing the Egyptian people as divorced from their pharaonic past and as active impediments to archaeological research (Meskell 2003). Since the eighteenth century, Egyptian villagers have confronted archaeologists as foreign intruders who have treated them as beasts of labor. Repeatedly, Western archaeologists or the Egyptian state has expelled villagers from their homes in the precincts of ancient ruins. The village of Gurna, in the ancient site of the Valley of the Nobles, near Luxor, has been a locus of such evictions. The shantytown of Gurna was unsightly and odorous and distracted the tourist's gaze from the splendors of ancient monuments. Attempts at forced relocation of the villagers have had limited success. In one attempt, police killed four people and injured twenty-five others (Meskell 2005:134). Tourist development in the area has focused on separating the local people from the tourists by using walls, aerial walkways, and gated tourist centers. The tourism industry has also constructed themed restaurants and faux Egyptian villages (Meskell 2003:163–164; 2005:140–144). Like the theme casinos of Las Vegas and South Africa, an improved version of Egypt allows tourists to visit without encountering the realities of poverty, unsanitary conditions, and exploitation that are typical of the real rural Egypt. In November 1997, Muslim extremists attacked tourists at the Temple of Hatshepsut, near Gurna, killing fifty-eight foreigners and four Egyptians (Meskell 2005:136–138). The terrorists identified heritage tourism as an attack on Islamic culture. They struck out at the most visible evidence of Western domination, the opulent bubble of tourism juxtaposed with the poverty and misery of communities like Gurna.

Some archaeologists have sought to subvert the culture industry and to burst the tourist bubble. Many have critiqued the experience of heritage tourism (Castañeda 1996, 2005; Joyce 2003, 2005; Meskell 2003, 2005; Ardren 2004; Rowan and Baram 2004; Duke 2007). A few others have sought to create cultural tourism that does not alienate local communities from their own heritage, economic benefits, or the visitors. This involves creating a heritage experience outside the tourist bubble. One of the best examples of heritage tourism that confronts alienation is on the Ruta Maya, at the site of El Pilar, in Belize.

Anabel Ford and her colleagues have sought to make El Pilar a place that promotes archaeological conservation, sustainable agriculture, and heritage tourism (BRASS El Pilar Project 2006). El Pilar project has worked with the local inhabitants and the government of Belize to design and manage El Pilar Archaeological Reserve for Maya Flora and Fauna. Key to the program is a community organization called Los Amigos de El Pilar. The project has worked with Los Amigos de El Pilar to develop gardens in the forest and to stop clear-cutting of forests for cattle grazing. The park has become a center for eco-tourism that links the tourist experience to the archaeology, the environment, and the local community. Community members run the Masewal Forest Trail, which introduces visitors to the gardens, local plants and Mayan lore. The community has also set up a café for visitors in the Be Pukte Community Center. El Pilar Archaeological Reserve for Maya Flora and Fauna bursts the tourist bubble to serve multiple interests and produce local benefits.

In many places around the modern world, certain social groups have used archaeology to advance their political interests, which has had real and significant consequences for the people in those societies: loss of land and jobs, starvation, death, and imprisonment. The seeming triviality of archaeology for political action has made it an effective pen for secret writings about nationalism and commodified heritage. Building an emancipatory archaeology is possible if we recognize the political nature of archaeology and eschew secret writings.

EMANCIPATORY ARCHAEOLOGY

Secret writing supports the powerful and the status quo. Positions that confront power and challenge the status quo must read secret writings aloud in order to question what they have made unalterable, given, and natural. Emancipatory praxis in archaeology seeks to recover memory and to confront the powerful with nonmythic histories of events placed firmly in time and space. Such histories reveal injustice rather than mythologizing or hiding it. The excavations of mass graves of the Spanish Civil War by Foro por la Recuperación de la Memoria Histórica are one example of such efforts (Gassiot 2005). Forensic archaeologists have also excavated mass graves to reveal the violation of human rights in many other countries, including Argentina (EAAF 2005), Bosnia (Stover 1998), and Mongolia (Frohlich and Hunt 2006). Archaeologists have excavated fascism's chambers of horrors to expose the secret writings of torture on human bodies at the Gestapo headquarters in Berlin,

Germany, and at the Clandestine Center of Detention and Torture (aka Club Atlético) in Buenos Aires, Argentina.

The Berlin Wall, built by the East Germans in 1961, ran through the heart of the city, a few yards away from the headquarters of the Nazi secret police, the Gestapo, at Prinz-Albrecht-Strasse 8. The basement of this building contained an infamous jail and torture center. During World War II, the Allies bombed the building to ruins, and by the mid-1950s, the City of West Berlin had leveled the remains. In 1985, a citizen's group called the Active Museum of Fascism and Resistance issued an appeal: "Let's dig. . . . Let no grass grow over it" (Meyer 1992:28). The group began an archaeological excavation to draw attention to the Nazi past and to recover the memory of the crimes of fascism in time for the celebration of Berlin's 750-year anniversary, in 1987. Many in Berlin and in Germany opposed the excavations, because they did not want this past memorialized or even revealed. Despite much opposition, the Active Museum of Fascism and Resistance continued its illicit excavation. By 1987, the group had uncovered the basement of the building with its cells and torture chambers. It then erected a temporary museum on the site, called Topography of Terror (Rürup 2002). The museum in the excavated basement consisted of interpretive panels that told the history of Nazi atrocities at the site. The panels listed the names of people whom the Nazis had tortured and killed there. In the museum's first year, over three hundred thousand people visited this impromptu exhibition.

When the Berlin Wall came down in 1989, the automaker Daimler-Benz proposed expanding its headquarters building over the site. Public support for the museum, however, grew. In 1992, the government of Berlin incorporated the Foundation Topography of Terror to build and administer a permanent museum at the site (Rürup 2002). This foundation, which included a number of communities, schools and churches, political parties, trade unions, citizens' groups, and history workshops, set up the Memorial Museum Department, which works with other groups and institutions seeking to recover the memory of Nazi atrocities throughout the German Republic. The foundation has conducted digs to uncover, preserve, and interpret other key Nazi buildings adjacent the Gestapo headquarters and the remains of bunkers and air defense trenches. Today the open-air museum in the excavated basement of the Gestapo headquarters is a popular tourist destination (Foundation Topography of Terror 2002).

Archaeologists in Buenos Aires, have undertaken a project similar to that in Berlin. A right-wing military dictatorship ruled Argentina from

1976 to 1983 (Weissel 2003:29–30; Acuto 2003). The dictatorship pursued the "Dirty War" to wipe out any and all left-wing opposition. Government agents took around thirty thousand people, known as *desaparecidos* (disappeared ones), to clandestine detention centers, where the military questioned, tortured, and killed most of them. The government released some individuals after torture, but its agents threw most from planes far out over the Atlantic Ocean or buried them in secret graves. The military opened the Clandestine Center of Detention and Torture, euphemistically referred to as the Club Atlético, in 1977. The center continued in operation in the basement of an old warehouse until 1980, when the building was leveled for freeway construction. The military government imprisoned and tortured about eighteen hundred people at the Club Atlético alone (Weissel 2003:29).

In the early 1990s, a survivor of the Club Atlético recognized the spot under the elevated freeway where the torture center had stood, and survivors and human rights organizations began to agitate for the excavation of the basement, to air the horrors that had occurred there. One of the survivors stated the goal of the project: "to recover what could have been forgotten, so memory is not lost and thus we can claim justice" (Acuto 2003:3). In 2002, survivors, relatives of the *desaparecidos*, human rights organizations, and the City of Buenos Aires began excavations in the basement (Weissel 2003:30). These groups set the agenda of the project and employed archaeologists as collaborators in the effort. The archaeological research focused on recovering artifacts and inferring the formation processes of the cellar so that the activities of the Club Atlético could be reconstructed (Weissel 2003:30). The materiality of the torture center, combined with the testimony of those who survived torment there, has made for a powerful public statement about the excesses of the military government. Archaeologists have undertaken similar excavations at other torture centers in the province of Buenos Aires, the city of Rosario, and the state of Tucumán. In Argentina and the rest of the world, the memory of the horrors of totalitarian dictatorship must be sustained so that such atrocities can never happen again (Weissel 2003:30).

Clearly, when archaeologists seek to make political action part of their practice, they step onto a very difficult topography. The history of nationalist uses of archaeology is at best checkered and at worst monstrous. The archaeology done in the service of commodified heritage for tourists has seldom been any better. Most Western archaeologists would probably agree with Trigger's stinging condemnation (2006:486) of indi-

viduals who deliberately invent or misrepresent archaeological knowledge for political purposes and his insistence that they should be decerti-
fied by the profession and criminally prosecuted if their actions help to
bring harm to people. But political archaeologies have also been emancipatory. The excavation of mass graves from the Spanish Civil War, the
Bosnian War, and the Dirty War of Argentina and of torture rooms in the
Gestapo headquarters and the Club Atlético has recovered the memories
of injustices and violations of human rights. Such recovered memories
have helped bring justice and closure to those who suffered as well as to
their families.

Scholars cannot resolve the dilemma of politics and archaeology by
invoking a sterile vision of archaeology as either science or politics. Two
decades of debate have shown us that archaeology is both science and
politics. The productive question is not, How do we make archaeology
one or the other? but, instead, How do archaeologists link science and
politics in our practice?

An honest, emancipatory political archaeology challenges the secret
writings that hide and justify injustice. Such archaeology is truthful about
its political content and confronts power and oppression. Neil Faulkner
(2000) and Yvonne Marshall (2002, 2004) have proposed that intellectuals can build an honest, emancipatory scholarship with a community
archaeology that is politically self-conscious and collaborative with local
groups of people. A candid, liberating archaeology has the potential to
develop a heritage tourism that benefits and advances the interests of
local peoples rather than the profits of multinational corporations
(Ardren 2004; Marshall 2002:214–215; Moser et al. 2002; Sen 2002;
Isaacson and Ford 2005:362). Such an archaeology disassembles secret
writing's myth of a single, common, national heritage. It reveals the
pieces that are hidden in this story to create a reflexive heritage that recognizes how social groups have differentially experienced a shared past
and the consequences of that difference (Scham and Yahya 2003). It
reveals how racial groups have experienced oppression and exploitation
in shared pasts. It helps their descendants reclaim their dignity, legacy,
and rights (Deloria 1993; La Roche and Blakey 1997; D. Thomas 2000;
Watkins 2000; McDavid 2002; Blakey 2003; Leone 2005; McNiven and
Russell 2005; Wiseman 2005). It transcends bourgeois interests to
include working-class communities (Gero 1989; Patterson 1995b, 1997;
Saitta 2005, 2007). A liberating archaeology transcends androcentric
bias both in the interpretation of the past and in the practice of archaeology in the present (Gero 1983, 1985; Conkey and Williams 1991;

Gilchrist 1999; Dowson 2000; Joyce 2004; Nelson 2004). In response to imperialism and global fast capitalism, emancipatory scholarship asks how we can build an archaeology that includes the colonized (Schmidt and Patterson 1995; Scham 2001; Lyons and Papadopoulos 2002; Given 2004; Schmidt 2005). The key to an honest, emancipatory political archaeology is praxis.

Marxist archaeologists are not the only archaeologists who have advocated a socially responsible scholarship that confronts inequality and oppression in the world (Fernández 2006). Processualists, feminists, post-processualists, indigenous archaeologists, and others have attempted to build archaeologies of political action. The theory that I use here is not the only starting point for a politically engaged archaeology. It is, however, the starting point for the praxis of archaeology that I develop in this book.

A MARXIST THEORY OF PRAXIS FOR ARCHAEOLOGY

Marxism differs from much other social theory because it has an explicit political intent. Marxism is first and foremost a critical study of capitalism that seeks to transform the social world. Modern Western Marxists recognize that exploitation, inequality, and oppression exist in capitalist social relations of gender, sexuality, race, and ethnicity. They use class as their entry point into an analysis that examines the intersection of these social relations, each with the others and with class (Sherman 1995:119; Wurst 2006). The alternative that these Marxists offer for capitalism is social democracy.

The relational dialectical method that I have adopted here is but one contemporary Marxist approach in archaeology. Archaeologists have also embraced classical Marxism and critical theory. These approaches share the ultimate goal of transforming capitalism but differ in the importance they give to knowing the world and taking action in the world. In chapter 2, I will compare how these approaches and non-Marxist approaches address praxis. Archaeologists who embrace classical Marxism also advocate a dialectical method, but it is a dialectics of nature rather than a Hegelian, or relational, dialectic. My discussion of the dialectic that follows in this chapter will elucidate the differences between these two dialectics.

Frederic Jameson (1997:175) defines Marxism as the science of capitalism or, more properly, as the science of the inherent contradictions of capitalism. This science begins with Karl Marx's radicalization of Enlightenment rationality into a critique of capitalism (Patterson

2003:7–32). Marx read history in class terms. That is, he looked at history in terms of social groups that have material interests. For Marx, the key to understanding that history lies in the struggle of these groups to create, maintain, or transform social relationships that advance those material interests. Social groups can act to advance their interests only if their members possess a shared consciousness—class consciousness—that encompasses their identity and interests. The Marxist study of the past seeks to reveal hidden social relations and to take up the perspective of the oppressed and dominated. Patterson (2003:8) has compared this process to peeling an onion: the scholar removes layer after layer to reveal its innermost structure and then reassembles the whole.

Praxis

Conscious, knowing human actors may seek the transformation of capitalism though a radical praxis (McGuire et al. 2005). Praxis springs from the realizations that people make the social world in their everyday lives and that they can also subvert and transform that world. A Marxist radical praxis necessarily involves three goals: to know the world, to critique the world, and to take action in the world. Without a praxis that integrates these three goals, individuals cannot fully realize their place in society or their capacity to transform society.

In order to change the world, people must have accurate knowledge of it. Action based on false or flawed knowledge can only lead to failure and error. Accurate knowledge does not, however, exist independently of the social consciousness of the individual. Rather, people produce knowledge in a complex dialectic between the reality that they observe and the consciousness that they bring to their observations. Knowledge becomes meaningful and important when the process of gaining it is intimately interconnected with both social concerns and the position and interests of people as social agents. Accurate knowledge, therefore, is possible only from a critical stance. If people do not question the ethics, politics, epistemology, and reality behind their knowledge, then their actions in the world will be unsound and may result in unanticipated consequences that can be counterproductive or even harmful. Marxist critiques challenge how people use the reality of the world, the social context they exist in, and their own interests in creating knowledge. These critiques involve a questioning of different visions or interpretations of knowledge and a self-examination of one's own perspectives. They must ultimately rest in the reality of the observable world, however, because if they do not, then they will only lead to self-delusion and fantasy. By the same token, these critiques should be coupled with collective action. Just as reality without critique equals self-delusion, critique without action produces only nihilism and despair.

Along these lines, Marxists argue that to take effective collective action in the world, individuals need to reflect on their larger social contexts. The political, ideological, and ethnic confrontations of the last three decades have led many social scientists to conclude that taking action in the world without concrete knowledge of that world inevitably leads to erroneous and pernicious results. In the same way, collective action that springs from knowledge and converts it into a rich platform for debate and critique avoids the tendency toward self-delusion and totalitarianism that lurk in isolated and unexamined knowledge or in absolute truths.

People realize praxis in the articulation of knowledge, critique, and collective action, all based in the concrete world. Praxis enriched by knowledge, critique, and action can exist only within real contexts of social relations, social struggles, social interests, and social agents. Praxis cannot exist in the abstract (McGuire et al. 2005).

A Dialectical Marxism

There is no simple or unambiguous way to define the dialectic, and disagreements about the nature of the dialectic define differences within Marxist thought (Ollman 1976:238–240; Sherman 1995:235–240). The Hegelian dialectic is just one of many concepts of the dialectic that exist in Marxism and in Western thought in general (Ollman 1976, 1992, 2003; Sayer 1987; Gottlieb 1989; Agger 1997; Roseberry 1997; Jacoby 2002). It is one of two concepts of the dialectic currently used in Western archaeology.

At least five major elements of a dialectical Marxism have important implications for a praxis of archaeology: a relational dialectical method; a relational theory of society; the concept of collective agency; an emphasis on knowing the world through the lived experience of people (everyday life) as opposed to the description of artifacts or a search for abstract models, laws, or theories of cultural change; and a self-reflexive awareness of archaeology's place in the modern world.

The Dialectic Although two different dialectical approaches exist in Western archaeology today, they share some basic concepts and definitions of the dialectic. These shared concepts include a holistic, relational view of society in which cultural change is an internal process driven by relational contradictions, a focus on the dynamics of quantitative and qualitative change, and the use of the dialectic as a method to study change rather than as a theory that explains change. The two approaches disagree over what is the proper object of a dialectical method. Classical Marxists in archaeology have adopted a dialectics of nature that applies the dialectic to nature and society. Dialectical Marxists use a Hegelian, or relational, dialectic that can be applied to the study of society but not to the study of nature.

The dialectic views society as a whole (Ollman 1976, 1992, 2003; Sayer 1987), as a complex interconnected web, within which any given entity is defined by its relationship to other entities, unable to exist in isolation. As Bertell Ollman has noted: "Dialectics restructures our notions about reality by replacing the common sense notion of 'thing' (as something that has history and external connections with other things) with the notion of 'process' (which contains its history and potential futures) and 'relations' (which contain as part of what it is its ties with other relations)" (2003:13). For example, you cannot have husbands without wives; each social entity (thing) exists because of the existence of its opposite. It is the underlying relationship of marriage that creates both husbands and wives. If the interconnectedness is broken (divorce), the opposites dissolve or, more properly, are transformed into something else (ex-husband and ex-wife). The dialectical method seeks to penetrate the observable reality of social entities such as husbands and wives to reveal the underlying social relationships that create these entities. This is the method that Patterson (2003:8) captures in his metaphor of peeling an onion.

In the dialectic, the entities that make up the social whole are not expected to fit comfortably together. They may fit, but the dynamics of change lie not in these functional relations but in the relational dialectical contradictions that spring from the fact that social categories are defined by and require the existence of their opposite. Thus, in the antebellum South of the United States, slavery defines both the master and the slave. The existence of masters requires the existence of slaves, yet the two are opposites and as such are potentially in conflict. Each participates in the relationship of slavery, but each has a different lived experience of slavery. For the master, it is an experience of wealth, freedom, comfort, and privilege. The master's experience depends on the slave's experience of poverty, want, and oppression. Thus, the slave and the master have different interests in the relationship that defines them both. Social change results from the conflict and contradictions inherent in such relations.

Change in these relations is never simply quantitative (changes of degree) or qualitative (transformative or revolutionary). Quantitative changes lead to qualitative change, and qualitative change necessarily implies a quantitative change. Conflicts that result from relational contradictions may result in quantitative changes that build to a qualitative change in those relations. Rebellion by slaves may lead the masters to enforce stricter and stricter controls, thereby heightening slave resistance until the relation of slavery is overthrown. The social relations that result from such a qualitative change are a mix of the old and the new; the old social form is remade, not replaced.

The dialectic does not explain or predict how change and interaction occur (Ollman 2003:12). Rather, it is a method that leads the scholar to understand change and interaction by providing appropriate questions. The test of the dialectic as a method is its utility (Sherman 1995:218): Does it help us choose important problems? Does it guide the researcher to the empirical observations needed to consider those problems? Does it provide a framework for evaluating those observations, a framework that helps the scholar solve the problems, formulate new theory and problems, and take action in the world?

Classical Marxists tend to accept Engels's (1927) concept of the dialectics of nature, applying the dialectic to the study of both the natural and the social world. Engels argued that Marxist concepts used in the study of society can be used in the study of nature. This perspective suggests that natural relationships such as that between cougar (predator) and deer (prey) can be understood in the same way as social unities such as the master and the slave. A dialectics of nature seeks the general laws governing the development of nature, science, society, and thought (Woods and Grant 1995:15). The role of the scholar is to gain knowledge of the world, then from this knowledge derive the laws of motion that drive social change and through this knowledge shape social change (Woods and Grant 1995:140).

In contrast, humanistic dialectical Marxists see the dialectic as a uniquely social phenomenon. A relational dialectic treats Marxism as a theory of relations and treats society as a complex web of social relations, within which the nature of any entity is governed by its relation to other entities. Dialectical Marxists argue that the dialectic between social entities, such as master and slave, depends on the entities having an underlying unity, which comes from their common humanity. Such a unity cannot exist in the study of nature. A master may become a slave, and a slave may become a master. The deer (prey), however, cannot become a cougar (predator). The study of nature produces scientists, but it does not produce nature; the study of geology creates geologists, but it does not create rocks. By contrast, the scholar may be the subject and the object of the study; it is the relationship inherent in study that creates scholars (subjects) and informants (objects). For humanistic Marxists, critique lies at the core of research. The scholar obtains knowledge of the world through observation but must be constantly critical of how and why that knowledge is accepted.

The unity of subject and object that characterizes the study of the social world exists even when archaeologists study people who are long dead. The dead cannot study the archaeologist, but it is their silence that allows many archaeologists to define scientific goals as objective, universal, or even in the interest of the dead. We cannot alienate the dead, but the assertion of an objective, universal, or true archaeology becomes a way to alienate the living from their past and to advance, justify, and maintain the inequities of today (McGuire 1992a; Watkins 2000; Fforde et al. 2002; Fforde 2004; McNiven and Russell 2005).

A Relational Concept of Society   The Hegelian dialectic makes social relations rather than social entities the key to studying society. The existence of individual humans necessarily implies the existence of society, and the existence of society necessarily implies the existence of individuals. A relational dialectic does not view the social world as made up of individuals (things) but instead sees the social world and individuals as products of underlying social relationships and processes. From the standpoint of a dialectical praxis, humans make history as members of collective groups.

A relational dialectic defines society as a network of interrelated differences. Difference is inherent in society, because underlying social relationships create social categories that are the opposite of each other, such as master and slave. Conflict is intrinsic in these social oppositions. Individuals negotiate identities, social characteristics, and consciousness through their relationship to others in these social networks. They do so within the social structures that these relationships create, but in doing so they also have the potential to transform the social structures. These individuals do not exist alone or outside the network of difference that is society, nor can they act alone in a transformative way. Thus, the important question for praxis is, How do individuals create a shared consciousness of group identity and interest that allows them to act as a group in a transformative way? In a relational view, the dynamics of social change cannot be reduced to the economy, human psychology, or action of individuals. A relational concept of collective agency allows us to understand how people make history.

Collective Agency   Society changes because of human action, but all human action is dependent on the existence of society. As Marx wrote: "People make their own history, but they do not make it just as they please; they do not make it under circumstances chosen by themselves, but under given circumstances directly encountered and inherited from the past" (1978:9).[3] Social structures, ideologies, and material conditions inherited from the past both enable and limit this agency, yet these same structures, ideologies, and conditions are products of conscious human action. People inherit the material conditions created in the past, and people will create the material conditions of the future. This dialectic between the past and the present creates a future through the dialectic of agency and structure. Understanding collective agency allows us to participate in the struggles of contemporary constituencies and creates the possibility of making the archaeological project part of transformational social projects.

Archaeologists have recognized that human agency is always social; thus, people never act simply as individuals (Silliman 2001). Even the act of being a hermit is social. Individuals can exist only in a web of social relations, and agency is realized through these relations. When individuals join together in collective action, their agency may transform these relations. Put another way, agency presupposes a web of social relationships and meanings, yet these social relations and meanings are themselves products of conscious human action.

Even the unintentional changes that fascinate practice theorists in archaeology entail goal-oriented social agency (Barrett 2000; Pauketat 2000; for a critique see Bernbeck 2003a). This is well illustrated by the classic case of unintended consequences, the tragedy of the commons (Hardin 1968; Pauketat 2000). In William Forster Lloyd's (1833) parable of the English commons, cattle herders personally gain greater income by grazing more cattle on the village commons, and each cattle herder makes an individual decision to maximize his or her income through this increased grazing. The unintended consequences of these individual actions is the overgrazing of the commons, resulting in the loss of all income by all herders and the loss of the right to the commons. This parable might appear to be an example of individual agency and unintended consequences, but it actually assumes individuals embedded in social relations acting as social agents. The right to the commons is a social relationship. Also, the only way that the herders could benefit from herding more cattle than the number for which they had use value was through the existence of a market in which to sell the cattle. That is, these herders had to engage in the social relations of the market in order to reach the decision to graze more cattle. Thus, social relations enabled and limited the decisions these herders could make, and the consequences of these decisions transformed these relations. The unintended consequences of individual agency may cause change, but this is not what brought about the demise of the English commons in reality.

Archaeologists, like many other scholars, have assumed that the tragedy of the commons was a frequent event in medieval and postmedieval England, but this belief is incorrect (Cox 1985; Neeson 2004). English law granted the right to commons only to members of the community or to individuals who provided services to a lord. Law and custom regulated who could use the commons and how many animals they could graze there, all in recognition of the carrying capacity of the land (Cox 1985:55). The social relations of the commons worked for hundreds of years in England and came to an end only through the praxis of the landed classes. Landlords enclosed or took possession of the commons. They increased their profits by applying improved agricultural techniques and selling wool to supply the mills driving the industrial revolution. Enclosure was a conscious and calculated movement by the landed classes (Neeson 2004). As part of this movement, they had to "reform" agricultural laws and discredit existing customs. Lloyd (1833) wrote his parable during the debates over the 1832 Enclosure Acts. The tragedy of the commons originated not as history but rather as an ideological myth to advance enclosure. It survives today as a right-wing fable that denies the efficacy of communalism.

Praxis implies something more than embodied practice, something more than practical consciousness, and something more than individuals simply making self-interested decisions. Agency becomes praxis only when social groups collectively seek transformational change to advance their interests (Gramsci 1971; Crehan 2002). Transformative praxis springs from communal action. One hand did not tear down the Berlin Wall, Martin Luther King did not march on Washington alone, the Stonewall riot did not involve a single rowdy homosexual, and Hitler did not by his own hand kill six million Jews.

People make history as members of social groups whose common consciousness derives from shared social relations and lived experiences and from common interests, cultures, and ideologies that link them to one another and oppose them to other social groups. They create this consciousness through their shared experience of day-to-day life. A shared consciousness exists when members of the group identify with other members of the group and develop an awareness of the relationship of their group to other social groups. The solidarity of lived experience may be based in class, gender, ethnicity, or race, or more commonly in some combination of these identities.

Antonio Gramsci (1971; Crehan 2002) argued that shared consciousness originates in common experience but that this experience does not automatically give rise to solidarity. Consciousness raising usually requires individuals acting as intellectuals, activists, organizers, and provocateurs to first mold the raw material of experience into consciousness. If group members recognize this consciousness as their own individual situation and if they are moved to act in solidarity, then collective agency will occur. The task of scholars is to produce knowledge and critique. For those scholars who seek to engage in praxis, that knowledge and critique should be based in a genuine understanding of the experience of the social group whose interest their scholarship serves. Praxis, therefore, flows from a dialogue or dialectic between intellectuals and the communities they serve.

The relationship of individuals to one another and to social groups is complex. Individuals participate in multiple relations within social groups, and they may participate in multiple groups. The inequality and exploitation that usually exist within social groups further complicate the relationship. Also, individuals may participate in various groups that have different or even contradictory social interests. People do not experience these relations and their multiple identities in isolation; rather, their experience flows from the interrelationships among social groups and identities in the social reality in which they participate. Furthermore, just because individuals participate in the same social reality does not mean that they will have the same experience. The lived experience in the coalfields of southern Colorado in the first decades of the twentieth century differed between husbands and wives, between company managers and miners. Thus, the axis of solidarity and experience that will be used to create a social consciousness will depend on the specific historical context of its creation.

Transformative collective agency will not always succeed. People may know what change they want, but almost inevitably their efforts to effect it will result in unintended consequences. Powerful groups within society will also actively seek to prevent such consciousness from rising in order to preserve their own interests. Social groups may also try but fail to form a collective consciousness and thus be ineffective agents. Competing identities and differences in experience may hinder the forming of group consciousness. Consciousness raising may succeed when struggle against a greater oppression transcends these differences or when groups with different interests can define mutual goals. Collective agency creates a very complex arena in which we as archaeologists seek to understand change and to build a radical archaeological praxis.

Knowing the World   Collective agency is both contingent and unpredictable. The prior conditions of a historical sequence, material relations, social structures, culture, and ideology define a range of possibilities for collective action. Which actions people will undertake, however, are not determined but contingent on both prior conditions and the subjective evaluations that people make of them (Roseberry 1997). The conditions that structure human action leave broad channels and lots of room for actions and consequences that cannot be known in advance. Small changes in events or circumstances, actions taken or not taken, can, over time, have dramatic and unforeseeable consequences for the course of history. Praxis occurs when people consciously try to chart their way through these channels. The starting point for praxis, therefore, is a historical understanding of society and prior agency to identify what the channels are, how they are bounded, and where they might lead.

The substantive analyses in this book begin with historical considerations of the prior conditions that channel praxis. The class structure of archaeology today is legitimated by a guild ideology of the discipline that reflects the history of the field rather than the modern realities. When we began archaeological research in Sonora, México, along the U.S. Mexican border, we stepped into preexisting social relations, social structures, economies, politics, and ideologies. The Ludlow Collective's study of the Colorado Coalfield War analyzes the collective agency and praxis of early twentieth-century miners to demonstrate why such praxis must be continued in the present to maintain the rights and dignity of working families. Following Marx, our analyses focus on the everyday lived experience of people in these cases.

Marx's method opens the way to the recovery of history, but it does not predict the course of that history (Sayer 1979:199). It provides a guide for how scholars can understand and analyze concrete cases of social change in order to make social change in the future. The key to this method is the study of real lived experience. In his own historical studies of transformational change, Marx (1978) started with real individuals, their actions, and the material (economic) conditions under which they lived, both those that they inherited from the past and those that they created through their actions. He examined how people acted within and on social, political, and cultural relationships, institutions, and structures, reproducing some and changing others (Roseberry 1997:30). In order to do this, these individuals had to have certain understandings, images, and beliefs about who they were and what they were doing. Marx undertook historical studies of transformative change because he rejected the idea that such changes are predetermined, inevitable, or predictable. He studied history to build praxis. His historical studies were commentaries on movements and attempts to shape them to change the world (Roseberry 1997:39).

A Marxist analysis starts with an analysis of economic relationships, focusing on the relations between classes and class factions (Wurst 2006). The method of Marxist class analysis can, however, be applied to any social groups that have common interests and consciousness (Bloch 1985:162–163). Any group of individuals who share an identity and interests and can form a group consciousness may engage in collective agency. This realization opens the door for complex analyses from multiple vantage points (Patterson 2003:12), including gender, race, ethnicity, sexuality, and age, in addition to classes and class factions. Regardless of these other vantage points, Marxist analyses always examine the lived experience of the oppressed, the marginalized, and the forgotten. The economic vantage point is essential to reveal secret writings. Marxism shares this vantage point with other approaches to emancipatory archaeology. We see it in the Argentinean studies of the Club Atlético (Weissel 2003:29–30; Acuto 2003), in Lynn Meskell's analyses of archaeology and violence in Egypt (2003, 2005), and in Rosemary Joyce's critiques of cultural tourism and the Ruta Maya (2003, 2005).

My substantive analyses in this book focus on communities and class factions that have not traditionally been included in archaeology. I read the secret writings aloud in order to build praxis. To include the oppressed, the marginal, and the forgotten in our analyses, archaeologists need to first be self-reflexive about the social and political positioning of archaeology in order to understand the power relations we exist in and contribute to.

Critiquing the World   Just as it is people who make history, it is also people who write history and do archaeology. As scholars, we are also social beings who live and work in a social context. Our social, cultural, and political point of view affects how we see the world, what questions we ask, what assumptions we make, what observations we value, and what answers we accept. Our understandings of the past must always fit the knowledge we have of its events and practices, but many explanations of these will always fit. A dialectical point of view urges us to accept that even though the past is real, our knowledge of it is always made in the present, and this knowledge is never a simple product of either past or present but a complex mix of both. Our assessments cannot be complete unless we also ask why we, as socially situated scholars, choose to raise the particular questions that we ask and why we might favor one possible explanation over another.

To answer these questions, we can study archaeology's history as a material social process (Trigger 1989a, 2006; Patterson 1986, 2003; Kehoe 1998). Our own history bequeaths beliefs and social relations to us as social beings and scholars. This inheritance conditions our scholarship, setting up paths of least resistance that we may travel without realizing why we took them or what the repercussions of our journey may be, for ourselves or others. A self-critical historical analysis reveals alternative paths and asks why the paths we are following appeared to us, why we should follow them, to what ends they can take us, and whose interests they serve? With such knowledge we can, hopefully, more wisely navigate our journey.

Recognizing that archaeology is a social product and process and that multiple stories, addressing different interests in the present, may always exist raises questions of what interests archaeology should serve and how these interests are best served. North American archaeology legitimately serves the academy, the people who pay for our work, the museum going public, indigenous nations, and many other communities. The interests of these various communities may be in harmony or in conflict or irrelevant to one another. Archaeologists have not given enough attention to identifying these interests or to building dialogues between those interests and us (Shanks and McGuire 1996; Faulkner 2000; Moser et al. 2002).

As socially engaged scholars, Marxists and other emancipatory archaeologists should remember that we cannot trust in "correct" theory or "true" knowledge of the world to direct our praxis. Critique must remain a constant and central part of what we do. We also need to avoid totalitarian theories. Social theories become totalitarian when they claim that their perspective identifies the determinants of social forms and thus serves as a way to engineer change in those forms. The feminist idea of entry point gives us a way to break this linkage by treating social theories as entry points to study social relations, with the recognition that, in any given case, multiple entry points will be possible and may give compatible interpretations that reinforce one another (Wylie 1991). A pluralistic praxis of alliance and common struggle can be built from these intersectionalities (Conkey 2005b).

Commentators have appropriately criticized Marxism for not adequately considering social factors such as gender, sexuality, race, and ethnicity (Hartman 1981; Sargent 1981; Taylor 1990). If scholars accept a totalitarian notion of Marxism (class is the root of all exploitation), or a totalitarian notion of feminism (gender is the root of all exploitation), or a totalitarian notion of queer theory (sexuality is the root of all exploitation), or a totalitarian notion of race theory (race is the root of all exploitation), then Marxism must be at odds with all of these other approaches. The feminist perspective of entry point, however, offers an alternative (Wylie 1991). If we are to take the diversity and complexity of oppression seriously, we must recognize that it derives from many relationships, including those of gender, sexuality, class, race, and ethnicity. Each of these provides an entry point to the study of social relations and oppression. Marxists enter the study of the social world with the analysis of class, and from this entry point we should examine its complex relationships with gender, sexuality, race, and ethnicity in the construction of oppression. Other socially engaged scholars use other entry points. For example, feminists begin their analysis with gender. As long as feminists seek a radical transformation of gender relations that must also address class, sexuality, race, and ethnicity (hooks 2000; Sanahuja 2002), and Marxists recognize that relations of class also involve relations of gender, sexuality, race, and ethnicity, then the intersection of multiple approaches can produce compatible and complementary praxis (Wurst 2006).[4]

Following from Antonio Gramsci (1971), the emphasis in this book is on how class is lived by people. That is, on how people experience class in their everyday existence (Wurst 1999, 2006). People live class as gendered, ethnic, sexual, and racial social beings (Crehan 2002:195). Addressing class as a social lived phenomenon means that all aspects of the social condition ought to be considered in the analysis and interpretation of history and the building of praxis.

The Marxist theory of relational dialectics that I have advocated here leads me to an emancipatory praxis of archaeology. This is not the only theory that may lead to political action. Indeed, archaeologists using other theories have sought to build praxis, sometimes with different goals and usually with alternative entry points. Multiple theories produce the debate and dialogue that help archaeologists better know the world, critique the world, and take action in the world. In chapter 2, I will compare processualist, post-processualist, Marxist, feminist, and indigenous efforts to build archaeological praxis. My theory of praxis builds on a foundation of these efforts and draws on the intersectionalities among Marxist, feminist, and indigenous archaeologies (Conkey 2005b).

NOTES

1. In Great Britain the term *traveler* refers to a variety of social groups who generally move around the country and have no permanent abode. This includes ethnic Gypsies, Irish tinkers, and, starting in the 1960s, a group of New Age travelers who formed around a free festival circuit that came to include Stonehenge.

2. The Navajo and Hopi nations have been engaged in a long-running dispute concerning control of land in northeastern Arizona. The dispute originated in 1882, when the president of the United States established the Hopi reservation and then later settled Navajo people on land originally assigned to the Hopi. The conflict continues today on the ground, in the courts, and in Congress. It has involved and deeply divided anthropologists and archaeologists who work with or for each nation (Benedek 1999).

3. The usual English translation of this quote begins "[Men] make history," but this translation is inaccurate. In the original German, Marx used the noun *Menschen*, which translates as "people," not as "men." The German word for "men" is *Mannschaft*.

4. I should note that all contemporary Western Marxists in archaeology do not agree with my advocacy of Marxism as a method for understanding social life as opposed to Marxism as an explanation of the social world or my advocacy of class as an entry point to study society as opposed to class as a determinant of the social world. Many times Marxist colleagues have told me that an approach that grants importance to social factors other than class is not really Marxist (Gilman 1993). Ultimately, the issue is changing the world, not defining what "Marxism really is." My reply to these critics can be found in the prologue of the reprinting of *A Marxist Archaeology* (McGuire 2002b) and in the totality of this book.

CHAPTER 2

Praxis

True knowledge is the reformer's most important weapon and
we should never surrender it.

Bruce Trigger (1995b:331)

This book is not the first attempt to develop an explicit praxis of archaeology that contributes to the transformation of society and, hopefully, to a more humane world. The theory of praxis presented here builds on a foundation of earlier efforts and from an ongoing engagement with current perspectives. My theory originates from a critical examination of these processes. It starts from the dialectical theory of Marxism that I presented in chapter 1 and draws on the intersectionalities between feminist and indigenous archaeologies (Conkey 2005b).

Praxis is a process of gaining knowledge of the world, critiquing the world, and taking action in the world (McGuire et al. 2005). Bruce Trigger charges us to base our praxis in "true knowledge" and to use critique to expose false consciousness and flawed knowledge. Yet, if our knowledge is always situated in social and political contexts, how can we talk of "truth"? The situated nature of knowledge means that truth will be overdetermined, not objectively discernable or separate from its context. If archaeologists accept this position, then critique is in and of itself praxis, because critique will evaluate the situatedness of knowledge. However, this leaves us no basis for alternative action, since it entails the nihilistic revelation that the world is not knowable. The nature of knowledge claims, therefore, is key to any theory of praxis in archaeology. A dialectical approach attempts both to know the world and to critique it, evaluating knowledge claims through a four-way dialectic among the four Cs: coherence, correspondence, context, and consequences.

Archaeologists laid the first stones of a foundation for praxis by the middle of the twentieth century. Those doing culture history assumed that knowledge lay in the ground, to be collected like so many potsherds. Although culture history remains a major effort in world archaeology today, current theoretical discussions recognize as naive the notion that data can exist independent of some kind of larger theoretical or social practice or both. One of the first archaeologists to acknowledge this was V. Gordon Childe, who adopted a modernist philosophy from classical Marxism that emphasized "true" knowledge. His discussion of the nature of knowledge presaged current debates by a generation. The range of positions that exist within contemporary archaeology run the gamut from those that seek true, or objective, knowledge to those that are overwhelmed by the situatedness of what we think we know (Wylie 1994; Bate 1998; Hodder 1999; Trigger 2003b; Meskell and Pels 2005; Fernández 2006).

The simplistic opposition between objective and relativist knowledge of the world lies at the heart of the debate between the two dominant theoretical threads of Anglo-American archaeology—processual archaeology and post-processual archaeology. Processual archaeologists have reduced the dialectic of knowledge, critique, and action to simply knowledge. They argue that critique must be tested against knowledge and that correct knowledge dictates action. In reaction to this positivist approach, the late twentieth-century postmodernist, post-processualist theorists of archaeology have emphasized critique as the purpose of archaeology. They attempt to critically demonstrate how social and political interests construct knowledge. Thus, in a post-processual archaeology, knowledge may become simply legitimation for action. The debate between knowledge and critique implies that we either know a real world or we make it up in our heads.

Different alternative archaeologies, Marxist, feminist, and indigenous, have wrestled with the relationships of reality, critique, and knowledge (Fernández 2006). Childe's modernist Marxist work inspired American archaeologists such as Bruce Trigger, Thomas Patterson, and Philip Kohl, as well as *la arqueología social* of the Spanish-speaking world. In the 1980s, some archaeologists followed Western Marxism and stressed critique and the construction of knowledge. This gave rise to a critical archaeology that developed in harmony with the post-processual critique. In some ways, these two Marxist emphases mirror the differences between processual and post-processual archaeologies. Marxist, feminist, and indigenous archaeologies differ from mainstream approaches, because, in all of them, critique, knowledge, and action remain interdependent in one form or another with praxis. Feminist archaeology began with a program of praxis that critiqued and sought to remake the field of archaeology. Indigenous archaeology emerged from the struggles over repatriation, and indigenous archaeologists have developed praxis to decolonize the discipline.

A dialectical theory of praxis critically engages and builds on all of these approaches. It springs from a view of Marxism as a theory of social relations. It intersects with feminist thought on how we know the world and with indigenous perspectives on how we collaborate with communities. Dialectical knowledge rejects both the optimism that we can objectively know the world and the trepidation that the world is ultimately unknowable. In place of this opposition, it proposes that scholars create knowledge in a complex dialectic between their observations of the real world and their own situatedness within that world. Knowing and critiquing the world come together in a four-way dialectic that evaluates the coherence, correspondence, context, and consequences of knowledge claims. Action comes from both knowledge and critique, and human action transforms the real world and the context of the scholar, thus perpetuating a dialectic of praxis.

V. GORDON CHILDE

V. Gordon Childe was undoubtedly the most prolific of the early modernist archaeologists and probably the most cited archaeologist of the twentieth century (Trigger 1980b). Childe had a great deal to say about the role and importance of knowledge both in the past and in the present. For Childe, praxis springs from knowledge and a correct understanding of how societies change.

Childe turned his attention to the nature of knowledge claims after World War II when the failings of the Bolshevism of the Soviet state became apparent to scholars in the West (McGuire 1992b:25–32). Bolshevists had argued that scholars using a scientific Marxist theory could come to a truer understanding of the world than intellectuals could reach using bourgeois theory. Marxists could ascertain the laws of motion that drive social change. Armed with this knowledge, intellectuals would become the vanguard party that would lead Russia to true communism. Faith in the vanguard party and the assumed prescience of its leadership justified horrible acts that led to the suffering of millions of people. The leaders argued such suffering was in the interest of the common good and was necessary for the attainment of the ultimate goal of a humane socialism. Bit by bit the vanguard party became a new ruling, bureaucratic class. When Stalin came to power in the Soviet Union, this class transformed Marxism into a repressive state ideology that alienated, dominated, and exploited the people and was antithetical to science (Klejn 1993; Sherman 1995:200–205; Trigger 1995a:326; Buchli 1999:77–98).

Childe (1989:15–17) would later call Stalinism "the Marxist perversion of Marxism" (Trigger 1989a:259–263). With this critique Childe became very concerned about the nature of knowledge and how we as scholars create it. He rejected notions of laws that determine social change. He saw "true" knowledge as complexly created and always subject to revision.

In "The Sociology of Knowledge," Childe (1949) argued that the function, structure, and content of knowledge is social and relates to action. The function of knowledge is social, since it provides rules for cooperative social action. The content of knowledge is social, since it provides a working model of the "real world" that must be accurate enough for a society to act. For Childe, the success of these actions proves the "truth" of these rules, and the test of this truth is practice. But a society's knowledge is not always progressive, and critique is necessary to reveal this. For Childe, the convergence between knowledge as a model of the "real world" and a society's means of production provides the measure of that society's fitness to survive.

Individual delusions or social illusions can hamper a society's knowledge or ability to act and progress (Childe 1956:115). In this sense, Childe distinguished between true consciousness as the operational and external correspondence of reality and false consciousness as the absence of this correspondence (Trigger 1980b:139). False consciousness may serve the particular interests of classes or specific groups and at the same time be a buttress to the authority of the ruling class (Childe 1949:308). Thus, individuals and social groups may transform knowledge and science into ideology, and this ideology becomes a brake on the progress of knowledge (Childe 1949:309). Childe saw the development of knowledge as a dialectic in which people achieve true knowledge through the negation of error (Trigger 1980b:141). Childe argued that all scientific knowledge is practical and must furnish rules for action (1979:93). Intellectual pursuits divorced from practical action are the primary impediment to progress and thus are not true knowledge (Trigger 1980b:141).

According to Childe, "The sociological limits of knowledge can be transcended if only so far as to guide the next step in practice. We need not predict what will happen thereafter when ideological distortions have been eliminated by the abolition of classes with class interests" (1949:309). For him, the ultimate goal of scientific history, or the accumulation of practical knowledge of the past, is to "enable the sober citizen to discern the pattern the process has been weaving in the past and from there to estimate how it may be continued in the immediate future" (1947:83).

Childe's ideas influenced archaeology during the second half of the twentieth century, but this influence took very different forms. The architects of the New Archaeology cited Childe as a forebear of their cultural evolutionary approach but did not read his works on history and knowledge. The authors of the manifesto of post-processual archaeology, *Symbolic and Structural Archaeology* (Hodder 1982), explicitly invoked the humanism of Childe as their precedent. For others in England, North America, Latin America, and Spain, Childe's work became the starting point for integrating Marxist ideas into archaeology.

PRAXIS IN THE DOMINANT DEBATE IN ANGLO-AMERICAN ARCHAEOLOGY

At the turn of the twentieth to the twenty-first century, the principal theoretical debate in Anglo-American archaeology is between the processual and post-processual archaeologies. For the last few decades of the twentieth century, a processual approach dominated the archaeology of the United States. The post-processual critique began in England, where Ian Hodder and his students at Cambridge University designed a postmodernist program of archaeology that they called post-processual archaeology.

Processual Archaeology

Processual archaeology developed in the United States and in England from the New Archaeology of the 1960s. Those who practice it embrace a positivistic epistemology science à la Hempel, and they advocate an approach to knowledge of the past based on objective science and nomothetic (lawmaking) deductive reasoning (Redman 1973; Plog 1974). New Archaeologists saw the past as a laboratory to test hypotheses that would produce generalizations governing human behavior. Their science had an

antiauthoritarian edge; that is, hypothesis testing, not the prominence of
the scientist, is what validated or negated a claim. The hypothetical
method made it possible for students to disprove the ideas of their professors or other superiors. The goal of a positivistic science was objective,
value-free knowledge of the past. Most New Archaeologists simply
wished to generalize about the past; however, some embraced the potential of this science to provide insights that could aid the contemporary
world and make it more humane. Such a political program never became
a major part of contemporary processual archaeology. The tension
between the somewhat naive understandings of science as apolitical and
the reality of some New Archaeologists' commitment to causes with
explicit political agendas soon became apparent (Wobst 1989).

Some New Archaeologists took up the 1960s search for "relevance."
They argued that archaeology, often viewed as an arcane practice, must
produce knowledge and insights that can be used by everyone, from aca-
demicians in various disciplines to "the common man" (Fritz 1973;
Redman 1973). They embraced the positivist science of archaeology to
strip away the major barriers to knowledge of the past. They claimed
that if archaeology were freed from narrow, subjective interests, the great
time depth that it entails could provide valuable insights into the present
and be a positive force for change toward a better world (Fritz 1973;
Plog 1974; Wobst 1989). They hoped that a scientific archaeology would
be able to provide tried and true solutions to the world's problems and
guides for future action.

The key to these solutions lay in the ability of archaeologists to dis-
cover the underlying laws of social process and cultural change.
Knowledge of these laws would allow scholars to predict cultural change
(Renfrew 1982:13; Watson et al. 1984:25–26). Armed with this knowledge archaeologists could become social engineers and alter the path of
cultural change to solve social problems (Minnis 1985:2, 14–15).
Despite much initial optimism, these attempts all failed to solve social
problems. Even processual archaeologists came to recognize the failure of
this program to generate general laws of cultural change (Renfrew
1982:8, Salmon 1982:140, McGuire 1992b:121).

New Archaeologists recognized that scholars are situated in a social
context and that individual archaeologists have a psychological desire to
be right. Processualists' anxiety about these biases tended to focus on the
psychological. They argued that the positivist method of hypothesis testing provides a way to control for or eliminate such biases (Hill 1970).
Merrilee Salmon (1982) recognized that social factors affect which

research questions scholars choose and that these social factors have an important effect on the direction and conclusions of research. But Salmon remained confident that the positivist method could provide an objective evaluation of hypotheses so chosen.

Archaeology at the service of humanity's problems requires an active engagement with the world that can hardly be devoid of political content. In order to control for this political bias, the New Archaeologists essentially separated knowledge and critique. Politically inspired critiques of the world led them to seek knowledge; however, given their positivist philosophy, that knowledge had to be independent of critique. The content of archaeological practice during this period remained in a very real sense politically neutral or at best reformist. These archaeologists identified problems, such as regional food shortages and urban overcrowding, that could be "solved" by understanding human behavior or environmental interaction or the two together. This focus ignored larger relations of oppression within a capitalist global system.

Martin and Plog's overview of Arizona archaeology (1973) contains one of the most extensive treatments of archaeology in the service of a better world. In an appendix, Martin and Gregory (1973) apply insights from Puebloan archaeology to the problems of poverty and violence in urban ghettos. After an impassioned discussion of these contemporary problems, the authors suggest that ghetto populations should disperse in the face of resource stress, as aboriginal peoples in the southwest United States did. While they recognize the modern limitations imposed by social prejudice and economic factors on contemporary conditions and future dispersal, they seem naively optimistic that the mere act of dispersal will help to resolve this oppression and the racism that feeds it.

Paul Minnis's archaeological study of food stress (1985) also focuses on practical universal solutions for a significant problem of contemporary global society. In that study, Minnis developed a theory of food stress and cultural change based on the prehistoric Mimbris culture of southwestern New Mexico. He presents this theory in the hope that it will have a practical application to all human groups. The theory successfully integrates ecological and social factors, but its stress on adaptation provides little insight into the global political factors that create food stress.

Although these two examples of praxis in processual archaeology probably do not exhaust such cases, a long list of similar examples is difficult to compose. It is also difficult to identify any specific instance in which policy makers actually applied archaeologically generated laws of cultural change to contemporary social problems. This is probably for the best. These interpretations of cultural processes are too tentative, insecure, and incomplete to use as a basis for decisions that directly affect the real welfare of people.

Some processualist attempts at relevance have had an impact on the world. Bill Rathje's garbage project used archaeological methods to study modern trash (Rathje and Murphy 1992). The project produced a wealth of practical insights about the composition of trash, household consumption practices, and the lack of decomposition of materials in landfills. These insights have helped to shape public policies about consumption, nutrition, and waste disposal. In Bolivia archaeologists excavated and reconstructed raised field systems in the 1980s and then cooperated with development workers to reintroduce this agricultural technique to a local indigenous peasantry (Swartley 2002). The use of archaeological methods to address practical issues in the Garbage Project and in Bolivia does have "relevance" and did create useful knowledge. But these projects did not produce the laws of social process and cultural change that processual archaeology sought. In the Bolivian example, farmers abandoned the raised fields within a decade, because the practice and social organization of the modern fields reflected preconceived notions of Latin American indigenous peoples (Swartley 2002:6). In the end, both projects' emphasis on practical knowledge was not transformative and, thus, not praxis.

Processual archaeologists' excursions into praxis had little or no real impact on the world. Probably for this reason, contemporary archaeologists have largely forgotten those excursions. Processualists did, however, establish a precedent for a politically engaged archaeology that seeks to effect a more humane world. But in following their precedent, we need to recognize the dangers inherent in the instrumentalist nature of their approach, when isolated problems amenable to modifications of human behavior require no major transformation in political and economic relations, just tinkering. The processualists did not build a critique that was informed by knowledge and united with action but, instead, sought instrumental solutions. Scientists use instrumentalist theory to gain power over what they study (Meskell and Pels 2005:4–10). Such theory gives those in power control of nature and people. Positivist social engineering presents the same dangers as those in the notion of the vanguard party. These dangers begin in the hubris that we can objectively know the world apart from our own position and interests in that world. Such hubris risks self-deception and has been used to justify actions that are destructive of people and society.

At the same time that the processual archaeologists were attempting to build a positivist praxis of archaeology, many scientists, international agencies, and nations had embarked on one of the most massive social engineering projects of the twentieth century. The "Green Revolution" sought to transform the Third World by exporting a scientific agriculture of irrigation, mechanization, and hybrid crops. In countries like India and Pakistan, these efforts were dismal failures that increased poverty, landlessness, and social inequality. Cultural anthropologists and others have criticized the Green Revolution for failing to take into account both the larger colonial context of the project and the specific cultures of the places it was implemented (Bodley 1983:141–144; Perkins 1998). As these criticisms grew, they became a more fundamental questioning of social engineering as at best paternalistic and at worst malicious (Poggie and Lynch 1974; Hobart 1993).

Post-processual Archaeology and Praxis

Post-processual archaeology developed in England during the 1980s. Like the larger current of postmodernism of which it is a part, it rejected any totalizing "metanarrative" and drew from an eclectic range of theories to arrive at a mélange of ideas (Fernández 2006:21–53). Post-processual archaeologists advocate a praxis of radical relativism. Their relativism is radical in two senses: it rejects the illusion of objectivity, or "true" knowledge, as the source of domination and oppression in the world, and these archaeologists hope it can transform the social relations of domination and oppression that exist in the world.

Post-processualist archaeology primarily focuses on critique. Christopher Tilley argued that "archaeology should not primarily be concerned with the past for its own sake and as a means of escape from the socio-political reality of the present, but with using the past as a basis for strategic intervention in the present" (1989:105). Post-processualist critique attempts to expose the situated nature of knowledge. Because knowledge is socially situated, multiple interpretations of the past exist and reflect the contemporary sociopolitical situation of each interpreter (Shanks and Tilley 1992). Thus, the interpretive process does not produce "true" knowledge but, rather, a revelation of the subjectivities of knowing.

Post-processualists reject the search for objective knowledge of the past and instead highlight the Western capitalist biases that pervaded the processual perspective (Shanks and Tilley 1992; Tilley 1989). They claim that archaeologists come to the data with a set of "prejudgments" that include things such as the definitions of terms, goals, assumptions, expected answers, tools, standards of measurement, methods, skills, and the social and political context of our research (Hodder 1999:32–33). These prejudgments matter and have a lasting effect on conclusions. Post-processualists reject the positivist notion that the method of testing hypotheses can create a moment in the research process that holds these prejudgments in abeyance (Hodder 1999:62–63). Archaeologists' starting points will always influence their conclusions and the directions of future research.

Processual archaeologists and classical Marxists have frequently accused post-processualists of an extreme relativism, in which political partisanship dominates the research process and no "true" knowledge is possible (Kohl 1985; Schiffer 1988; Renfrew 1989; Thomas 1990; Trigger 1995a, 1995b). To make such accusations is to kick a straw dog. The post-processualist movement began with critiques of objectivity that overstressed the relative nature of knowledge (Hodder 1984; Tilley 1989). More recently, however, post-processualists have turned to considerations of the role of reality in knowledge claims. Most post-processualists would acknowledge that archaeological data place limits on all interpretations, and Hodder has argued that interpretations should be "theory led" (1999:62–63). Post-processual archaeologists fit theory and data together in a hermeneutic circle, linking knowledge, theory, and ethical or moral standpoints to arrive at interpretations (Hodder 1999:62–65). The claim that contemporary post-processualists espouse an extreme relativism that makes all interpretations of the past acceptable is, therefore, incorrect. However, even though their hermeneutic circle is more data led than many critics allow, the role of data remains weak. The weak role that the post-processualists give data in interpretation may not allow for the most effective praxis of archaeology.

Post-processualists advocate multivocality as the key to praxis (Hodder 1999). They argue that many different ways of knowing the past exist and that power relations play a greater role than data in which of those interpretations are heard. Thus, praxis lies in giving voice to the voiceless or in letting all voices be heard. Praxis becomes radical if the voices that are heard are the suppressed voices of the disenfranchised. Multivocality requires that archaeologists surrender their authority and claims of privileged knowledge. With this surrender of authority and privilege, no social engineering or vanguard party can occur, and therefore, our efforts will not have pernicious consequences.

A post-processual praxis can be divided into two parts (Hodder 1999). First comes the critique that breaks down the authority of the archaeologist as a knower of the past and that eliminates the scholar's hegemonic control of the archaeological process. This creates a stage and an opportunity for other voices. Second comes the archaeologist's provision of multiple representations of the archaeological record that can be read in various ways. This provisioning of representations involves more than just a compendium of data, because for the post-processualists data do not exist separately from interpretation. Interpretation begins at the trowel's edge. Thus, the only way to let multiple voices speak is to involve them from the very beginning and at every stage of the research process.

The post-processual notion of praxis has much of value, but in the end it does not work as an emancipatory praxis of archaeology. The post-processualists' goals of empowerment and transformative practice share much with the goals of this book. The dialectical knowledge that I espouse builds on the critiques that the post-processualists have made of the subjectivities of knowledge. Dialectical knowledge also parallels the process of "fitting" that Hodder advocates to evaluate correspondence in knowledge claims (1999:30–66). But, the post-processualists underestimate the complexity of the craft of archaeology and overestimate the ability of individuals not trained in that craft to make sense of the representations that archaeologists produce. Their theoretical focus on the individual does not lead to effective action, and it unwittingly reinforces the dominant ideology of twenty-first-century capitalism (Fantasia and Voss 2004:9). Radical relativism and multivocality give little guidance on how to decide between competing voices. Different voices exist in relationship to one another and to social contexts. Some voices seek to silence others and maintain the powerful, while other voices challenge inequities. In the absence of relational criteria to distinguish one voice from another, multivocality may be harmful, because it leaves the stage open for oppressive voices.

Perhaps the best example of an attempt at multivocality and of the problems that it can create is Ian Hodder's project at Çatalhöyük. Hodder (1998, 2000, 2006) has made the Neolithic site of Çatalhöyük in Turkey the high-tech showplace of excavation for post-processual archaeology. This site is well known in Europe as one of the earliest towns in the world. Eco-feminists and goddess worshipers regard it as an ancient center of the cult of the goddess. The project seeks to produce a multivocal archaeology that includes the perspectives of various archaeologists and of a global general public. It attempts to do this by making available all possible data and interpretations so that each individual can derive his or her own conclusions about the site. The Çatalhöyük Web site (http://catal.arch.cam.ac.uk/catal/catal.html) contains reams of archaeological data that even a professional would be hard-pressed to make sense of. This would seem to inhibit rather than enhance the ability of individuals and groups to use these data to create empowering interpretations. Moreover, even if nonprofessional individuals and groups could read and interpret archaeological texts, again, how do they choose between the competing texts?

Several aspects of the post-processualists' theory seem to inhibit or limit their goal of empowerment. Most post-processualists have embraced a mixed bag of postmodernist theory that has led them to focus on questions of individual agency and identity. This spotlight on the individual has led to a literature littered with statements about why the individual matters (Meskell 1999, 2002b; Hodder 2000; Shanks and Tilley 1987; Johnson 1989). This literature often identifies the active individual as the only force capable of creating cultural change. Although the goal of post-processualist archaeology is to empower people in the present through critique and the provision of space for multiple interpretations, post-processualists' focus on individuals seems to deny these abilities. Individuals are truly empowered only through solidarity and collective agency. Postmodernist and post-processual theorists would have us believe that their positions are radical and transformative of capitalism (Shanks and Tilley 1987). However, since postmodern theorists have accepted one of the most important foundational myths of capitalism, the autonomous individual, this approach cannot be radical or transformative (J. Thomas 2000, 2004:122). Some authors have argued that the postmodernist focus on the individual fits rather nicely as a component of the dominant ideology of globalization and fast capitalism (Eagleton 1996; Harvey 2000; Larrain 1995; Zavarzadeh 1995; Wurst and McGuire 1999; J. Thomas 2000; McGuire and Wurst 2002; Agger 2004; Fantasia and Voss 2004:9). Others have been more outspoken, claiming that the postmodern foundation of post-processualism is the dominant ideology of twenty-first-century fast capitalism and globalization (Jameson 1992; Hawkes 2003:10; Hardt and Negri 2000; Žižek 1994:17).

Archaeologists often find themselves confronted by conflicting voices about the past. The post-processualists provide us with little guidance in how to choose among these voices (Wylie 2002:190–191). Barbara

Bender's dialogues with Hodder about her involvement in the travelers' protests against their exclusion from Stonehenge illustrate this quandary (Bender 1998). Hodder essentially questions whether this is really important political action. Bender's response, that we have to start somewhere, is somewhat unsatisfying. Hodder has also questioned the use of archaeology in relation to goddess worship and the men's and eco-feminist movements, which frequently only seem to reaffirm contemporary middle-class searches for identity and self-fulfillment (Hodder 1999; see also Bender 1998; Meskell 1998). Here we meet the central irony of post-processualist archaeology: the tension between its goals of interpreting individual agency and identity in the past, and its focus on critique and multiple interpretations, which question the authority of the archaeologist as interpreter. Divorced from any theoretical metanarrative that would provide insight into the relevance of competing knowledge claims, post-processualist archaeology is devoid of the power to contest interpretations that uphold existing conditions.

Archaeologists should not wish to let every voice speak (Kohl 2004:297–298). Some voices are pernicious, such as those that spoke in the Nazi Gestapo headquarters and in the torture rooms of the Club Atlético, in Buenos Aires. Multivocality has the danger of denying or masking the power of the powerful. We must be able to judge some voices as pernicious, because the real human cost of not doing so is too great. A relational multivocality that critically examines the power relations among voices and the consequences of each voice speaking offers a means to decide which voices are pernicious. In a relational multivocality, archaeologists will retain some authority to say when interpretations are in error or immoral. Yet in making these judgments, we must also avoid the dangers of social engineering and the vanguard party.

ALTERNATIVE ARCHAEOLOGIES AND PRAXIS

The dominant debate in Anglo-American archaeology does not encompass the full range of theoretical positions that exist on praxis in archaeology. Marxist, feminist, and indigenous alternative archaeologies have also engaged this issue. In the dominant debates, participants may simply lump these alternatives under the mantle of post-processual archaeology (Redman 1991; Hegmon 2003). This lumping obscures the variation that exists in these positions and ignores the contributions they can make to the debate. These alternative archaeologies provide some of our best examples of praxis and starting points for resolving the opposition between relativism and objectivity that so befuddles the processualists and post-processualists (Fernández 2006). Classical Marxists in the Hispanic and Anglophone worlds take a modernist position that emphasizes objective knowledge of the world but also address the subjectivities of knowing that affect the creation of knowledge. Critical archaeologists engage in a critique of knowledge creation but also test their critique by evaluating how effectively it influences human action. Feminist archaeologists engage in a gendered praxis that struggles to transform the discipline of archaeology and society. Indigenous archaeologists confront colonialism and seek to decolonize archaeology.

Praxis in Hispanic Archaeology: La arqueología social

Hispanic archaeologists created *la arqueología social* as a reaction to both the descriptive cultural historical approach that dominated Latin American and Spanish archaeology in the late 1960s and Anglo-American processual archaeology (McGuire and Navarrete 1999, 2004; Benavidas 2001; Politas 2003). They argue for a scientific approach and increased rigor both in method and in the formulation and testing of research questions. Their science, however, has been based in a Marxist materialist dialectic and not in positivism (Bate 1998; Lull 2000; Lumbreras 2005). They criticize the New Archaeology for its functionalism, its unilineal evolutionary theory, and its lack of political consciousness (Gándara 1980; Castro et al. 1992).

In Latin America, *la arqueología social* began with the question, Archaeology for whom? (*Arqueología para quien?*) (Panameno and Nalda 1978). This group of archaeologists expresses a profound concern for the social and political roles of archaeology, and they seek to build a Marxist praxis in archaeology. They stress the development of methods, categories, and concepts to gain a scientific understanding of the past from the archaeological record. Like the North American processualists, they began with the scientific conviction that the transformation of social relations in the present depends on a true knowledge of the past and of general historical processes.

Practitioners of *la arqueología social* found their inspiration for archaeology as a social science in the work of Marx and V. Gordon Childe, but they realized that these works could not be applied directly to the aboriginal history of Latin America (Lorenzo et al., 1976:6; Vargas and Sanoja 1999:60; Lumbreras 2005:28). Marx had formulated his concepts in the study of European capitalism, and Childe had developed theories to account for European prehistory and the development of the classical world. The culture history of Latin America varies from these examples in levels of development, in modes of production, and in historical specifics. Because of this, the Latin Americans have developed an elaborate scheme for categorizing cultural differences and social change in order to apply Marxism to the aboriginal history of Latin America.

The purpose of this scheme is to gain a "true" knowledge of the past. *Arqueólogos sociales* value knowledge of the past as the base for a critically informed effort to transform the present. As Vargas and Sanoja state, "The fundamental aim of social archaeology is the critical study of history as a dialectical process, considering the past as that which determines the present and, conversely, the present as the source of the manipulation of the past" (1999:70).

A pragmatic and programmatic emphasis on praxis springs from the substantive theory of Latin American social archaeology built on a classic vision of historical materialism. This view gives primacy to the material conditions of life over social consciousness. It emphasizes social and technical relations of production as determining the form of society and how it changes. From this perspective, the ability of humans to transform nature is the basis for change in all social processes and in all historical moments. By linking the theory of the past with a critique of the present, these scholars seek to demonstrate that contemporary class inequality and imperialism are connected to that past. More important, they argue that just as people changed their social conditions in the past, so too can people change these conditions in the present (Vargas 1990).

Between 1984 and 1987, Mario Sanoja and Iraida Vargas developed the Museo del Hombre Venezolano within the Universidad Central de Venezuela, in Caracas, as a form of praxis (McGuire and Navarrete 1999, 2004). The museum proposed an alternative history of Venezuela that stressed social processes more than events, social groups more than heroes, struggles and contradictions more than accomplishments, and progress and the construction of national identity more than legendary anecdotes. The first and only exhibition, "Three Cultures, One Nation," sought to challenge the official state history. The exhibit emphasized the continuity of processes over an immense span of time, and it represented a clear break with elitist, Eurocentric, official, hegemonic history.

In the end, however, the museum was not a success, because it failed to capture the interest of the public. The exhibit also suffered from insufficient critique. Even though the exhibit explicitly confronted the hegemonic national history of Venezuela, some of the concepts embedded in the exhibit and in its title, "Three Cultures, One Nation," ran the danger of reinforcing nationalist notions of creolization (McGuire and Navarrete 1999:101–102). European elites of Latin American countries have used the ideology of creolization to co-opt and diminish the political potential of racial groups (Badillo 1995; Sorensen 1997; Alonso 1995). Although the exhibit presented an explicit critique of creolization, implicitly it continued to spread the same ideology of cultural and racial equivalence by asserting that Indian, European, and African cultures formed a single nation.

La arqueología social has profoundly affected Latin American archaeology but has had less success in its goal of praxis (McGuire and Navarrete 1999, 2004). La arqueología social has had a substantial impact on academic archaeology in the autonomous universities of Latin America (with the exception of those in Chile and Argentina) and some limited influence in North America (McGuire 1992b; Patterson 1994; Ensor 2000). In the autonomous universities, la arqueología social has trained several generations of students who today dominate Latin American archaeology and intellectual circles. Outside the university, however, Latin American states control the presentation of archaeology as part of a national heritage and as a tool of nationalist ideology (Patterson 1995a). Critiques of this nationalist archaeology by arqueólogos sociales have not resulted in its transformation (Gándara 1992).

In Spain, the death of the dictator Franco in 1975 and the subsequent collapse of the Fascist Party allowed for the development of Marxist approaches in archaeology. As in Latin America, Marxist archaeologists formulated their theory in reaction both to an entrenched cultural historical approach in their country and to the Anglo-American New Archaeology (Vázquez and Risch 1991). Marxism became a major theoretical movement in Spanish archaeology, with research groups in three Spanish universities (Gassiot et al. 1999; Gassiot and Palomar 2000). One of the most creative and internationally influential of these groups has been at the Catalán Universitat Autònoma de Barcelona.

The research group in Barcelona adopted an explicitly scientific archaeology that focused on the history and evolution of socioeconomic formations, the levels of development of productive forces, and the complexity of relations of production (Vázquez and Risch 1991:37). In this work, they have integrated Marxist and feminist approaches into a theory of the production of social life (Castro et al. 1998; Sanahuja 2002). This theory begins with the assumption that social life requires the existence of three objective conditions: men, women, and material objects.

They use an all-inclusive notion of production that views men and women as both the products and the producers of society. Their theoretical framework is highly structured with a typology of production that includes basic production of human beings, object production of food and other products intended for consumption, and maintenance production that increases the social value of things without altering their use value. The Cataláns posit a dialectical relationship between production and property, a relationship that forms the internal dynamic that drives social transformation.

Like *la arqueología social* of Latin America, the Spanish Marxists regard a correct knowledge of the past as the necessary basis for praxis. The first generation of Spanish Marxists struggled to transform Spanish universities from ideology factories of the Fascist state into centers for the critical study of the social world. They confronted right-wing ideology in the traditional intellectual settings of the university classroom and the museum and in the published word. They proposed alternative interpretations of the ancient past that reveal the errors in the established discourse and in the written critiques of the social and political context of its production (Estévež and Vila 1999, 2006).

The contemporary generation of Marxist Catalán archaeologists have taken their archaeology to the masses in a popular praxis of archaeology. This praxis parallels the approach advocated in this book, as the Cataláns seek to undertake archaeological research that serves the interests of specific communities. For example, in the late 1990s, university students worked with Barcelona citizens to identify, map, and record Spanish Civil War bomb shelters in order to sustain the communal memory of the resistance to fascism. Currently archaeologists from the Universitat Autònoma de Barcelona are launching a program of forensic excavation in mass graves from the Spanish Civil War to document the atrocities of that war and to return the bodies of the victims to their families (Gassiot 2005; Gassiot et al. 2005).

In Nicaragua, Catalán archaeologists have worked with the Unión Cooperativas Agropecuarias de Miraflor and the Universidad Nacional Autónoma de Nicaragua, in Managua, to develop an academic research program that is integrated with the interests of the agricultural cooperative at Miraflor (Gassiot and Palomar 2000). The project has involved collaboration with the cooperative members in the design, execution, and interpretation of archaeological research. The Miraflor project builds a popular heritage for Nicaragua. It uses archaeology to integrate the interests of Nicaraguan intellectuals and *camposinos*, to reinforce and support the Nicaraguan cooperative movement that is under assault by conservative forces.

Classical Marxism and Praxis in North America

Childe influenced a generation of archaeologists who have continued his focus on Marxist theory in North America (Trigger 1984b, 1985, 1993b; Muller 1997; Patterson 2003). From Childe they have taken the idea that praxis should follow from correct knowledge of the world, as well as the realization that such knowledge is always tentative. They have critiqued both the processual and the post-processual archaeologies.

North American Marxist archaeologists reject the basic tenets of the New Archaeology. In the works of V. Gordon Childe, the late Bruce Trigger (1978) found the critical dialectic between history and evolution, theory and data, and mentalism and materialism that he thought lacking in the New Archaeology. In the early 1960s, Thomas Patterson (1973, 1989) came in contact with Marxist political thought in Peru. He increasingly saw it as a useful theoretical perspective for archaeology. By the 1970s, Marxism had attracted the interest of only a handful U.S. archaeologists (Gilman 1989:63). Among these was Phil Kohl, who, in the 1970s, turned to Marx as an alternative to processual archaeological approaches to exchange and production (Kohl 1975).

These North American Marxists reject the New Archaeology's separation of critique, knowledge, and action, recognizing the subjective nature of knowledge and the political role knowledge plays in human affairs (Trigger 1995a:328–329). They have written numerous critical historical analyses of archaeology that discuss how archaeological thought developed in social and political contexts and served specific interest (Patterson 1986, 1989, 1994, 1995b, 2003; Trigger 1980b, 1984a, 1989a, 2006). They see Marxism as a theory that can explain human behavior and provide guidance for a revolutionary praxis to transform the world. Kohl (1985:115) argues that archaeology can capture a real past, but only through an active dialogue that involves a critique of our research and of the social and political context of that research. This process arrives at knowledge through a never-ending series of approximations. Praxis then follows from this knowledge.

Among these scholars, Bruce Trigger most explicitly considered the linkages among epistemology, critique, and praxis. Trigger described himself as a moderate realist (Trigger 1989b, 1995a, 2003b). He recognized the subjectivities of knowledge that arise from the situatedness of knowing in social and political contexts. He rejected the positivist notion that social scientists can use method to control and moderate these subjectivities. For Trigger, scholars can attain "true" knowledge only if they overtly challenge these subjectivities as part of the research process.

Trigger wrote much on the subjectivities of archaeological research and knowledge. He critically examined how North American archaeologists' assumptions of unchanging Indian people mislead them in their interpretations of the aboriginal past (Trigger 1980a). He identified three global approaches to archaeology that are determined by a country's position in the capitalist world system: nationalist, colonialist, and imperialist (Trigger 1984a). In each approach he demonstrated how archaeology incorporated the aspirations, fears, and goals of the dominant classes of the society. In both editions of his historical opus, *A History of Archaeological Thought* (Trigger 1989a, 2006), he linked the development of archaeology to the rise of the bourgeois classes in the West. The bourgeoisie embraced archaeology as a means to create mythic charters that legitimate both the nation-states they have created and the notion of a Western civilization superior to other civilizations (see also Patterson 1997). In these critiques, Trigger sought to reveal the false ideology that has shaped archaeological thought and knowledge, so that scholars can strip it away and find "true" knowledge.

Trigger's historical analysis shows scholars that archaeology reflects the interests of specific classes or communities. This revelation debunks the processualists' definition of archaeology as a method to obtain objective (that is, context-free) understandings of the processes of cultural change. Some archaeologists have used this revelation to create archaeologies that serve the interest of communities other than the bourgeois classes and thus weld archaeology as an instrument to challenge the powerful rather than legitimate them (Shanks and McGuire 1996). Archaeologists have developed feminist (Hays-Gilpin and Whitley 1998; Franklin 2002; Conkey 2005a), indigenous (Watkins 2000; Smith and Wobst 2005), and working-class (McGuire and Reckner 2003; Shackel and Palus 2006; Saitta 2007) archaeologies, among others. Trigger ultimately sought to transform the social world through his scholarship (1993a, 1998:192–193, 2003a, 2003c). He urged scholars to struggle for a society that is technologically advanced, culturally diverse, egalitarian in both its economy and its politics, and in which all people share in both the rewards and the responsibilities of living on this earth.

Trigger (1989b:790) had confidence that as long as social scientists do not ignore it, "true" knowledge will prevail over ideology. His confidence comes from the belief that the weight of true knowledge works against ideology: true knowledge resists the subjectivities of knowing. For Trigger, scholars attain true knowledge in a two-part process: they critically identify the subjectivities of knowing, and they accumulate data that will challenge the pernicious uses of history that come from those subjectivities. Like Childe, Trigger realizes that the material world of archaeology and the data we generate do not exist independent of thought. Only by struggling to find a fit between our views of reality and the material world can we generate data and true understanding. Trigger recognizes that this is an inexact and imperfect process. The social, political, and ideological subjectivities of knowing heavily affect the process, but the process remains capable of generating, and being shaped by, our cumulative knowledge of the past.

Trigger's last ten years of scholarship culminated in his book *Understanding Early Civilizations* (Trigger 2003c). He argued that humans in small-scale societies are not inherently altruistic but rather that they maintain egalitarian relations through ridicule, gossip, and fear of witchcraft. Thus, hunter-gatherer societies demonstrate that social and political egalitarianism is possible in human societies, but they do not provide a blueprint for the future. Trigger's historically comparative cross-cultural study of early civilizations indicates that these small-scale mechanisms fail with a scalar increase in social complexity. He argued that institutionalized political, social, and economic inequality inevitably results from social evolutionary changes that necessitate high-level decision making. Trigger maintained that this necessity, however, does not explain why managerial elites appropriate heavy surpluses for their own use. He concluded that people cannot create more just societies by simply removing the corrupting influences of a mode of production such as capitalism. Rather, social scientists have to imagine and design control mechanisms that will work in technologically advanced large-scale societies in a manner analogous to the role of ridicule, gossip, and fear of witchcraft in small-scale societies.

Critical Archaeology and Praxis

Independent of the classical Marxists' reading of Childe, a new generation of North American archaeologists read Western Marxism in the 1970s and 1980s. These archaeologists differ from the classical Marxists in their wish to build praxis through critique and consciousness raising rather than from a "true" knowledge of the world. The critical archaeology developed at the same time as and with much fruitful interaction with post-processual archaeology. Mark Leone's critical archaeology derived from an understanding of French structural Marxism and the Frankfurt School (Palus et al. 2006).

Leone began his critical archaeology with the problem of ideology. Following Althusser, he wondered why our taken-for-granted assumptions about the world permeate every aspect of daily life and why they work so effectively to uphold dominant interests while making true knowledge of class interests difficult. Leone sought to expose the workings of ideology in modern capitalist society: "to understand the past in order to create a consciousness of modern society" (Leone 1986:431). He hoped to raise the consciousness of people about the ideological nature of capitalist society so that they would struggle to change it: critique and knowledge lead to action. As Leone and Little state, we need to understand "things historically to be able to know consciously or criticize the society we live in now" (1993:162). Leone and Potter (1999) continued this mission in *Historical Archaeologies of Capitalism*, which expresses one of the clearest and strongest statements about American historical archaeology as political action. In that same volume, Wylie (1999) passionately argues that we have to study capitalism in order to comprehend a present that is based on exploitative social relations and to provide alternatives to those relations.

To move from theory to praxis, Leone (2005) used the Annapolis project, which, in 1981, began questioning the ideological construction of Annapolis, Maryland. Protestant English colonists established Annapolis in 1650 C.E., and throughout the eighteenth century it was an important sociopolitical and cultural center of the North American colonies. It has been the capital of Maryland since 1695, and numerous important figures of the U.S. Revolution lived in or visited the city. Today the city uses this history to attract tourists, making heritage tourism its major industry. The Annapolis project sought to reveal the contradictions and social inequalities that the hegemonic history of the city obscured on paper, in reconstructed and restored buildings, and in the ground (Leone et al. 1987; Leone 1995). The project organizers sought to create a participatory experience that would engage tourists in a critical reflection of the colonial history of the United States.

Reading the popular history of Annapolis, project scholars concluded that this history is fragmented and that it reflects a nationalist ideology (Palus et al. 2006). The popular history sunders the temporal and cultural continua of the city from the eighteenth and nineteenth centuries and obscures the relationship between Euro-Americans and African Americans. This dismembering reinforces a static and harmonious vision of the U.S. past and justifies the inequalities of the modern community. These archaeologists took up Althusser's (1969) notion of a dominant ideology that creates a false consciousness for all members of society. They sought to challenge this ideology by demonstrating to the tourists that the history and the "historic" Annapolis that they encounter has been "falsely" constructed. The project used guided tours of the historic center of the city and of project excavations to demonstrate how the hegemonic history has been constructed and to reveal the inequalities and exploitation of the past (Leone and Potter 1984). The archaeologists stressed how industrialization led to the increased consumption of goods and created the division between those who could acquire such goods and others who were marginalized in this consumption. They also emphasized how common goods used in daily life served to establish and enforce social divisions in the formation of the United States.

In the end, the Annapolis project's challenge to the hegemonic history of the city failed to sweep away the official history and the cultural and social relations that produce it (Potter 1994; Leone 1995). The tourists generally responded to the alternative vision that the project offered by reinterpreting this vision in terms of their preconceptions derived directly from the ideology under critique. The archaeologists wanted to demonstrate the relationship between past inequalities and contemporary relations of discrimination. The visitors, however, were fascinated by the exotic and odd features of the past. Their responses focused on the unusual, the monumental, and the extraordinary and expressed assumptions directly derived from a capitalist ideology. Tour participants were preoccupied with the value of objects, the time necessary to produce goods, and their availability in the market.

This range of responses should not have been surprising, given the background of the tourists who visit Annapolis and the types of historical interpretations that they have already internalized. In general, people engaged in heritage tourism are members of the professional middle classes of U.S. society (McGuire 1992b). The fact that Annapolis is a high-end tourist destination only amplifies this trend. This example demonstrates that relationships of power affect the distribution of knowledge within society. Leone, following Lukács (1971), noted that a hegemonic ideology reifies and distorts the history produced for the mass of people. This history naturalizes and makes universal the inequalities and forms of exploitation that exist in the past and the present. Clearly, in Annapolis, the privileged classes of U.S. society did not question hegemonic history even when presented with alternatives.

As a result of this experience, Leone (1995, 2005) adopted Habermas's (1984) notion of communicative action. He recognized that the people who were alienated by the contradictions, inequalities, and exploitation in society would be the most open to alternative histories. He therefore shifted the focus of the research in Annapolis to an African American community within the city and to a project that actively incorporates members of that community (Leone 2005). Archaeologists did not assume that they knew the interests of the community. Instead, the archaeologists actively worked with its members to develop an alternative historical discourse that meets the interests of both parties. This process of cooperation revealed to the archaeologists how African Americans also assume the symbols and beliefs of the hegemonic ideology but on their own terms and only after giving these symbols and beliefs their own meaning (Mullins 1999).

Feminism and Praxis

Feminism has the capability to transform society (Mohanty 2003). As Maria Franklin has stated, "The point of employing feminist theorizing in general is to produce scholarship that leads to social change" (2001:114). Like Marxists, feminists evaluate the structures of power and ideology that exist in society (Conkey 2005a). Feminists, however, ask, "How much of what is going on here is caused by the workings of patriarchy?" (Enloe 2004:7). Through this question, they critically seek to understand how male privilege springs from controlling women or mobilizing their complicity or both (Enloe 2004:7). This understanding then becomes a starting point for a praxis to challenge and eliminate the control and complicity of patriarchy and thus transform society.

Feminism has been a significant locus of praxis within the discipline of archaeology (Conkey 2005a). For a feminist archaeology to exist, it had to first confront a powerful androcentric bias in archaeology and provide alternatives to it. Today we might ask why archaeologists did not seriously take up the study of gender until the 1980s (Conkey and Spector 1984), long after such research had become commonplace in cultural anthropology, history, and sociology. Throughout human history, social relations have always been gendered, because human societies must include both men and women. How could archaeology, with its studies of long-term change in human societies and its comparative methods, ignore gender? There is really only one answer to this question, and it has to do with the powerful androcentric bias of the field (Gero 1983; Wylie 1991; Gilchrist 1994:1–4; Gamble 2001:30–31).

Androcentric bias has pervaded both the interpretation of the past and the practice of archaeology (Sanahuja 2002; Voss 2006). Archaeological interpretation has largely focused on the image of active male hunters, chiefs, kings, builders, and farmers in opposition to the image of passive female gatherers, child bearers, food processors, and homemakers (Gero 1983; Conkey and Spector 1984). Archaeologists have created and reinforced these images of active men and passive women, which have in turn reinforced broader gender stereotypes in U.S. society. Before the mid-1970s, many male professors actively and explicitly discouraged women from entering the field of archaeology, because they saw women as unprepared for the rigors and physical demands of fieldwork (Kehoe 1998:ix). Instead, they encouraged women to become cultural anthropologists or to stay in the laboratory (read kitchen) (Gero 1985). Ivor Noel-Hume, in a rare published example of these attitudes, wrote: "Digging is, after all a masculine occupation, and while more women than men are likely to do well in the pot washing shed or in the laboratory, shovel wielding women are not everyday sights in Western society" (1969:60). This bias directly affected the ability of women to advance in the field (Gero 1985).

Conkey and Gero (1991:5) have identified three goals for a feminist archaeology: to expose gender bias in archaeological inquiry; to find women in the archaeological record and to identify their participation in gender relations, gender ideologies, and gender roles; and to challenge underlying assumptions in Western culture about gender and difference. This is a program of praxis that calls for a radical transformation of archaeology.

Processual archaeologists ignored gender in the past by assuming that gender relations are given in nature, that is, that male and female roles originated with the biological evolution of the human species and that they have been unchanged from that point on (Conkey and Williams 1991). The processualists assumed that men would always hunt (engage in productive activities) and women would always gather (engage in reproductive activities) (Gero 1985). They also assumed that changes in men's productive activities (hunting, farming, building, etc.) drove cultural change and evolution, while the tasks of reproduction (cooking, caring for children, and cleaning) remained basically unchanged. The neo-evolutionary theory that they embraced made gender inequality a

given and unchanging facet of human existence. One of the most popular evolutionary sequences in processual archaeology is Morton Fried's
(1967) sequence of egalitarian, ranked, and stratified societies. Fried
defines an egalitarian society as one in which the only inequalities that
exist are those of sex and age. That which does not change (in this case
universal gender inequality) does not require study and becomes the
unexamined category (women) in research.

Feminist archaeologists challenged the assumption that gender is given
in nature through critique and by seeking knowledge based on that critique (Gilchrist 1994, 1999; Sanahuja 2002). Much of their first volley of
work pointed out the strong androcentric bias in archaeology (Gero
1983, 1985; Conkey and Spector 1984; Conkey and Williams 1991). At
the same time, feminist scholars undertook many case studies to reveal
variation in gender roles in the past and the active participation of
women in the course of cultural change (Sanahuja 2002). Brumfiel's
(1991) demonstration that women's work of tortilla making and weaving was central to the formation and maintenance of the Aztec state is a
classic example.

Recently some archaeologists have enlisted queer theory to study sexuality as a shaping essential of social life (Schmidt and Voss 2000; Joyce
2004; Voss 2006:121–122). Like gender, sexuality is an omnipresent
aspect of social life that archaeologists have largely ignored (Dowson
2000). The first step to an archaeology of sexuality has been to propose
our common knowledge of sexuality as a topic of research. Scholars
enlisting queer theory argue that archaeologists need to consider sexuality in all of its variations and to challenge the assumption of heterosexu-
ality as the given or natural variant (Meskell 2002a:283).

Feminist critiques of science and the subjectivities of knowing contributed to the critiques of positivism. Feminist archaeologists asked, If
the positivist method is value free and self-correcting of error, how is it
that the processual archaeology was so riddled with gender stereotypes
and androcentric biases (Wylie 1991, 2002:185–199)? Like the post-
processualists and Marxists, feminists recognized that scholars with different standpoints as a result of their gender, race, or class position in
society will draw different conclusions to produce knowledge (Wylie
1991; Gilchrist 1999:17–30). Some feminists have argued that a female
standpoint privileges the study of gender (Harding 1986; Taylor
1990:35; Mohanty 2003:231–232).

Wylie (1991) has questioned this privileging of standpoints, because it
assumes a universal standpoint (i.e., a universal womanhood) that can-

not really exist. Each person exists in a social space defined by multiple social relations and contradictions. No specific standpoint can encompass the social whole or even the social position of an individual scholar. She argues that instead of privileging specific standpoints, scholars need to embrace a diversity of points of view. With this diversity some standpoints may give a clearer understanding of a specific issue than others, but no one standpoint will give a complete or "true" picture of the world. We thus gain by including multiple standpoints in our construction of knowledge. She also asks us to consider entry points, which determine the social questions addressed by different approaches and theories and may also lead to different answers to those questions. But if in their questioning, Marxists' consideration of class includes its relationship with gender and sexuality, feminists' reflection on gender includes its relationship with sexuality and class, and queer theorists bear in mind the relationship of gender and class in their focus on sexuality, then their answers should be complementary and not necessarily at odds with one another.

The feminist demonstration that nature does not determine gender relations calls into question the gender inequalities within archaeology. Feminist archaeologists have identified the power structure of archaeology as part of the problem. They have actively sought to critique and transform our discipline into a more equitable practice. Kramer and Stark (1994) began addressing issues of gender inequality by collecting and analyzing data on the effects of gender on professional careers. Leslie Wildesen (1994) did the first such study and published it in the *Anthropology Newsletter*. In the 1990s a plethora of further studies collected and examined more data (Chester et al. 1994; Spencer-Wood 1994; Beaudry 1994). Nelson, Nelson, and Wylie (1994) drew many of these together in the Archaeological Papers no. 5 of the American Anthropological Association. These studies consistently show that women have lower status in the profession than men. Women hold fewer positions of leadership, publish fewer books, advance more slowly up the academic ladder or not at all, receive fewer research grants, hold fewer positions at prestigious universities, earn less money than men, and are subjected to other more subtle forms of gender discrimination (Nelson and Nelson 1994; Association Research, Inc. 2005:C1–C5; Baxter 2005).

Women and men have organized to address these inequities, for instance, forming the Committee on the Status of Women in the Society for American Archaeology (SAA) and the Committee on Gender Issues in the Society for Historical Archaeology. Less formal networks have included the Historical Archaeology Women's Caucus, the Women in Archaeology Interest Group in the SAA, and a host of even less formal and often unnamed groups. At regional, national, and international meetings, archaeologists have organized workshops and roundtables to discuss issues of gender inequality in the field and ways to change it.

In many ways feminist archaeology has been the most productive praxis of archaeology, although much remains to be done to eliminate gender inequalities in our discipline. With feminism we see the integration of critiquing the world, knowing the world, and taking action in the world with a well-defined political agenda: the elimination of gender bias in archaeology. The gross and explicit inequities that characterized archaeology before the 1970s have become less common. Archaeologists rarely, publicly, express overtly sexist attitudes like those of Ivor Noel-Hume. But in some ways, contemporary sexism is more subtle and circumspect and thus harder to confront than the overt pronouncements of a generation ago (Baxter 2005). Women now receive slightly more than half the Ph.D.s awarded in archaeology (Zeder 1997:205). Quantitative increases in the status of women have also occurred within archaeology, but those increases have not been adequate to eliminate gender bias (Zeder 1997:203–207). Despite improvements over the last three decades, women continue to be paid less, have less success at receiving both grant and CRM funding, hold a lower number of CEO positions in private firms than men, and make up a smaller percentage of the tenured professoriat (especially at research universities). Women in archaeology continue to face a plethora of challenges surrounding life roles and decisions that are quite different from those faced by their male colleagues. These challenges spring from continuing gender inequalities in society as a whole. Clearly, a feminist praxis needs to continue to confront the more subtle biases, social patterns, and domestic issues that perpetuate gender bias in twenty-first-century archaeology.

Indigenous Archaeology and Praxis

The struggle of indigenous peoples for the repatriation of the remains of their ancestors gave birth to indigenous archaeology (Lippert 2005:63). In settler states of the world, including North America (McGuire 1992a; Nichols and Andrews 1997), the southern cone of South America (Endere 2002; Barbosa 2002), New Zealand (Tapsell 2002), Australia (McNiven and Russell 2005), Scandinavia (Levy 2006), and southern Africa (Parsons and Segobye 2002; Nemaheni 2002; Ouzman 2005), archaeology has been a fundamentally colonialist enterprise, the study of the ancestors of the conquered by the descendants of the conquerors. Indigenous archaeology sprang from the attempts by archaeologists, both native and nonnative, to decolonize archaeology (Atalay 2006).

In the 1970s and 1980s, indigenous peoples informed archaeologists that the pasts we study are the heritages of living peoples and that archaeological practice forms part of their oppression (Deloria 1993; D. Thomas 2000; Watkins 2000; Fforde 2004; Wiseman 2005). An example illustrating these confrontations occurred in Fort Collins, Colorado, in the fall of 1971, when members of the American Indian movement (AIM) took over the Colorado State University physical anthropology laboratory. They handed out "citizens arrest warrants" to field school students who had excavated Native American burials the summer before. I was one of the students they issued a warrant. The AIM members then gathered up human bones that the Department of Anthropology had purchased from scientific supply houses for the university's teaching collection. They later exchanged the teaching collection in return for the field school burials. Another example occurred in Australia in 1982, when Ros Langford (1983) delivered a broadside attack on archaeology at the meetings of the Australian Archaeological Association. She spoke as a representative of the Tasmanian Aboriginal community. Langford asserted that Aboriginal pasts belonged to Aboriginal Australians and that they alone had the right to control these pasts. In reaction to her comments, the meeting passed a motion that recognized Aboriginal ownership of their heritage and called on archaeologists to seek permission from Aboriginal owners to do their research (McNiven and Russell 2005:189). Indigenous people see archaeology in the historical context of colonialism. In this context, the archaeologists' control of native pasts is simply one more facet of native life that has been taken from them. Most archaeologists have been honestly troubled by the dark images reflected at them from the mirrors that indigenous people held up. They see their actions in terms of their own intentions, debates over national heritage, a scientific search for knowledge, and the particular history of archaeology.

Eventually, it took legislation to force settler state archaeologists to confront and change the colonialism of our discipline (Watkins 2000:176). In the United States, the Native American Graves Protection and Repatriation Act of 1990 (NAGPRA) legislated that Native Americans would have a voice in the disposition of their ancestors' remains. In Australia, the Mabo decision of the High Court of Australia in 1992 recognized native title to lands in Australia. This decision and subsequent

legislation greatly expanded the ability of Aboriginal Australians to control their lives, lands, and heritage (McNiven and Russell 2005:197). A
patchwork of laws regulate repatriation in Australia, but their impact on
archaeology is similar to NAGPRA in the United States (McGiven and
Russell 2005:189). In New Zealand, the Resource Management Act of
1991 and the Te Ture Whenua Maori Act of 1993 have enabled Maori to
become increasingly active in repatriation and control of their heritage
(Watkins 2000:163). Also in 1993, apartheid ended in South Africa.

In all of the settler states, the struggle over repatriation was part of
larger movements to grant indigenous peoples greater independence and
control over their lives, lands, culture, education, and heritage. In the
United States, the federal policy of self-determination has allowed Native
American nations to take over functions that were performed by the
Bureau of Indian Affairs. Many Native Americans have taken control of
the management of heritage on their reservations. The first two Indian
nations to do this were the Navajo, who set up the Navajo Nation
Cultural Resource Management Program in 1978, and the Zuni, who
established the Zuni Archaeological Program in 1978. In 1996, twelve
Native American nations established Tribal Historic Preservation Offices
(THPOs), thus taking control of the implementation of federal historic
preservation legislation on their lands. In 2006, fifty-eight Native
American nations had THPOs (NATHPO 2006). As a result of these
changes, Indian nations now employ archaeologists who work for the
best interests of the nations (Two Bears 2006). This has also created a
pool of jobs for Indian people who wish to become archaeologists.

At the end of the twentieth century, more indigenous peoples in settler
states had the opportunity and preparation to attend universities (Deloria
1997:216), which has resulted in a small but increasing number of
college-educated indigenous professionals. Some of these professionals
are archaeologists. Indigenous archaeologists find themselves in an awk-
ward and often conflicted position (Lippert 1997, 2005; Watkins 2000;
Russell 2001; Isaacson and Ford 2005; Two Bears 2006). On the one
hand their "objectivity" may be questioned by other archaeologists, and
on the other hand their motive may be distrusted by indigenous people.
This position makes them highly aware of the social and political context
of archaeology.

Although native peoples have been at the heart of the creation of an
indigenous archaeology, this archaeology is not defined or limited by
race or ethnicity. "Indigenous archaeology is a methodology or a theoretical approach, rather than a culturally or biologically based activity"

(Lippert 2005:63). Key to this approach is the desire to behave respectfully with regard to the cultural sensibilities of native peoples. Indigenous
archaeology is archaeology informed by native values and agendas. It is
archaeology conducted by and for indigenous peoples (Smith and Wobst
2005). Ultimately indigenous archaeologists strive to help native peoples
build vibrant communities in full control of their pasts, presents, and
futures.

Four facets are key to the praxis of indigenous archaeology. First, it
serves the interests of native communities. Second, the method of working with these communities is collaboration. Third, collaboration
requires that many voices be heard. And finally, this kind of archaeology
should be of use to indigenous peoples. An indigenous approach to
working with communities goes beyond the tenets of community archaeology (Marshall 2002) to become partnership archaeology (McNiven
and Russell 2005:232–242), emphasizing that the native community is a
full partner in the archaeological process. Indigenous archaeologists view
members of a native community not as simply another voice but rather
as the owners and regulators of their own heritage. For example, in
Australia, archaeologists need permission from the Aboriginal, traditional owner of an area before they can work there (Wiynjorroc et al.
2005). In the fullest application of this approach, scholars do archaeology as guests of the community.

Collaboration requires working jointly with the community to benefit
all participants in the process (Colwell-Chanthaphonh and Ferguson
2004:6; Atalay 2006:293–294; Martinez 2006). The colonialist history
of archaeology makes establishing collaboration between archaeologists
and indigenous communities a process fraught with problems. Scholars
must overcome long-standing prejudices against archaeologists. For the
archaeologist, the first step to doing this is to be humble (Zimmerman
2005), and the second step is to respect the community that he or she
works with (Lippert 2005). Indigenous archaeologists reject mechanical,
bureaucratic processes of consultation that focus on single events and
acts. Collaboration implies sustained action and springs from a long-
term commitment to the community (Colwell-Chanthaphonh and
Ferguson 2004:23; Isaacson and Ford 2005:361). This commitment, by
its very nature, bridges private and professional lives. The archaeologist's
commitment to an indigenous community must go beyond issues of
archaeology and the archaeologist's needs.

Collaboration leads archaeologists to include multiple voices and perspectives in their research. Indigenous knowledge and tradition are most

commonly contained in oral traditions. A partnership archaeology respects oral tradition and includes it in research. Virtually every indigenous community has suffered oppression and exploitation. For this reason, an indigenous archaeology rejects a hyperrelativistic multivocality that lets all voices speak, because its practitioners know that some voices are pernicious. Indigenous archaeologists simultaneously embrace multivocality and seek objective understandings (Colwell-Chanthaphonh and Ferguson 2006:159). They produce multilayered narratives of the past that mediate between the physical and social world and recognize the connection between these worlds and meaning and belief.

Native communities have little reason to collaborate with scholars unless the community has some use for the archaeology. Indigenous archaeologists seek to be allies with communities (Wobst 2005:25). Our praxis can address real issues for communities, including land claims, tourism, and education, and can help to facilitate cross-cultural communication (Isaacson and Ford 2005). A long-term commitment to be of use to communities also leads the scholar to assist in community interests beyond the craft of archaeology.

Indigenous archaeology has grown rapidly in the first decade of the twenty-first century. Myriad examples of collaboration between archaeologists and indigenous communities exist, far too many to cite here (Nichols and Andrews 1997; Watkins 2000; McNiven and Russell 2005; Smith and Wobst 2005; Colwell-Chanthaphonh and Ferguson 2006). These collaborations represent some of the strongest examples of praxis in modern archaeology, a praxis that is transforming the field and supporting native interests.

DIALECTICAL KNOWLEDGE AND PRAXIS

Earlier archaeological attempts to contribute to the transformation of society and, hopefully, to the creation of a more humane world provide a foundation for building a praxis of archaeology. My dialectical, relational theory of praxis eschews the polar opposition between objectivism and relativism that has characterized contemporary theoretical debate in archaeology. It rejects an instrumentalist approach that seeks to engineer society. It also rejects critical and relativist approaches that strip the scholar of any authority to take and support transformative action. A dialectical praxis of archaeology begins with a relational theory of knowledge that offers an alternative to the objectivist and relativist epistemologies that create these poles.

The real question facing a praxis of archaeology is not whether archaeological knowledge should be objective or subjective but, rather, how we relate the subjectivities of knowing and the realities of the world in our construction of archaeological knowledge. Such knowledge is a very complicated thing. Prior knowledge, conventions, methods, and cultural understandings both enable and restrict empirical observations, and the whole process of constructing archaeological knowledge is situated in social and political processes. It is little wonder that relativists avoid these complexities by letting all voices speak or that positivists put their faith in empirical observations and try to control or ignore the rest. In a dialectical approach, the evaluation of knowledge involves a comprehensive dialectic among what I have called the four Cs: coherence, correspondence, context, and consequences.

The alternative that I present here attempts to chart a route down the middle of the opposition between subjective and objective knowledge. This perspective gives equal weight to the subjectivities of knowing and the realities of the world but does not reduce knowledge to either. This is not a particularly easy or comfortable route, because it disallows the security of true knowledge as well as the complacency of hyperrelativism. I argue, however, that this discomfort and tension provide the means to avoid the dangers of either extreme.

Hodder (1999:24) has noted that the debate over how to plot such a path quickly becomes a matter of emphasis and language and that scholars resolve the tension between the subjective and the objective only in practice. My emphasis and language follow here, but the true measure of my alternative lies in the praxis discussed in chapters 3, 4, and 5.

The idea of dialectical knowledge springs from a realist philosophy of science (Keat and Urry 1983; McGuire 1992b:106–115; Wylie 2002). Realism accepts that a real world exists independent of our senses and that scholars can gain empirical knowledge of that world. Our knowledge of the world, however, remains imprecise, faulty, and diverse, because we can know the world only through human minds. Knowledge is, therefore, constructed in the dialectic between our consciousness and the reality of the world. Neither is it an honest reflection of that reality, nor is it simply fabricated.

To understand and evaluate knowledge, archaeologists have to look at its coherence with theory and logic, its correspondence with our observations, the context in which we have created it, and the consequences that it has for humanity. Our research occurs in social and political contexts that shape what questions we will ask, how we will ask them, and what meaning we will give the answers. Our knowledge of the world should be coherent in a logical sense and consistent with the theory that guides our research. But coherence does not guarantee that knowledge will correspond to the empirical observations we can make of the world or that it will not have harmful consequences. We can construct coherent knowledge that lacks an empirical fit with reality, and we can produce coherent rationalizations for malicious actions. By the same token, correspondence with empirical observations is not, as the processualists would suggest, an adequate measure of knowledge.

Usually multiple interpretations fit a set of empirical observations, and when an interpretation does not correspond to empirical observations, scholars habitually modify the interpretation to fit. In the end, an interpretation may buckle, groan, or even collapse under the weight of empirical observations, but multiple alternatives virtually always remain. Since we may practically never be able to come up with one "empirically correct" interpretation, we cannot justify accepting one interpretation simply because it fits. As socially responsible intellectuals, we should critically consider the consequences of the different interpretations that do fit our empirical observations. This critique should include both assessment of the subjectivities of knowing that lie behind that knowledge and the social, political, and ideological consequences of that knowledge.

A four-part dialectic between coherence, correspondence, context, and consequences makes the evaluation of knowledge claims quite complex, contentious, and changeable. In a dialectical relationship, no one of these criteria is adequate or privileged. Moreover, the critique does not reduce to a simple sequential comparison of one to another but instead requires a dynamic, recursive consideration of how each informs and creates the others.

Coherence

It perhaps goes without saying that our interpretations of the past must be coherent. They should be rational; they should not be tautological or filled with logical contradictions. But coherence implies more than just logical consistency. It also implies theoretical coherence.

Interpretations should be consistent with our social theory. Social theories entail assumptions about the world, entry points for studying the world, objectives, critiques, terminologies, conventions, and styles of discourse. They not only define what is important to study in the world;

they also circumscribe the questions we can ask and the observations we can make. They enable us to make sense out of the enormous variability that exists in the social world, but they also restrict what aspects of that variability we can study. The melding of different theoretical stances and concepts through an in-depth process of synthesis can produce a coherent interpretation. Synthesis requires that we consider the compatibility and incompatibility of various entry points, objectives, and assumptions. Failing to do the hard work of synthesis results in muddled interpretations. The willy-nilly use of theoretical concepts, terms, or goals to construct knowledge results in confusion, blind alleys, and both conceptual and substantive contradictions in interpretation.

One of the main purposes of theory is to define the questions we ask about the social world. These questions define the phenomena that we study and simultaneously enable and limit what we can understand of the social world. Our interpretations should also be theoretically coherent and comprehensive in terms of the questions we ask. Better interpretations take into account more aspects of the phenomena we wish to understand (Sayer 1979:117).

Correspondence

Archaeologists can make empirical observations of the world, and these observations may be regarded as evidence or data. Examples of such observations include the following: the Native peoples of the Mesa Verde region of southwestern Colorado grew corn in 1100 C.E.; the climate of Europe was considerably colder in the Pleistocene than it is today; the Great Pyramid at Giza was built in the third millennium before the common era. Such observations are not reality, nor do they exist prior to or outside dialectical knowledge. As observations, they are the products of conscious human action. They necessarily entail the prior knowledge, conventions, methods, categorizations, and cultural understandings that people must bring into play to observe the world in a coherent way.

Empirical observations take on meaning, become knowledge, only within a socially constructed discourse about the world. In the absence of such meaning, observations such as the examples listed above are trivial. We must give meaning to observations; they cannot simply speak for themselves (Leone 1981:312). These meanings are made in the present and reflect social and political interests. Thus, all knowledge must be social and political. But, as Agger observes, "Just because we recognize that truth is a matter of perspective doesn't mean that we shouldn't pursue it, especially where the alternative is to accept the present ('facts') as eternity" (2004:47).

I have carefully chosen the word *observations* here as opposed to *facts, data,* or *truths.* As Hodder (1999:84) has pointed out, empirical observations are dialectical from the start. He would argue that we can have no knowledge of the world independent of the "prejudgments" we must have to be able to observe the world. Accepting this point, however, does not mean that observations necessarily correspond or fail to correspond to reality (Eagleton 2002:103–109). For example, consider empirical observations comparing the length of two projectile points, one four centimeters long and the other six centimeters long. Many aspects of these observations, such as why we make them in the first place and our choice of systems of measurement (metric or English), are cultural understandings. However, the reality remains that one point is longer than the other. Empirical observations entail a culturally constructed awareness of how to make sense of the world, but the fact that they do or do not correspond to the reality of the world means that even these cultural understandings can be considered empirically (Eagleton 2002:103–109).

Evaluating correspondence requires that archaeologists retain some authority over the production of knowledge (Colwell-Chanthaphonh 2006:23). Archaeology is a craft that entails heart, hands, and minds (Shanks and McGuire 1996). The archaeologist's craft is the skill to use material remains to interpret past experiences and situations. As a craft, archaeology is more than just a set of theories, methods, and techniques. It is, instead, a practice with a range of endeavors from the technical to the interpretative, from the practical to the creative. Our authority lies in our craft. Mastering the craft of archaeology requires special training and skills. Not all people can think archaeologically, have acquired the background knowledge necessary for archaeology, or have mastered the motor skills to do archaeology. These things are learned. The craft of archaeology is a process of interpretation at all levels, from the first spade in the ground to the last period of the final report (Hodder 1999). But to say that archaeology is interpretation does not mean that it is merely subjective or that just anyone can do it.

Estimating a radiocarbon date provides an example of this. The collector must have prior knowledge that includes how the process of radiocarbon dating works, how samples may be contaminated, what the advantages and problems are of dating different materials, and how to identify these materials in the field. He or she will also need to have the background knowledge necessary to interpret archaeological contexts, both the stratigraphic and the horizontal. The collector must make judgments as to what materials to take and where to take them. Collectors often disagree on the type of material to take, the identification of types of material, and, more likely, the nature of the context to take the sample from. Exposing the sample and removing it involve knowledge of procedures and specific motor skills. When results come back from the lab, the archaeologist needs to understand issues such as the correction of radiometric dates and the conventions of how dates are reported. Once a chronometric date is derived from lab results, its relevance to the chronology of the phenomenon being dated must be interpreted in terms of the stratigraphic and horizontal relationships between a host of archaeological objects (layers, artifacts, and features). In this process, multiple interpretations will exist at every step, but not all interpretations will be correct and not all individuals are equally capable of making such interpretations.

Our interpretations need to fit the empirical observations that we make of reality. They should correspond to the artifact distributions, dates, events, and practices that we can interpret from the archaeological record using empirical methods. In looking for this correspondence, we must remember that these observations are not reality. They are the results of both a reality that existed before our research and the conceptual schemes, methods, and prior knowledge that governed the inquiry that found them. As such, they are in the same moment both real and social.

Context

Archaeologists practice their craft in social and political contexts. Postprocessual, feminist, indigenous, and Marxist critiques of the last twenty years have emphasized the importance of understanding the impact of these contexts on knowledge production. Once archaeologists abandon the illusion that our discipline is an objective science, we have to seriously consider these contexts, the interests that our craft serves in them, and how these interests influence the knowledge that we produce. My consideration focuses on the relationship of our craft to the "public," to actual human communities, and to archaeology itself.

Much discussion has occurred in archaeology about the need for our discipline to serve the interests of a "general public." This discussion has frequently proceeded without asking key questions: Who is this public? Do they need or want to listen to us? The first step in answering these questions is to recognize that there is no such thing as the general public. Archaeologists speak to many publics, including the educated middle class, school children, Native Americans, college students, and scholars. At the most general level, a discourse on how we interact with these publics is useful (Pyburn 2005; Schmidt 2005). The praxis of archaeology, however, will most fruitfully occur on a much more local level in a dialogue with actual human communities. Archaeologists should ponder how our praxis relates to global issues and broadly defined publics, but the realization of that praxis will be local.

I use the term *communities* here to refer to groups of people who share a common lived experience and who, because of this experience, have common interests and the potential to engage in collective agency. This shared experience may be based in a variety of social factors—class, gender, age, sexuality, residence, race, and ethnicity—and most commonly in complex combinations of them. In the modern world, such communities may or may not share a common geographic space, but shared experience does imply individuals who interact with one another.

Communities in the sense that I have defined them here are not hard-bounded objects. Individuals are normally members of multiple communities, and they form, manipulate, and perform identities within and among them. These processes also transform the community, making community boundaries and membership dynamic and fluid. People are also members of communities that exist at different scales. For example, unionized workers in southern Colorado form a definable and self-conscious community that acts in solidarity. Most of these workers are members of the United Mine Workers of America, which forms a larger community, which in turn is a subset of the labor movement in the United States. Finally, each community exists in relationship to other communities with their own interests and different abilities to realize those interests. The conflicts, collaboration, and clashes among these communities transform them all.

By my definition, members of a human community share a lived experience and share common interests as a result of that experience. But this does not mean that a community is a homogeneous mass. Because individuals participate in multiple communities and communities almost always encompass multiple social factors, all members of a particular community do not participate the same in that lived experience or share interests equally. Power relations exist among communities and within communities. Inequalities, discrimination, and oppression usually exist within communities; therefore, alienation may exist both among com-

munities and within communities. An emancipation that confronts
oppressive relations among communities cannot be fully successful if it
ignores alienations of class, gender, sexuality, or what ever else exists
within communities.

Zimmerman (2005) discusses the complex politics he encountered in
defining indigenous communities during his direction of the Crow Creek
Massacre Project in 1978. He had thought he would have to deal with
two distinct communities: the Lakota of the Crow Creek Reservation,
where the archaeological site was located, and the Arikara community
that was descendant from the occupants of the site. Instead, he found
that multiple social groups, varied interests, and internal hierarchies
existed within these two communities. More important, it became apparent that serving some interests compromised others. In the end, the project was able to negotiate among these interests.

Human communities do not exist in the abstract. Archaeologists in a
given social context cannot assume a priori what the nature or composition of the communities will be, how they will be delimited, or what their
internal inequities or interests will be. General or global understandings
of social factors such as gender, race, class, ethnicity, and sexuality aid us
in understanding the local context. But answering the questions of who
the communities are and whether they want or need to listen to us
requires archaeologists to examine actual lived experience and our relationship to it within that context.

I would argue that our consideration of contexts should begin by
identifying the communities involved, their interests, their internal relations, and their relationships with other communities, especially the community of archaeology. In many cases, such as with Native Americans
and Egyptians, the archaeologist enters a context in which the community already has an established relationship with archaeology and well-
formed opinions on the need to listen to us or not (Pullar 1994; Moser et
al. 2002; Meskell 2003, 2005; Zimmerman 2005). In other cases archaeology may be something new to a community. These relationships affect
where archaeologists can do research, what methods they can use, what
questions they ask, and what answers they consider.

Archaeology as craft can be put to the service of multiple communities. Archaeology is part of the social capital that defines the middle class
and has historically served the needs of that class, as well as traditionally
serving the needs of a community of archaeologists that is by and large a
subset of the middle class. However, some archaeologists have entered
into active dialogues with feminist (Hays-Gilpin and Whitley 1998),

indigenous (Watkins 2000; Smith and Wobst 2005), Third World (Schmidt 2005), and working-class communities (McGuire and Reckner 2003; Shackel and Palus 2006), among others. I advocate that archaeologists actively dialogue with different communities to forge common interests and acknowledge different interests with mutual goals (Marshall 2002). Successful dialogues entail a give and take that can transform both archaeology and the community involved.

Archaeologists must, however, always be in dialogue with the community of archaeology itself. It is here that our craft lives and where it is developed, modified, assessed critically, and enhanced. The community of archaeology possesses the prior knowledge, conventions, methods, categorizations, and cultural understandings that allow us to practice our craft and to make interpretations of the world. It is also this community that reviews, validates, and critiques our specific practice of the craft of archaeology. In the absence of this review and critique, our individual practice of archaeology can have no authority.

Most archaeological work serves the community of archaeologists. The majority of archaeologists seek to increase archaeological knowledge for this community and to assess and improve the craft of archaeology (Hodder 1999). This is good and essential, but it is not all that archaeology should be. Marxists, critical archaeologists, feminists, indigenous archaeologists, and post-processualists have all critiqued the ideological aspects of the knowledge we produce. These critiques make archaeologists more aware of the political role of archaeology in society as an ideology factory and of archaeology's potential use as a tool of oppression. The knowledge that we create also serves the social and political interests of other communities, and some of us need to engage this process as praxis.

The community of archaeology forms a social context that is embedded in larger contexts. As the feminists have demonstrated, our praxis of archaeology must critically evaluate and attempt to transform archaeology when inequities and abuses exist within our community. The social and power relations of archaeology have real consequences for archaeologists. Again, as in the gendered praxis of archaeology, these social and power relations usually replicate and participate in broader societal relations. Thus, a praxis that transforms archaeology both necessitates and participates in praxis to transform society. By the same logic, our praxis with other communities should encourage a critique of archaeology and affect our practice as archaeologists.

Communities, in the sense that I define them here, are made. A shared consciousness of community is essential to transformative change, because only with this consciousness can collective agency be realized. Powerful groups within a society actively seek to prevent such consciousness from rising in order to preserve their own interests. But through struggle and negotiation, individuals can establish a shared consciousness of community and engage in collective agency. Communities that fail to form a collective consciousness become ineffective agents. Archaeology has taken an active role in the dialogue to create this consciousness.

Archaeologists who enter into such a dialogue must give up some of their privilege (Marshall 2002). The privilege that we surrender should not be the authority that comes from our craft. The craft of archaeology gives us the ability to make observations, interpretations, and knowledge of the world that cannot be made by those who are not archaeologists. Without such authority, we speak only as the propagandists for political interests. Without this authority, why should anyone believe us? More important, why should we believe ourselves? Rather, we should give up the programmatic privilege to exclusively define the questions, the substance, and those aspects of the archaeological record that we apply our craft to. These things should be established through a dialogue with the community we work with. Only then can we make a meaningful contribution to praxis.

Dialogue and humility are the tonic against the hubris of social engineering and the vanguard party (Zimmerman 2005). By allowing the community that we serve to help define our research questions and goals, we can do research that is relevant to that community. This process of negotiation ought to continue throughout the research process. We should not impose our goals, conclusions, or solutions on the community; we must negotiate them. Because archaeologists and the communities we work with bring different skills, interests, knowledge, and experience to the discussion, the dialogue may often be conflictual. It should also be transformative of archaeology, the community, and knowledge.

Consequences

By and large all the approaches to knowledge in archaeology have avoided making the consequences of knowledge criteria for evaluating it. This issue is a political hot button. Those approaches that stress objectivity want to fall back on "data" as the arbiter of knowledge. For archaeologists that promote such approaches, weighing the consequences of knowledge gives the political agenda too much power to subsume "true" knowledge (Trigger 1995b:331). The approaches that stress relativism lack any metatheory to critically evaluate the consequences of knowing. Thus, Hodder (1999:155–156) finds it difficult to distinguish between the archaeological curiosity of New Age goddess worshipers and the heritage claims of indigenous peoples. The key to evaluating consequences lies in the critical appraisal of the social interests and the communities that archaeology serves.

If we accept that archaeology has always served the interests of communities and that it is desirable to expand beyond the traditional community of the middle class, then we must consider the issue of how we decide what interests to serve. I propose that archaeologists need to answer three questions when evaluating potential interests that they might serve: Whose interests are served and how? How do those interests and their consequences relate to other communities and to the internal relations of the communities we serve? How do those interests correspond to our knowledge of the world?

I will examine each of these questions in turn. They raise issues that archaeologists have been reluctant to discuss explicitly but have always been implicit in our research. Answering these questions is the hardest and most fraught step in a dialectical praxis.

The Chosen Interests and How They Are Served   It is always difficult to know what the costs, benefits, and unintended consequences of human action will be. We should not, however, use uncertainty as an excuse to ignore the potential consequences of our research and the interests to which it might be put. By the same token, we ought not embrace a multivocality that lets all voices speak regardless of the consequences of that speech. Rather, we need a relational multivocality that examines whose interests will be served and whose voices we will support, ignore, or challenge (Colwell-Chanthaphonh and Ferguson 2006). Part of the process of examining interests involves looking beyond the specific issues of archaeology to a broader political picture.

Considering the consequence of our research demands that we have a good understanding of the political stage on which we perform (Deloria 1997; Lilley 2006). Archaeologists frequently confront the politics of heritage, but we rarely consider the full canopy of political issues in which our work is embedded. This canopy includes powerful historical relations of race, gender, ethnicity, sexuality, and class that our craft and we are part of. For example, several archaeologists have advocated interpretations of the aboriginal history of ancestral Pueblo peoples that stress the importance of violence, warfare, and even cannibalism (LeBlanc 1999; Turner and Turner 1999). They propose these ideas as an antidote to the stereotype of Pueblo peoples as peaceful, noble savages. These archaeologists have failed, however, to examine how their arguments reinforce simplistic oppositions between good and bad Indians and how their stance participates in and reinforces a current political backlash against Native American rights (McGuire 2002c; McGuire and Van Dyke, forthcoming).

We need to evaluate interests primarily by social rather than psychological and emotional criteria. In other words, we should prioritize the social, political, and material consequences of community interests as opposed to simply asking how well these interests fulfill the emotional and psychological needs of community members. People may derive emotional and psychological satisfaction from the pursuit and realization of interests that alienate others and, thus, are contrary to emancipation. For example, many Germans were emotionally moved by the Nazi Party's Nuremberg rally of 1934. They left the rally feeling that the experience had given them a stronger sense of what it meant to be German. Indeed, a movie of the rally, *Triumph of the Will*, remains an emotionally stirring experience, perhaps even more than the actual rally because of our knowledge of the events that followed it (Kershaw 1987). The Nazis used rallies, films, and other ideological devices to give people a redefined and emotionally satisfying sense of what it meant to be German at that time. This fascist sense of German-ness alienated and dehumanized millions of Jews, Gypsies, gays, disabled people, and dissidents, thus justifying and making possible their murder (Gellately 2002).

In a post-processual radical relativism, archaeologists often invoke emotional and psychological criteria to justify multivocality. Hodder (1999:155) questions archaeologists' right to challenge the beliefs of goddess worshipers. These largely bourgeois, European cultists embrace the nineteenth-century evolutionist notion that the first religions were all based in a belief in the goddess. They cite female figurines at Çatalhöyük as evidence that this town was a center for the worship of the goddess (Meskell 1995, 1998). Hodder notes that he has seen people emotionally moved by visiting goddess sites and in a side bar states, "Many of these people are women. Who are you to say that discovering the goddess does not help them gain a stronger sense of what it means to be a women after millennia of subjugation?" (Hodder 1999:155). Goddess worship does not have the harmful consequences of nazism. Emotional considerations may justify archaeologists simply ignoring this bourgeois play. I am not, however, sure that goddess worship at Çatalhöyük is without problems. When goddess worshipers arrive at Çatalhöyük, they arrive as privileged members of a dominant, secular Western culture. They enter a social context torn by struggles between a secularized, urban, Turkish elite and a devout, Islamic, rural peasantry (Hodder 2000). Much of this struggle focuses on gender, and the European feminist view of gender that the goddess worshipers bring conflicts with the views of the devout Muslim inhabitants of the area (Hodder 1998). The consequences of these actions must be carefully considered.

The Relationship between Different Communities   Marxist theory charges us to examine how the gain for some will come at a cost to others. We cannot evaluate consequences without looking at the relationships between communities and interests, which exist in social contexts that are the historical products of cooperation and struggle. In order to look at these relationships, scholars need to understand the histories that created them, as well as their present situations and contexts (Mohanty 2003).

People form communities for various reasons, including the advancement of different kinds of interests. My focus here is on communities that share social, political, and material goals, rather than those that exist primarily or solely to serve individual psychological and emotional needs. Individuals may form communities principally to fulfill these needs by creating identities for themselves, such as the U.S. organization known as the Society for Creative Anachronism, whose members gather to take on medieval personae. In capitalism, these individuals tend to be from the bourgeois and middle classes, who have sufficient resources and free time to engage in such play.[1] The vast majority of the people in the world, however, do not have the liberty for such amusement. They are too intently engaged in the struggle to survive. Communities may arise from such recreation, but they rarely engage in transformative change, because their focus is on individual self-realization.

Identity creation that may be harmless bourgeois play in one context may be domination in another. The mainly white, middle-class members of the Society for Creative Anachronism take on medieval personae, engage in mock combat, feast, and create an imagined society in which they spend a significant portion of their lives (Price 2002). The Society for Creative Anachronism represents unabashed romanticism, but their activities do not appear to enter into power relations with other communities or compromise the interests of other communities.

However, the same cannot be said for all bourgeois play. The New Age movement has many devotees in the southwestern United States and elsewhere. These people seek spirituality through a pastiche of "primitive" beliefs and rituals drawn from various sources, including Native America. The government, missionaries, schools, and private interests in the United States have a long history of suppressing Native American culture and denigrating Native religion. New Age devotees thus operate, often unwittingly, in a powerful arena of social struggle. These members of the dominant society express white dominance and subordinate Indian peoples by appropriating aspects of Native religion and desecrating Native sacred sites with trinkets and made-up rituals (Finn 1997).

Navigating the complex maze of interests among and within different groups is one of the thorniest tasks of a self-conscious praxis of archaeology (Zimmerman 2005). Social groups constantly negotiate and struggle to advance their interests vis-à-vis other groups. Archaeologists who engage in praxis that is radical and transformative should address interests that serve the needs of the subordinate and challenge the privilege of the dominant. Relations of power and oppression, however, are usually multifaceted, cross-cutting, and contradictory. A single "oppressor" with a clear relationship of dominance to other groups almost never exists. Relations of power may seem clear when scholars compare only two communities or only look at them from a global perspective. When viewed as part of a larger set of social relations and in detail, however, these power relations rapidly become confusing and confounding. Subordinate groups may have oppressive internal hierarchies of power. A group that is subordinate in one context or relationship may be dominant in another.

Archaeologists also need to keep in mind that, in much of the world, archaeology has been a colonialist or imperialist enterprise (Trigger 1984a), which is most assuredly the case in North America and Australia (McGuire 1992a; Watkins 2000; McNiven and Russell 2005). In most of the rest of the world, it has been a tool of nationalism (Trigger 1989a; Kohl and Fawcett 1995; Meskell, ed. 1998; Kane 2003; Galaty and Watkinson 2004). Archaeology may be part of the problem in any of these cases.

Knowledge of the World   Sometimes the interests of social groups may be based on a conception of the world that lacks correspondence to our empirical observations or conflicts with our existing knowledge. This is where archaeologists must retain the authority of our craft. We cannot support alternative group interests if they do not correspond to our empirical observations and knowledge of the world. We need to retain the authority of our craft to reject such interests. That said, archaeologists must also be critical of our own observations and knowledge when challenged by alternative conceptions.

Within cultural anthropology, many scholars have adopted an advocacy position that challenges anthropology to "speak truth to power." One quandary in such a position is what to do when fictions support the subordinate and challenge the dominant. Can we ignore a lack of correspondence with knowledge and wield convenient falsehoods in our struggle? I would join others to argue that we must not (Conklin 2003)! If archaeologists advocate ideas or perceptions that do not correspond to our knowledge of the world, then archaeology loses any authority to speak truth, and we abandon the dialectic between the empirical and the political. With this abandonment comes self-deception and the rationalization of harmful acts. More important, we lose the ability for self-reflection and the capability to critically evaluate power relations within the groups we work with.

This is all to suggest that in our knowledge claims, archaeologists need to have some independence from the social groups and interests that we serve. The basis for this independence resides in our craft and in our obligations to the community of archaeologists. It is, therefore, almost inevitable that our knowledge claims will come into conflict with the claims of the communities we work with. I view this situation as good. Such contradictions create tensions that force each community to critically examine its own dialogue as well as the other's. This critique may have many consequences, such as modifying the perceptions and interests of the archeologists or the community or both and revealing social relations and ideologies that were previously unknown to one or the other or both. Of course, these contradictions also carry the real danger of rupturing the relationship.

Different ways of knowing the world and different kinds of knowledge can be gained from these epistemologies (Colwell-Chanthaphonh and Ferguson 2006). When archaeologists work with communities that do not share a Western secular way of knowing, tensions are inevitable (Watkins 2000; Smith and Wobst 2005). Any U.S. archaeologist who has worked closely with Native Americans appreciates this. I have numerous experiences of visiting an archaeological site with Indian people and being struck by how differently we see things. Archaeologists and Native Americans often give importance to dissimilar types of empirical obser-

vations. Native American ways of knowing involve different notions of
time, evidence, and proof (D. Thomas 2000; Deloria 1997, 2002;
Colwell-Chanthaphonh and Ferguson 2006). Indigenous epistemologies
are not archaeological. At this point, positivists would dismiss the Native
voice as metaphysical. At this point, relativists would claim that letting
each voice speak is a radical praxis. In a dialectical praxis, however, we
should ask how these voices have been historically created in relations of
power and how we may use an archeological way of knowing to confront this inequality.

CONCLUSION

Trigger worried, like many others, that doing archaeology in the service
of politicized interests is dangerous. They worry that archaeology will
only produce mythic charters to validate these interests unless the discipline makes "true" knowledge the ultimate arbiter. But archaeology must
be more than a bourgeois practice in order for true knowledge to have a
transformative impact on the world. Put more simply, an archaeology
that speaks to and for the bourgeoisie will not be transformative, because
the bourgeoisie have no interests in transformation; witness the failure of
Leone's critical archaeology in Annapolis. Trigger worried that political
partisanship will dominate our efforts and that, with a loss of objectivity,
archaeology will become simply a prop for preconceived ideologies, as it
did in the Soviet Union. He feared that such an archaeology risks self-
deception. He wanted us to stand aside from the game and serve more as
referees than as players. Yet, it was Trigger who laid out the process by
which this anxiety may be alleviated.

Trigger (1989a; 2006) made the convincing case that modern archaeology has resulted from the development of the capitalist middle classes
and that archaeology has served the interests of that class. He also
argued, however, that the accumulation of knowledge by archaeology
has resisted bourgeois ideologies despite the class basis of archaeological
practice. He identified the key to this process as a focus on empirical reality and a reluctance to dismiss lightly any evidence that does not support
current political beliefs. Thus, he argued that to consider the political
nature of archaeology is to arrive at a more objective understanding of
the world.

I agree and support these efforts within the community of archaeology, but I argue that there is more to be done. As Trigger recognized,
what knowledge archaeologists accumulate depends in large part on

what questions and interests we bring to our research. I wish to allow communities other than the middle classes to define the interests and questions of archaeology. In doing so, I resist simply providing other communities with mythical charters that justify their existence, interests, aspirations, and authority. Instead, I wish to examine these questions critically and empirically, to arrive at knowledge that will transform the political struggles of our world, in terms of both advancing nonbourgeois interests and critically assessing the interests and beliefs of the communities that archeologists work with. Such a praxis of archaeology stands to be the best hope of contributing to a change in society for the collective good of a majority of human beings.

The praxis of archaeology involves a dialectic among knowing the world, critiquing it, and taking action in it. Effective praxis is possible only if archaeologists abandon the opposition between objectivity and subjectivity and give equal weight to knowing the world and to critiquing it. When critique, such as that of feminists or the indigenous, reveals that archaeology is part of the problem, we need to take action to transform archaeology. By critically examining what interests our craft serves in the world, we can put that craft to the advancement of interests that have the potential to make the world a more humane place.

NOTE

1. In this book, I am using a Marxist relational concept of class that differs from the common popular usage of class in the United States. In common usage, class position is equated to income (lower, middle, and upper class) or to the type of work done (blue collar, white collar, pink collar). In a relational concept of class, a person's class position is defined by his or her relationship to the means of production and to other class positions. In capitalism, there are minimally three class positions: the bourgeoisie, who own the means of production; the workers or proletariat, who actually produce goods and services; and the middle class of managers, professionals, and administrators, who mitigate between the bourgeois and the workers.

CHAPTER 3

Class

WITH MARK WALKER

> In Marxist terms, one doesn't advocate class struggle or
> choose to participate in it (common bourgeois misconcep-
> tions). The class struggle, representing the sum of the con-
> tradictions between workers, broadly defined, and capitalists,
> simply *is,* and in one way or another we are all already
> involved, often—as we come to discover—on the wrong
> side. On learning about it and where we fit into it, we can
> now decide to stop acting as we have been (the first decision
> to make) and what more or else we can do to better serve our
> own interests. What can be chosen is what side to take in this
> struggle and how to conduct it.
>
> Bertell Ollman (2003:20)

Class and class relations permeate all aspects of capitalist society, and as a part of that society archaeology embodies these relations. Archaeologists approach the study of the past from a discipline that has traditionally served middle-class interests. This discipline also has its own dynamic class structure, and this structure is becoming increasingly exploitative both in the academy and in cultural resource management (CRM). Bertell Ollman (2003:20) reminds us that we are all already part of the class struggle. By learning about the struggle and where we fit in it, we can decide which side we are on. Too often we learn that we are on the wrong side of the struggle. This knowledge gives us the ability to change our conduct to support the other side.

The authors' lived experience of class affects our understanding of class struggle in archaeology. Randall McGuire is a tenured full professor of anthropology at Binghamton University. He worked in contract archaeology during the halcyon days of CRM in the 1970s, starting as a field technician and eventually becoming a project director. He came to Binghamton University as a visiting assistant professor in 1982. His stint as a gypsy scholar was brief, because he acquired a tenure-track position the next year. Since then he has lived the guild model, rising to the rank of full professor. He is a member of the United University Professionals, a faculty union affiliated with the AFL-CIO. Mark Walker's professional career has been almost entirely within CRM, with a stint in graduate school. He worked as a transient field tech in the early 1980s and, after obtaining a master's degree, achieved a steady position as a project director. Returning to graduate school at Binghamton University, he worked on the research-oriented Colorado Coalfield War Project. He is currently a project director at the Anthropological Studies Center of Sonoma State University, a university-based CRM group. Mark is a member of the California State Employees Association, which is affiliated with the AFL-CIO. We published an earlier version of this chapter as an article in *Historical Archaeology* (McGuire and Walker 1999).

Attempts by archaeologists to transform the social context of our discipline are not new. In the last decade archaeologists have published explicit comments on the gender foundations (Chester et al. 1994; Nelson and Nelson 1994; Spencer-Wood 1994; Beaudry 1994; Zeder 1997; Association Research, Inc. 2005: C1–C5; Baxter 2005) and racial foundations of our practice (Barbour 1994; Leone 1995; Blakey 2003; Watkins 2000). Concerns with gender and race are essential to an emancipatory archaeology, and feminist and indigenous critiques of archaeology have contributed much to freeing archaeology of sexism and racism. Even with these contributions, however, much remains to be done, and we would argue that an explicit concern with class must be added to these efforts.

The class structure of archaeology has remained largely a hidden issue, which should not surprise us, because the denial of class and class differences has long been a fundamental aspect of American ideology (Domhoff 1983:3–6; Fantasia and Voss 2004:167; Durrenberger 2006). Despite this denial, class remains one of the inherent relationships that structure modern capitalist America. By denying or overlooking its existence, we ignore an important factor that affects the histories that we write and structures the audiences whom we write for. Finally, by denying class, we conceal the class struggles that exist within our own discipline.

Archaeology is a locus of contemporary class struggle. In the universities, downsizing, declining employment opportunities, restructuring, and decreasing funding levels have proletarianized the life of the mind (Aronowitz 1997; Nelson 1997a; Yates 2000; Nelson and Watt 2004). A reserve army of part-time professors and gypsy scholars now performs more than 40 percent of the teaching. Class struggles have erupted among teaching assistants, professors, and administrators (Nelson 1997b). In cultural resource management, a group of managers formed a trade association, the American Cultural Resource Association (ACRA), and numerous field technicians banded together in the United Archaeological Field Technicians (UAFT), a union affiliated with the AFL-CIO. These struggles involve all archaeologists in one way or another, and they are profound forces shaping our discipline.

Archaeology exists in a tangled web of class relations. In our effort to untangle the strands, we have found it useful to distinguish between archaeology as a discipline and the various occupational structures that archaeologists labor in. The discipline of archaeology is a branch of learning grounded in a distinctive craft that can be used to study the world (Shanks and McGuire 1996). Individuals who master this craft and who apply it to research in the world are archaeologists. Archaeologists have different professions or careers, and they labor within various occupational structures. For most of the twentieth century, professional archaeologists primarily practiced their trade in the academy (museums, colleges and universities), and amateur archaeologists did archaeology as a hobby or as an avocation. Today, archaeologists still ply their craft in these two contexts, but the vast majority of professional archaeologists labor in CRM, where most are employed in either the governmental or the private sector (Patterson 1995b; Zeder 1997; Fagan 2006). Archaeology as a discipline has a class position and class interests. As a profession or occupation it has a class structure in which class struggle occurs.

Archaeology is part of the intellectual apparatus (composed of things such as schools, books, magazines, organizations, and arts) that produces the symbolic capital (including things such as esoteric knowledge, shared experience, certification, and social skills) that individuals need to be part of the middle class (Ball 2003). This apparatus, archaeology included, developed as part of the historical struggles that created the capitalist middle class (Trigger 1989a, 2006; Patterson 1995b). Because archaeology is set in the middle class, it attracts primarily a middle-class following and often does not appeal to working-class audiences. Archaeology also uses the intellectual apparatus of the middle class to reproduce itself. Ideally this reproduction follows the guild model of apprenticeship and mastery. In the idealized guild model all archaeologists are either middle-class or apprentices moving toward that status.

In our current era of fast capitalism, all archaeologists are not simply either middle-class or apprentices with a reasonable hope of becoming masters. Hypercompetition among capitalist firms erodes workers' rights, reduces workers' security, and corrodes working conditions (Agger 2004; Fantasia and Voss 2004). Archaeology is no exception; fast capitalism has transformed its class structures. The guild of apprentices, journeymen, and masters does not exist in the academy or in CRM. These occupations entail permanent class divisions that exploit subordinates and do not provide them with a living wage. In the academy, class divisions have arisen as a result of changes in the function of the university in reproducing the middle class. In CRM they arise from the competitive, profit-driven nature of contracting and have led to the practice of employers paying skilled archaeologists at lower wage rates than those applied to unionized unskilled laborers. In both cases the ideology of the guild model obscures the realities of exploitation.

What, then, is to be done? The first step to class praxis in archaeology is to learn how archaeologists live class and how class interests limit the audience of the discipline and exploit individuals within it. With this knowledge, archaeologists can see where they fit in the struggle and decide whose side they are on. Those of us who are in a privileged position, whether we be tenured faculty or project directors, can question that privilege. This questioning could include how we remake our practice to mitigate the exploitation we find. Finally, those in subordinate positions, whether they are field technicians or adjuncts, need to organize to represent their own interests and struggle on their behalf. Our focus in this chapter is on archaeology in the United States, but similar processes and struggles are occurring in archaeology throughout the core capitalist states of the world.

THE DISCIPLINE OF ARCHAEOLOGY AND CLASS INTERESTS

The prevailing middle-class nature of archaeology manifests itself in the history of our discipline and in the audience for archaeology (Trigger 1989a, 2006; McGuire 1992b; Potter 1994; Patterson 1995b). The dominance of middle-class interests and ideologies in archaeology encourages archaeologists to see middle-class perspectives as universal and to disdain other class interests and perceptions of the past. The discipline of archaeology reproduces itself in the middle-class setting of the academy.

The Middle Classes

In the United States, the popular usage of the term *middle class* equates this class either with middle income or with white-collar occupations (Keller 2005). In contrast to this common usage, we speak of class as a structural phenomenon defined by the relationship of a social group to the means of production (Foster 2006; Wurst 2006). In modern capitalism, the middle classes . . . are composed of those individuals who stand between the owners (or controllers) of the means of production and the workers who do the labor of production (Braverman 1974:403–409, 1989:42; Ehrenreich and Ehrenreich 1979; Ball 2003). On average this group (e.g., managers, administrators, and professionals) earns considerably more than mean or median income and makes up no more than about 20 percent of the population of the United States (Ehrenreich 1989:12). Most of these individuals have white-collar occupations, but many other white-collar occupations (e.g., clerks, secretaries, and bank tellers) are not considered middle-class in terms of class structure. The middle class is not a uniform mass, and some authors even write about it in the plural, that is, *the middle classes* (Patterson 1995b; Ball 2003). For instance, individuals who make their living primarily through their command of a specialized body of knowledge form the professional middle class, as opposed to the managerial middle class, which is composed of individuals who make their living primarily by managing the labor of others (Ehrenreich 1989; Ball 2003). We can also define class factions on the basis of regional, racial, and cultural differences (Patterson 1995b).

Classes reproduce themselves over time. Self-reproduction is an essential characteristic of classes that distinguishes them from strata (Foster 2006). Indeed, many sociologists have argued that scholars should speak of classes as being made up of families rather than individuals (Sennett and Cobb 1972; Domhoff 1983, 1996). The process of reproduction entails both maintaining the structural position (the occupations and relations among them) and socializing the next generation to take up roles within that class position.

In modern capitalism, the reproduction of the middle class is the most insecure of the class positions (Frykman 1987; Ehrenreich 1989:12; Sullivan et al. 2001; Ball 2003; Lareau 2003). Working-class occupations minimally require the ability to do physical labor or, in many cases, sets of skills that can be acquired from a parent or with modest education. Bourgeois families (the owners of the means of production) usually have capital resources (wealth, stocks, property, etc.) that allow them to ensure that their children will be able to maintain the class position of their parents (Mills 1956; Domhoff 1996). Middle-class families, however, typically lack the capital resources to guarantee their children's class position and instead seek to provide them with a formal education to equip them with a body of esoteric knowledge, social skills, shared experience, and certification that will allow them to become middle-class adults in the future. Formal education gives middle-class children the technical skills necessary for middle-class occupations, but of equal importance it entrusts to them the social skills and symbolic capital of the middle classes (Ball 2003; Lareau 2003). Middle-class status derives primarily from the control of this symbolic capital.

For most of the twentieth century and now in the twenty-first, entry to the middle class has typically necessitated a college education, and this need has been a major barrier to working-class individuals who sought to enter the middle class (Wolff 1969:151; Ryan and Sackrey 1996:101–109; Aronowitz 1997:190; Jancius 2006). Higher education commonly separates learning from doing (Potter 1994:148–149; Leonhardt 2005), which creates a hurdle for working-class individuals, who must sustain work to maintain themselves and their own families. These people are limited to learning as part of their work or in their time off from work or to rapidly learning technical skills that they can directly apply to work.

The separation of leaning and doing also permeates the relations of labor between the middle and working classes. The work of the middle class is by and large intellectual labor, the application of formal knowledge or principles commonly to tasks that working-class individuals execute. Middle-class ideology puts a high value on the intellectual apparatus of capitalism, especially educational institutions, because the class reproduces itself through this apparatus and because much of the class finds employment in it. Working-class ideology tends to resent this apparatus as elitist, because it hinders their own class mobility and because in the work place their experience and skill are usually subservient to formal knowledge (Ryan and Sackrey 1996:106–109). Thus, middle-class individuals tend to value book learning in contrast with the working-class appreciation for knowledge based on experience (Sennett and Cobb 1972; Frykman 1990; Ball 2003).

The segmentation of learning from doing, of intellectual labor from physical labor, and of knowledge workers from manual workers lies at the heart of modern capitalism (Braverman 1974). This segmentation is the culmination of over a century of class struggle. The discipline of archaeology was both a tool in and a product of this struggle (Trigger 1989a, 2006; Patterson 1995b).

Class and the History of Archaeology

Archaeology is a distinctive product of Western civilization that emerged in the mid-nineteenth century (Daniel 1981:212). Trigger (1989a:14; 2006) links the appearance of archaeology with the rise to power of the middle class in Europe and argues that archaeology broadly expresses the ideology of that class. The middle class found in archaeology a tool to build a common identity, to legitimate their power and privilege, to create mythic charters, and to justify historical events that served their interests. This process involved an alliance with the bourgeois classes that defined the broader interests of capitalist society and initially funded most of the work. Archaeology has also been a weapon wielded in those struggles among class factions within the middle and bourgeois classes (Patterson 1995b).

The rise of the middle class took place in a context of nation-state formation (Anderson 1983). The new middle class manipulated the process of nation creation by inventing traditions that define and reenforce the culture, language, and heritage of the nation (Hobsbawm 1983; Harris 1990). They also established national institutions of education and learning (such as museums) to manipulate these traditions and to educate their youth. Archaeology fit into these new institutions as a way to confirm middle-class notions about history and human nature (Trigger 1989a:14; Wallace 1996:4–32, 178–186). In the middle of the nineteenth century, the first professional, middle-class archaeologist, Jens J. A. Worsaae, received his training and employment in one of these nationalist institutions, the Museum of Northern Antiquities, in Denmark (Trigger 1989a:81).

At the beginning of the nineteenth century, the new nation of the United States faced a fundamental contradiction in the ideology that justified its existence as a nation. The people of the nation-state were not the indigenous people of the continent, but rather the interlopers who had forcibly taken the territory from those who were already here, the Native Americans. Competing class factions of bourgeois and middle-class interests developed rival ideologies to reconcile this contradiction (McGuire 1992a). An urbane East Coast elite steeped in Enlightenment thought argued that Native Americans were the first Americans, a race of noble savages who could not withstand the vices of civilization and who, as they vanished, had passed legitimate ownership of the continent to the new Americans from Europe. Bourgeois individuals such as Thomas Jefferson and George Washington asserted that the great mounds of the Midwest and South demonstrated the accomplishments of the first Americans. Through the nineteenth century, middle-class professionals in eastern institutions, including Henry Schoolcraft, Samuel G. Morton, and John Wesley Powell, conducted research to support the first American point of view (Kennedy 1996:238). A rural midwestern and southern elite, including presidents Andrew Jackson and William Henry Harrison, embraced a more fundamentalist notion that Americans were God's chosen people and that Native Americans were not part of the nation. Midwestern middle-class individuals such as Ephraim G. Squire, Edwin H. Davis, and J. W. Foster did the leg work to support the idea that a race of civilized Mound Builders had built the mounds only to be overwhelmed by red savages who destroyed them (Patterson 1995b:28; Kennedy 1996:238). Cyrus Thomas disproved the Mound Builder myth in 1894, four years after the last official battle of the Indian Wars at Wounded Knee made moot the legitimacy of a European nation on the American continent. The ideological battles of the class factions had shifted to other terrain.

By the turn of the century, the bourgeois class of the United States had created a complex intellectual apparatus that included colleges, universities, and museums (Patterson 1995b:46–47). They staffed these institutions with technicians, scientists, and other professionals, including archaeologists. These intellectual fractions of the middle class mastered the techniques and know-how that created and maintained capitalist culture, and they argued that this mastery justified their control of that culture and of knowledge production. By the second decade of the twentieth century, these institutions were becoming the defining locus of class reproduction for the middle class (Patterson 1995b:58; Aronowitz 1997:190). The intellectual middle class manufactured the symbolic capital necessary to join the middle class and controlled who gained access to it. Archaeology formed part of this symbolic capital that a well-educated, that is, middle-class, person had to possess.

In the universities and colleges, archaeologists taught bourgeois- and middle-class students an official history that primary and secondary teachers distilled and simplified for schoolchildren. Until the 1960s this history tended to deny cultural change in Native American pasts and thus reinforced the idea that static Native American cultures had to fade away in the face of dynamic, inventive Europeans (Trigger 1989a:128–129).

After 1960, archaeologists spoke of culture change in Native American history in theories that made a managerial elite (a primitive middle class?) the prime movers or, in terms of environmental cautionary tales, that reinforced then-current middle-class concerns with ecology (Trigger 1989a:314–315). In the 1980s, Native Americans confronted archaeologists, challenging this control of their pasts and asserting their own histories, which they had not forgotten (Patterson 1995b:115). This challenge shattered the complacency of archaeology and confronted us with the fact that we do not simply produce objective knowledge for a widespread audience.

The Audience for Archaeology

Most archaeologists see their audience as broad and diverse (DeCicco 1988; Lynott 1990; J. Jameson 1997). The limited studies that have been done of the constituency for archaeology suggest that this is not the case and that, in fact, the middle class forms the primary audience for archaeology. In general, visitors to all types of museums, other than school groups, strongly tend to be middle-class, with open-air museums drawing a slightly broader audience (Falk and Dierking 1992:20–24; Hooper-Greenhill 1994:65–66; Wallace 1996:25). Trotter's study of visitors to Wupaki National Monument in Arizona (1989:2) found that most of them have been well-educated, middle-class Anglos. Likewise, Merriman's study of visitors to archaeology museums in England (1987, 1991) found that they too have been predominantly well-educated and middle-class. The vast majority of the readers of the popular magazine *Archaeology* come from the middle and bourgeois classes, with over 60 percent having college degrees and over 80 percent being professionals, administrators, or managers (Archaeology 1996). *National Geographic* has a broader audience with a higher proportion of working-class readers, but still the magazine's readers are primarily middle-class individuals (Lutz and Collins 1993:222).

People who participate in professionally led field programs in archaeology also seem to be predominantly middle-class. Few high schools in the United States include archaeology in their curricula, and those that do are usually suburban, predominantly middle-class schools. Consequently most people who obtain formal training in archaeology do so only in college. Archaeology is always well represented in Earth Watch's expeditionary programs that allow individuals to participate in scientific field projects. More than 94 percent of Earth Watch participants are in, or retired from, middle-class occupations (college students, professionals, managers, and administrators). Merriman's study of volunteers in archaeological field projects in Great Britain (1987) suggests the same.

Segments of the middle class make up the primary audience of archaeology for many possible reasons. Members of this class generally have leisure time and money that can be used for such pursuits. Many working-class jobs do not provide sufficient quantities of either of these resources to allow the pursuit of archaeology. The middle-class interest in archaeology clearly flows from the emphasis on education and formalized learning that characterize the class. Middle-class individuals are socialized to respect, value, and appreciate expert knowledge, while the life experience of working-class people encourages them to distrust, spurn, and disparage such knowledge (Ryan and Sackrey 1996:105–107). Archaeology also resides in the institutions of the middle class, so its children gain familiarity with archaeology from an early age. Finally, the themes and interests of archaeology have paralleled those of the middle class throughout this century (Trigger 1989a; Patterson 1995b). For example, Trigger (1989a:313, 319–320, 355) has argued that the scientific evolutionism of 1960s archaeology, with its emphasis on progress and the humanities' ability to solve problems and make life better, reflected the self-confidence and faith in technology of a prospering U.S. middle class. This prosperity began to wane in the early 1970s, leading to greater insecurity and pessimism in the middle class (see also Ehrenreich 1989; Patterson 1995b:104), and archaeologists began advocating a "cataclysmic evolutionism" that stresses how technological change forces people to work harder and how technology degrades the environment.

Archaeology and Working-Class Interests

Archaeology's tendency to represent middle-class interests as universal fits easily into a larger American ideology that says we are all middle-class, except for a very small number of wealthy and poor individuals (Sennett and Cobb 1972; Domhoff 1996; Fantasia and Voss 2004:167; Keller 2005; Durrenberger 2006). Thus, archaeologists often represent those individuals who hold different interests in the past or use the past in different ideological ways as being ignorant, pernicious, or motivated solely by greed (Lynott 1990). They have rarely considered that these differences in attitudes may be class based. Nowhere is this more evident than in the archaeologist's abhorrence for pothunters, or looters (not to be confused with amateur archaeologists who are part of the discipline).

Archaeologists approach their database with a reverence uncommon in other disciplines. From the first introductory course to the conclusion of the Festschrift, we sanctify the archaeological record. We justify it as a source of knowledge and, more important, as our heritage. We stand in a unique relationship to our data; unlike the investigations of most other disciplines, ours destroy that which we wish to study. Furthermore, the archaeological record is given and finite; what we destroy cannot be replaced. Thus, in the ideology of our discipline, the archaeologist exists to serve a higher goal, the search for knowledge, but archaeologists must also serve the archaeological record. This ideology includes a strong notion of self-sacrifice, of economic gain and even well-being, to achieve knowledge and to protect the archaeological record. Such self-sacrifice embodies middle-class ideals of the sanctity of learning.

•   •   •

Looter: An individual who plunders archaeological sites
to find artifacts of commercial value, at the same time
destroying the evidence that archaeologists rely upon to
understand the past.
                Wendy Ashmore and Robert J. Sharer (1993:616)

A strong animosity to pothunters, or looters, runs through archaeology. Archaeologists argue that looters destroy the archaeological record in order to recover objects that can be bought and sold. This process both denies the archaeologist the material necessary to the production of formal knowledge and violates the archaeologist's sense of reverence for the archaeological record. Archaeologists portray looters as being needy or greedy, as lacking an appreciation of the past and any understanding of the intellectual value of the materials that they seek. Most archaeologists seem to agree that we need to educate looters to appreciate the record, to see things our way (Lynott 1990).

Our data on who loots archaeological sites and why they do it are every bit as meager as our information on who appreciates archaeology. Even limited knowledge does suggest, however, that the looters come predominately from working-class backgrounds. The distinction between middle-class archaeologists and working-class pothunters goes back at least to the 1930s (Duke and Matlock, n.d.; Patterson 1995b:59). Hodder (1984:29–30) noted that the antagonism between treasure hunters and archaeologists in Britain has been rooted in broader class differences. Merriman (1987) surveyed metal detector users who looted archaeological sites in Great Britain and found that the majority of them were working-class individuals with slightly above average incomes. Potter (1994) has argued that we need to recognize the cultural differences between looters and ourselves and ask why these individuals engage in these activities and what needs of theirs they fulfill. Only then can we engage in a dialogue with these people that might change both their and our behavior.

Clearly those people who loot archaeological sites and advocate cult archaeologies have a concept of the value of the past that differs from ours as archaeologists. We would argue that these differences are not the manifestations of simply greed or ignorance. If a class difference separates archaeologists from looters, then each group approaches the past with very different beliefs about formal knowledge and intellectual labor. The programs that archaeologists have developed to educate the public—exhibits, site tours, magazines, classes, tours, and pamphlets—appeal more to middle-class individuals, who look to books and authorities for knowledge, and less to working-class people, who stress practical know-how. Hodder's (1984) and Merriman's (1987) studies suggest that many working-class people have a deep interest in the past, but they feel alienated from an archaeology that they identify as elitist. The charge of elitism is not unwarranted, since the traditional process of reproducing archaeology seeks to remove archaeologists from the day-to-day world of work and to imbue them with a sense of membership in an exclusive group. Chapter 5 discusses an attempt to link archaeology to working-class interests through the study of the 1913–1914 Colorado Coalfield War and the Ludlow Massacre.

Reproducing Archaeology

The discipline of archaeology traditionally reproduced itself in the university through a guild model. This process involved a long apprenticeship (graduate school), journeyman status (untenured faculty), and finally the security of master status (tenure). In theory at least, these stages related to age, maturity, and proficiency. Apprentice, journeyman, and master formed a class structure, but, again in theory, it was a structure of mobility. Not all apprentices became masters, and exploitation did occur, but all apprentices had the opportunity to become masters, and all masters were once apprentices.

In this idealized model, teams of scholars conducted archaeological fieldwork. Senior members of the teams were established researchers with publications and recognition. Junior members were apprentices, there to learn and to acquire the skills and eventually the status of their mentors. The participants in this process saw it as a noneconomic one in which they received only as much money as was needed to support the higher goals of the research. They eschewed the ethos of the market and instead stressed archaeology's goal as honest, disinterested, and competent research (Moore 2006:30). They saw their rewards in the process as advancement through the guild.

Until the late 1970s, the vast majority of archaeologists labored in the academy. Today a person must still pass through the academy to become an archaeologist. The B.A. is usually a minimum requirement for regular employment, and supervisory or managerial positions virtually always require at least an M.A., if not a Ph.D. (Fagan 2006). The academy remains the locus of socialization for archaeologists. In this context, they are taught a reverence for the resource base, to sacrifice economic well-being for research, the guild model of hierarchy, and the mental and practical skills of the discipline.

Unlike fields such as business, engineering, and nursing, archaeology traditionally did not train undergraduate students to take up professions. Rather, archaeology as part of a liberal arts education, served to reproduce the middle class through undergraduate programs and to reproduce itself through apprenticeship by a small number of individuals in graduate programs. Archaeology was part of the socialization process of the middle class in undergraduate programs, giving them shared experience and knowledge (symbolic capital) that were not easily obtained outside the university by working-class individuals. Individuals who were drawn to master archaeology (to become university professors) traditionally were people who searched for a life of the mind and who wished to escape the day-to-day world of capitalism (Kehoe 1998:86). The growth of contract archaeology has greatly changed this situation, creating a professional arena that employs the vast majority of archaeologists in the day-to-day world of capitalism. However, it is very much our impression that the majority of students who pursue apprenticeship in the academy have the traditional longing for a life of the mind and seek to emulate their professors of archaeology (Zeder 1997:16–17).

Archaeologists, like most middle-class Americans, have had little awareness of the class structures within which they work and live. The vast majority of archaeologists come from middle to bourgeois socioeconomic backgrounds, and a Society for American Archaeology survey of the discipline by Zeder (1997:13) suggests that the imbalance may be increasing. Archaeologists have also been, by and large, white Anglos; more than 98 percent come from this demographic, according to the SAA survey (Zeder 1997:13). Few African American, Asian American, Latino, and Native American individuals have entered the discipline. The racial imbalance in part reflects the white predominance in the American middle class. It is also the case that the class position of middle-class people of color is more precarious than that of the white middle class, because people of color must also deal with racism and discrimination. Middle-class people of color tend to direct their children to more practical, stable, and financially secure professions (Barbour 1994:12; Franklin 1997:800; Lippert 1997). They also direct their children away from archaeology, because they often identify it with the racism and discrimination that they experience in modern American society (Hill 1994; Pullar 1994). Thus, most archaeologists share a common social background, and they see one another as the same. The common experience of the university reinforces this sense of sameness, and the guild model tends to obscure from archaeologists the class nature of archaeological interests and also the class structure within the profession.

Traditionally, therefore, archaeology reproduced itself as a discipline by training individuals to take up a very specialized niche, the university professor, in the reproduction of the middle class. This traditional training, however, does not meet the realities of archaeology as an occupation in our present era (Bender and Smith 2000; Whitley 2004; Fagan 2006). Fast capitalism shapes archaeology, both in the academy and in CRM, to an ethos of market exchange and corrodes the guild model of the university. More important, in both the academy and in CRM the guild model has become an ideology that is used to mask or hide class relations and exploitation within the occupational structures of archaeology.

FAST CAPITALISM

The current state of the class struggle in archaeology today springs from and is embedded in the fast capitalism that has shaped the turn of the twenty-first century (Agger 2004:9). The consequences and driving forces behind fast capitalism have been the erosion of worker's rights, the reduction in worker's security, and the deterioration of working conditions (Agger 2004; Fantasia and Voss 2004). The middle class has not

escaped these consequences, because fast capitalism has increasingly proletarianized professions such as archaeology.

After World War II, the worldwide capitalist economy soared, especially in the United States. By 1970, this growth began to slow down and
even stall, leading to hyperinflation and declining profits by the end of
that decade (Foster et al. 2002). The election of Margaret Thatcher in
Great Britain and Ronald Reagan in the United States and the growth of
the so-called New Economy in the 1980s did not reinvigorate capitalist
economic growth, but they did usher in fast capitalism. In government
policy, liberal ideas of social contract and social welfare lost sway to
right-wing ideas of free trade, individual responsibility, and noninterfer-
ence by governments in economic affairs. The end of the twentieth century witnessed shifts in the class structure of the core capitalist countries,
with declining working-class wages, more wealth concentration in the
bourgeois classes, and a squeezing of the middle class (Domhoff 1996).
What has emerged in the United States since the 1980s is a split economy
with relatively fewer secure well-paying jobs than before and more insecure low-paying jobs (Patterson 1995b:104). The production of durable
consumer goods that drove capitalism since World War II has declined
and much manufacturing has shifted from core states to the peripheries.
The essence of the New Economy engaged economic sectors most closely
associated with the revolution in digital technology and the growth of the
Internet. The rapid convergence of information technologies (including
computers, software, satellites, fiber optics, and the Internet) has altered
the economic landscape (Foster et al. 2001). These trends have produced
an accelerated fast capitalism.

In chapter 2, I discussed how multinational firms have commodified
heritage through cultural tourism. The same processes have worked to
transform education and archaeological knowledge into profit genera-
tors. Education has many social goals, including social development,
democratic empowerment, advancing the general well-being of societies,
increasing economic competitiveness, and sharing knowledge and personal growth (Noble 2003). The commodification of education ignores
the social and transforms education into a private (individual) good that
can be bought and sold. Commodified education focuses on certification
rather than learning. The measure of education becomes the cost of the
degree relative to the market value that it has. Governments have used
the idea of education as a private good as a justification to cut funding
for public education, bringing the pressures of fast capitalism to the
academy. In a somewhat different way, cultural resource management

has commodified archaeological knowledge (Tilley 1989:106–107). CRM treats archaeological sites as units that must be managed. "Each has a price-tag and, when the demands of business efficiency raise questions about who can do the requisite work for the least money the past may be tagged with competing prices" (Tilley 1989:107).

The watchwords of fast capitalism are *speed* and *flexibility* (Holmes 2000; Agger 2004). The technology of computers, software, satellites, fiber optics, the Internet, and the container ship make fast capitalism possible. Fast capitalism is a fully global capitalism in which any task can be broken down into its component parts and deskilled. The least skilled components can be outsourced to the other side of the world, so computer programmers in Boston lose their jobs to workers in Bangalore. Manufacturers need not own factories but instead can contract with agents from around the world for delivery of goods on demand.

Fast capitalism creates a hypercompetitiveness that rewards an enterprise's adaptability, dynamism, and continual reskilling/learning. The first victims of fast capitalism were high-wage core-state manufacturing workers who lost their jobs to low-wage countries on the peripheries of the capitalist system. But the processes of fast capitalism penetrate all levels of the economy, from manufacturing to service to management to education. In this way, fast capitalism proletarianizes traditionally middle-class professions. In order to maintain their competitive edge, employers demand total commitment from their workers. Economic acceleration and increasing demands on employees drive down the quality of life. People suffer increased levels of stress, reduced time spent with friends and families, and overall dissatisfaction with their lives (Agger 2004; Fantasia and Voss 2004). Fast capitalism celebrates temporary and fast-changing networks, including those of coworkers, businesses, friends, and families (Holmes 2000). People come together for a given project and then disperse when products, projects, and services change in the hypercompetitive and fast-paced environment of fast capitalism. These ephemeral networks erode stable communities of people with shared histories and long-term commitments (Agger 2004).

The bourgeois classes have fared well under fast capitalism. This is very clear in the United States. In 1980, the compensation for CEOs was 42 times that of the average worker in the corporation. By 2003, the compensation for CEOs had risen to 245 times that of the average worker (Fantasia and Voss 2004:15). Between 1983 and 2001, the top 1 percent of wealth holders in the United States received 28 percent of the increase in national income, 33 percent of the total gain in net worth, and 52 percent of the rise in financial worth (Foster 2006). The acceptance of great disparities in compensation has permeated society, justifying a star system of disproportionately high compensation in business, entertainment, sports, and the university.

Fast capitalism's mantras of speed and flexibility have meant greater insecurity for people who work for a living, so the working and middle classes have not fared so well in the New Economy. Real wages, controlled for inflation, peaked in 1973, declined until the Clinton administration, recovered slightly then, and are now falling again (Fantasia and Voss 2004:12; Magdoff and Magdoff 2004). The reserve army of the unemployed has increased under fast capitalism through underemployment, illegal immigration, and decreases in welfare support (Magdoff and Magdoff 2004). A large reserve army of the unemployed drives down wages at the bottom of the scale. Finally, workers are laboring more hours, often at multiple part-time jobs. The bifurcating effects of fast capitalism have created a split wage scale, with the rich getting very much richer and the working and middle classes getting relatively and absolutely poorer (Fantasia and Voss 2004; Magdoff and Magdoff 2004).

Fast capitalism has been hard on unions. In the boom years from the 1940s to the 1970s, "business unionism" dominated organized labor in the United States (Fantasia and Voss 2004:57). Under this model unions abandoned the social change agendas of organized labor in the first half of the twentieth century to focus on winning higher wages and benefits for their members. Union members, principally white and male, worked primarily in manufacturing, construction, and transportation. Business unionism won its workers the highest wages and benefits in the history of the United States. In 1955, union membership peaked at 35 percent of the labor force (Fantasia and Voss 2004:54). The focus of most unions on gaining compensation for their primarily white male members often put unions at odds with social movements to improve the conditions of African Americans, women, and immigrants. Business unions were highly hierarchical, with top-down control and widespread graft and corruption (Fantasia and Voss 2004:78–119). Starting in 1980, business began a concerted effort to break unions. Fast capitalism undermined union occupations with its emphasis on flexibility, outsourcing, and hypercompetitiveness. An industry of consultants, attorneys, and accountants developed to aid corporations in union busting. Finally, conservative legislation eroded workers' rights and the ability of unions to organize workers. By 2002, only 14 percent of the U.S. workforce belonged to a union (Fantasia and Voss 2004:19–20).

In the 1980s, many of the rank and file in the AFL-CIO called for reform and organized to democratize their unions (Fantasia and Voss 2004:98–119). At the AFL-CIO national convention in 1995, this reform movement took control with the election of John Sweeney as president of the organization, ushering in the current era of "social movement unionism." This new model of unionism emphasizes the organization of service, public, and information workers. These organizing efforts and the continued decline of manufacturing in the United States have increased the percentage of people of color in the union movement. The movement has embraced a progressive social program of social justice and social change. In addition to stressing the organization of service workers, the AFL-CIO moved to organize more middle-class professionals, such as teachers, college professors, and doctors. Despite these welcome reforms, union membership and power have continued to decline. At the 2006 AFL-CIO convention, a group of four large unions broke from the organization. The implications of this split for the future of labor in the United States are not clear yet.

WORKING AS AN ARCHAEOLOGIST IN AN ERA OF FAST CAPITALISM

Fast capitalism has transformed archaeology as a discipline and as an occupation. Today bifurcated working conditions and compensation exist in both the academy and in cultural resource management. Increasing numbers of archaeologists are trapped in class positions that do not pay them a living wage or grant them the respect that their mastery of the craft of archaeology deserves. In both of these professional situations, this denigration of archaeological labor threatens a deterioration of standards and quality in the archaeological product.

Even though the occupational structures of the academy and cultural resource management are distinct, the two spheres remain interconnected and will always be so. Archaeology still reproduces itself in the academy, and almost all archaeologists share the experience of the academy. Also, even though a core of higher-level, established professionals (professors, managers, project directors) exists in each sphere, the two share a common pool of aspiring archaeologists. These aspirants move back and forth between the two spheres until they land a permanent professional

position in one or the other, resign themselves to a life in the new archaeological proletariat, or drop out of the discipline altogether.

The Changing Relationship of Class and the Academy

Fast capitalism has proletarianized the academy both in its role in the
reproduction of the class structure and in its occupational structure. The
democratization of the university in the postwar United States transformed it from an exclusive portal to the white middle class into the
training ground for the middle class and a technically skilled working
class. This has eroded the symbolic capital of the middle class, because,
although middle-class status still virtually requires a university degree, a
degree no longer ensures that status. Concurrently, the occupational
structure of the academy has been transformed from a guild of masters
and apprentices to a knowledge factory dependent on a reserve army of
underemployed teaching assistants and lecturers (Yates 2000).

In the United States in the 1960s and 1970s, a massive expansion of
colleges and universities occurred because of the demographic bulge of
the baby boom and the ever-increasing percentage of young people entering college. In 1947, eighteen hundred colleges and universities existed in
the United States with 2.3 million students. By 1990, the number of institutions had risen to thirty-two hundred and the number of students to
12.5 million (Aronowitz 1997:190–191). This expansion fueled a massive increase in the number of anthropology departments in the country
and provided jobs for an unprecedented number of archaeologists in the
academy (Patterson 1995b:81; Roseberry 1996:9).

Thousands of people from working-class backgrounds flocked to the
more open universities, seeking a stepping-stone to the middle class
(Aronowitz 1997; Menand 1997). The university ceased to be the sole
preserve of the middle and bourgeois classes. In 1947, 10 percent of high
school graduates went on to higher education. This number increased to
40 percent in 1960, to 50 percent in 1980, and to 62 percent in 1994. At
the end of the twentieth century, most of this increase was fueled by the
entry of students of color (African Americans, Asian Americans, Latinos,
and Native Americans) into higher education (Menand 1997:48). During
the period in which the economy was still expanding, a significant portion of new graduates could gain access to the middle class. The economic downturn that started in the 1970s and the resulting New
Economy changed this situation. The economic decline halted expansion
in the number of academic positions, and by 1975 new Ph.D.s in anthro-

pology hit a solid wall of fully employed departments (Patterson 1995b:17–108; Roseberry 1996). Individuals graduating with bachelor's degrees hit similar walls, and since the 1980s a university degree has not guaranteed entry into the middle class, although it remains a requirement (Jancius 2006). Fifty percent of the workforce today enters college, but only about 20 percent of the jobs available are middle class (Menand 1997:48). In the 1980s, social science enrollments, including anthropology, plunged as students sought more practical training in business and professional colleges (Givens and Jablonski 1996:5). At the same time, real working-class wages declined, so we have witnessed an ever-widening gap between working-class and middle-class lifestyles. The insecurity of the middle class has increased as the material costs of failure in reproduction—that is, of their children slipping into the working class—have escalated (Ehrenreich 1989; Ball 2003; Lareau 2003).

Starting in the 1980s, the academy came under a concerted and sustained attack by the political right (Roseberry 1996:17). Members of the right saw the academy as one of the few areas of modern society that had not succumbed to a fast capitalist ethos of market principles. The right sought to "defund" the left by actively interfering with governmental endowment and funding agencies and by attacking the privilege of the professoriat (Bloom 1987; Sykes 1988). These attacks found widespread support within the middle class, in part because of the changing relationship of that class to the university. As the university student body has increasingly become more proletariat and less white, the support of the white middle class for the university has declined (Aronowitz 1997; Nelson 1997b; Nelson and Watt 2004). In a climate of increased middle-class insecurity, rising university costs, and a decreasing efficacy of university credentials in the reproduction of the class, middle-class individuals have wanted universities to be more practical and cost effective (Ehrenreich 1989; Ball 2003; Lareau 2003). Working-class families facing declining real wages and increasing university costs, which have limited their children's access to the essential credentials for class mobility, have responded warmly to right-wing attacks on latte-drinking, brie-eating, Volvo-driving intellectual elites, especially university professors.

Two consequences of these shifts have been an effort to restructure the university and a crisis of employment in the academy (Roseberry 1996:17; Yates 2000). Fast capitalism has turned schools into workplaces (Agger 2004:83). For students at all levels, the emphasis has switched from learning to earning credentials, grades, and test scores (Agger 2004:98). The guild image of the university as a community of scholars in pursuit of knowledge does not fit well with a fast capitalism that demands constant flexibility and constant reskilling of employees (Siegel 2006). Many aspects of the traditional university, such as a liberal arts education, tenure, theory, philosophy, personal fulfillment, and humanism, do not fit well with fast capitalism's emphasis on rote learning, skill acquisition, and value-added accountability (Agger 2004:98; Siegel 2006).

Colleges and universities have become degree factories that employ a significant portion of the U.S. workforce (Aronowitz 1997:188; Noble 2003). In 1991, colleges and universities in the United States employed 2,662,085 workers (Kelley 1997:146). In many communities, colleges and universities are the largest employers and landlords in the area (Kelley 1997). A hierarchical system of higher education has developed in which the class and racial exclusivity of the traditional academy exists only at the highest tiers, in private schools, and in state flagship universities, while the lower tiers train proletariat workers (Leonhardt 2005). Elite private schools have become the new guarantor for middle-class status, and the competition to enter such schools has soared. One of the reasons for the establishment of community colleges was to provide a stepping-stone to four-year schools, but increasingly a community college degree is a terminal degree that gives access to a working-class occupation (Aronowitz 1997:189).

In the academic factory, the autonomy and the privilege of college and university teachers have declined, except among an elite stratum of stars (Yates 2000). University workers at all levels increasingly find themselves facing the same challenges and difficulties (Nelson 1997b:6). One of the few growth areas for unions in the 1980s was in colleges and universities. As of 1997, 25 percent of full-time faculty at colleges and universities in the Unites States were unionized, as opposed to 14 percent of all workers in the economy (Aronowitz 1997:188, 204).

In the 1990s, the federal and state governments cut funding to the academy, and administrators began actively downsizing the professorial staffs of colleges and universities. As a result, the number of full-time tenured and tenure-track positions in the academy has declined. Universities have responded to these cuts by replacing tenured faculty with graduate assistants and adjuncts to teach more and more classes. In the 1970s, about 25 percent of faculty were part-timers. This figure rose to about 45 percent during the late 1990s (Pratt 1997:265) and fell slightly to 43 percent in 2003 (Jacobe 2006:46). Even among full-timers, the percentage of non-tenure-track faculty went up from 12 percent in 1984 to

20 percent in 1996, then dropping a bit by 2003, to 17 percent (Jacobe 2006:46). Including full- and part-time faculty (but not graduate student teaching assistants), over 50 percent of the faculty teaching in U.S. higher education are nontenured today (McKenna 1997:6–7; Yates 2000; Jacobe 2006:43); only 28 percent of university teachers in the United States have tenure, and another 12 percent are on the tenure track (Jacobe 2006:46).

Academic standards and quality have suffered in this process. Declining numbers of faculty have meant increasing class sizes and notions that equate academic productivity with higher and higher student-faculty ratios. At Binghamton University in the last decade of the twentieth century, the student-faculty ratio in the department of anthropology went from 14:1 to 25:1 and has not declined since. Such ratios are much higher in teaching colleges around the country. We have also been pressured by administrators to lower entrance standards for graduate students and the requirements for a master's degree in anthropology to increase the number of graduate students that we enroll. Students are not necessarily well served when overworked, underexperienced graduate students or transitory adjuncts teach many of their classes.

The Ideology of Apprenticeship as Exploitation in the Academy

Archaeologists who labor in the academy are battered by fast capitalism's erosion of the benefits of university employment. This erosion has transformed teaching assistants and adjuncts into an academic proletariat. Anthropology departments, where most archaeology programs reside, have not been as hard hit as departments in the humanities, especially English (Nelson 1997a). Even so, anthropology departments have marshaled the ideology of apprenticeship to justify and obscure the existence and exploitation of the academic proletariat. Departments have increased the duties and responsibilities of graduate students and adjuncts even as the support and rewards for these individuals have declined.

The apprenticeship of graduate studies has grown longer and longer, because the university increasingly asks apprentices to do more and more work not necessarily directly related to their own preparation for mastery (Kennedy 1997; Pratt 1997). They also have no guarantee that they will be able to move to mastery (a tenured professorship) or even to journeyman status (a tenure-track position) after graduation. Without the availability of jobs, the whole logic of apprenticeship collapses, and graduate students simply become exploited labor (Nelson 1997a:169). As a result graduate students have come to see their status as that of employees, not as that of students. One consequence of this shift has been increasing struggles by graduate student teaching assistants to unionize (Joseph and Curtiss 1997; Nelson 1997b; Kennedy 1997; Kelley 1997; Kadir 2006).

Presently, only a minority of graduate students can hope to land tenure-track jobs (Jacobe 2006). For example, of Harvard's 1995 Ph.D. class, only 27 percent had found teaching positions by 1997 (Menand 1997:49). National statistics are comparable. Since 1971, only about 33 percent of new Ph.D.s have obtained tenure-track jobs, and the chance of a new Ph.D. earning tenure and staying in the profession has been less than one in ten (Nelson and Watt 2004:23). This is also true in the specific case of anthropology and archaeology (Fagan 2006). The number of Ph.D.s granted in anthropology has been about four hundred a year since 1974; yet, in the last decade of the twentieth century, the number of tenure-track academic positions open in the field never reached one hundred per year (Evens et al. 1997). In response to legions of applicants, those few departments with tenure-track positions have increased their expectations of applicants, excessively raising requirements for obtaining such a position. Job ads in the *Anthropology News* for assistant professors seek candidates who are established scholars with proven records of research, publication, and teaching. It was not so long ago that these were the requirements for tenure, not employment. This inflation of requirements is common throughout the academy (Nelson and Watt 2004:50). Tenured faculty tell graduate students that they must complete the requirements for their degrees, teach for their departments, and publish meaningful research if they hope to get the tenure-track job. With so few such prizes available, the student is like a jogger on a treadmill, running faster and faster to go nowhere. Such is fast capitalism.

Most graduate students who seek an academic position end up in a continuing series of temporary and adjunct positions (Joseph and Curtiss 1997; McKenna 1997). Traditionally, the academy used temporary and adjunct positions to fill in for absent faculty, to offer exotic courses, and to host visiting faculty. Individuals accepted these positions as a step in their movement to mastery, to supplement employment outside the academy, or because they were married to a full-time faculty member. Adjuncts were the auxiliaries of the academy, but as positions have been cut and demands on faculty time increased, administrators have increasingly used adjuncts to perform core teaching functions in the university. Tenured faculty have acquiesced to or even supported this shift in order to maintain their own privilege and position (Nelson 1997a:1–3; Nelson and Watt 2004:24–26).

Today, individuals often cannot escape this adjunct status, and it has become a career track. One or two adjunct positions convey experience, but at some point the candidate becomes damaged goods, undesirable, because departments wonder what personal failing has kept him or her from a tenure-track position (Nelson 1997a:159–161; Nelson and Watt 2004:25 Jacobe 2006). Moving from town to town each year or semester, adapting to a new campus, and teaching four or five courses on multiple campuses to make ends meet do not leave adjuncts the time to nurture their own intellectual life or produce the kind of research that will lead them to a tenure-track job (DiGiacomo 1996). As graduate students, they ran fast to stay in one place. As adjuncts, they run faster to fall further behind. These "gypsy scholars" receive lower pay (25 to 35 percent of regular faculty pay) (DiGiacomo 1996:5) and fewer benefits than regular faculty if they receive any benefits at all. They satisfy fast capitalism's demand for lowered labor costs and leaner, more competitive enterprises. They arguably form a lesser class within the professoriat and are often regarded and treated as such by the tenured faculty (DiGiacomo 1996; McKenna 1997). Gender also plays an important role here; this new class or reserve army of labor is disproportionately female, both in general (Thompson 1997:278; Sullivan 1997; Jacobe 2006) and in archaeology (Zeder 1997:16). These people are arguably middle-class but in a fractional position quite distinct from and disadvantaged in relation to that of the tenured or tenure-track professor.

Fast capitalism demands flexibility, and the gypsy scholars provide this in higher education. They allow the college or university to shift its course offerings more quickly than it can with tenured or tenure-track faculty. The university can meet an increase in student demand for Introduction to Microeconomics by not rehiring the adjunct that taught Introduction to Archaeology last semester and instead hiring an economics adjunct to teach microeconomics. The easy dispensability of the gypsy scholars gives the college or university flexibility in other situations as well (Nelson and Watt 2004:49). The administrators of the State University of New York system dramatically demonstrated this following the tragedy of 9/11. In 2002, the State of New York drastically cut funding for the university system, claiming financial exigency as a result of the attack on New York City. The system absorbed the cut in budget by increasing class sizes and not rehiring the vast majority of adjuncts who had taught the year before.

As Roseberry (1996) points out, within anthropology this shift has greatly increased the differential between "elite" Ph.D. programs that place a higher percentage of their students in tenure-track positions and "commoner" programs that supply the individuals for the adjunct and temporary appointments. Within the academy, tenured faculty often justify the position of the gypsy scholars by claiming that they are inferior researchers (DiGiacomo 1996). These ideologies of achievement and prestige from a past when each apprentice had a chance to become a master obscure the fundamental structural change in how the academy now reproduces itself as a class-stratified community. Our view of the current situation for archaeologists in the academy is grim. We fear, as Nelson (1997a:5) points out for the discipline of English, that the present situation is not temporary and that it represents a structural change in academic labor. We can only echo his warning: "Again, I write on behalf of every job candidate to tell you the academic profession is sick and broken and in need of change. In the meantime, take Mao's advice: dig tunnels deep, store grain everywhere" (Nelson 1997a:170).

Archaeology has weathered the storms of fast capitalism better than many of the other social sciences because of the coincidental development of contract archaeology or cultural resource management (CRM). In the 1970s, as academic employment hit the wall and then shrank, employment in the contract sector grew enormously. This growth slowed or stopped in the 1980s when the creation of new positions lost speed and petered out (Moore 2006). But even today archaeologists have an option for employment in their field that is not open to many other social scientists, such as historians and sociologists. However, contract archaeology has matured in fast capitalism, and it has opened up new dimensions of class struggle that were not traditionally part of our profession.

The Class Structure of Cultural Resource Management

CRM archaeology evolved along with fast capitalism. Initially in the 1970s, universities and museums provided contract archaeology, usually using an academic approach to research that stressed archaeological goals (Moore 2006:31). These institutions were not-for-profit entities. They often grafted the CRM onto exiting programs of apprenticeship training.

The academic guild model did not fit well with the increasingly market-driven requirements of CRM. Training apprentices interfered with the accelerated requirements for on-time completion of projects and efficiency. Academics accustomed to working with little money but unlimited time often failed to meet compliance requirements and deadlines.

Today, private companies devoted exclusively to contract-based archaeology have largely replaced universities and museums as the providers of services, a shift that was evident by the close of the 1970s (e.g., Fitting and Goodyear 1979). A market model, in which the results of archaeological research are commodified as a "deliverable" produced for a client and priced within competitive market conditions, replaced the disciplinary ideal of "pure research" (Shott 1992:9–11; Fitting and Goodyear 1979). In this model, profit derives from the difference in the price paid for the product and the labor and material costs to the contractor.

Economic efficiency has become a necessity as more and more companies compete for scarce contracts. Like all other enterprises in fast capitalism, increasing competition has made CRM purportedly more efficient and flexible. Many companies survive by doing archaeological work as quickly and cheaply as possible. In general, the purchasers of required archaeological services are unconcerned with the quality of the work, except insofar as it gets them through various permitting "hoops." The overall result of this is a pressure to relax the quality of archaeological work. Standards and guidelines of state historic preservation offices and regulatory agencies have become not the minimum standards but, for many contractors, the only standards. The implications for the quality of CRM research as a whole have been addressed elsewhere (Lacey and Hasenstab 1983; Shanks and McGuire 1996). The need to be competitive prods CRM companies toward minimum effort, standardized research, greater flexibility, and increased production (more contracts executed in less time for less money). These same pressures depress wages and erode working conditions.

CRM companies, and the archaeologists within them, must work within a set of tensions between the demands of the disciplinary ideals of archaeological research and the often-incompatible economic demands of fast capitalism. How CRM companies and archaeologists work within these structural tensions varies tremendously, depending on the policies and "cultures" of the individual companies, the size of their contracts, and the commitment of the employees. Some companies choose to compromise the discipline for the sake of business efficiency, while others sacrifice profitability to do interesting research. The people within the companies may likewise respond in different ways. Principal investigators may produce a report with the minimum effort necessary for it to meet standards or, as is more often the case, exploit themselves, working long hours in order to do research that makes a contribution to the discipline. An enormous amount of important work in archaeology has been done within the context of CRM. More often than not though, individual investigators have accomplished this work through self-sacrifice, in spite of the economic realities of CRM. In this way, the general trend of fast capitalism to make work omnipresent by blurring the boundaries between work and home, leisure and productivity, is realized in archaeology (Agger 2004:60–82).

The escalating competitive pressure on CRM companies has also resulted in increasing discordance between the disciplinary ideals of research and the lived experience of the CRM labor force, the workers in the field projects and laboratories (de Boer 2004). The maximization of profit and the minimization of cost have propelled CRM on a trajectory typical of most capitalist industries, and, like most other industries, it finds itself confronted with labor problems. Sporadic attempts to organize field technicians in response to the proletarianization of fieldwork have failed.

Almost all archaeologists in CRM are trained in the academy and are often ill prepared for the realities of research within a profit-driven business (Blanton 1995; Schuldenrein 1992, 1995; Bender and Smith 2000). Many archaeologists working in CRM have expressed dissatisfaction with their university training, claiming it did not give them realistic expectations as to the careers available to them or adequately train them for the jobs that they now have (Zeder 1997:13, 17; Whitley 2004). But even as these archaeologists adjust to a market and profit-driven archaeology, they still retain assumptions and expectations that derive from their disciplinary backgrounds. These assumptions and expectations enter CRM labor relations as an ideology that emphasizes the academy-derived guild-based, or "apprenticeship," ideal of career advancement. In this ideal, the position of field worker is temporary, an interlude of acquiring skills and putting them into practice for a couple of years after graduation. After a period of time, the field worker, by now probably a crew chief, is expected to leave the field and enter graduate school, where he or she will acquire the necessary accreditation to become a director and eventually a principal investigator, leaving the working class of CRM and joining its middle class. In this ideology, long-term or permanent field workers are an aberration, trapped only because of their own failings or lack of ambition in a position that should be temporary. Like adjuncts in the academy, the discipline blames them for their lack of advancement.

We should note that this ideal of career advancement is not a lie promulgated by managers to deceive their workers. It does, in fact, reflect the lived experience of many managers, most of whom entered CRM in the boom years of the 1970s. Reminiscences of this experience are a common trope in communications from managers to field staff. However, the vast majority of individuals entering CRM since the end of the 1970s have not shared the experience of advancement. Staffing in CRM reached a plateau by the 1980s, and the individuals who gained positions during this rapid growth phase by and large have yet to retire (Moore 2006). A constant turnover of entry-level individuals means that field technicians' positions continue to open up, but, without the requisite degrees, field technicians are unable to advance to supervisory positions. This ideology also ignores the skyrocketing costs of education (Schuldenrein 1995) and the insufficient salaries in CRM for paying off extensive student loans (McGuire 1984).

The guild ideal also emphasizes a vertical corporate identity rather than a class-based solidarity. In this way, CRM participates in fast capitalism's disruption of social distinctions, particularly those based on class. The ideal proposes that we are all archaeologists, bonded through our mutual concern for the preservation of the archaeological record. Archaeologists should pursue economic well-being and quality of life as secondary considerations to the preservation of this record and the knowledge that we gain from it. Managers portray economic demands by, in this case, field technicians as endangering the discipline, because they "are rocking the Section 106 boat" (Kintz 1996).

Managers fear that increased wages will drive up the costs of projects, ultimately increasing corporate opposition to cultural resource legislation, an alarming prospect in the current political environment. The values enshrined in cultural resource legislation are not market values. They run afoul of the ethos of fast capitalism that has encroached on all aspects of social life. Thus, CRM faces an explosive contradiction. As an enterprise within fast capitalism, it must adapt to demands for flexibility, hypercompetition, and accelerated production. Yet, fast capitalism seeks to corrode the values that justify CRM and to erode and eliminate the legal structure that generated CRM as an economic enterprise.

The CRM Labor Force

Field workers in CRM daily confront the contradiction between the ideology of the discipline of archaeology and the economic realities of the industry (de Boer 2004). In both the academy and CRM, archaeologist workers are usually taught that the discipline of archaeology requires skill, professionalism, and detailed, meticulous work. Teachers and supervisors expect them to comport themselves as skilled professionals, achieving mastery for their advancement in the discipline. As apprentices, they are expected to sacrifice their livelihood willingly for the sake of the discipline. Yet, field technicians hear many managers arguing that fieldwork (i.e., the excavation of the archaeological record) is a job for unskilled or, at best, semiskilled labor (Wilson 2001a, 2001b).

Compiling a picture of the CRM labor force is not easy. We have a general impression from the people who have worked on our projects. Trent de Boer's zine *Shovel Bum* (2004) augments this impression. We use these subjective impressions without apology, since few quantifiable data are available. We would certainly encourage a full-scale survey of archaeological field workers as a valuable project. We have drawn mainly on three surveys of field workers from the mid- to late 1990s: one compiled by the editors of the *Underground* newsletter in 1995 (Kintz 1995), another published by the United Archaeological Field Technicians (UAFT 1996), and a third done by Michele Wilson (2001a, 2001b) in 1997. The *Underground* editors made the raw data from their survey available to us. For wage information, we have used a survey of CRM companies done by the *Grapevine* newsletter and posted on the Web by ACRA (1996). Wilson's survey (2001a, 2001b) is the largest (thirty-six field technicians and nineteen managers) and most systematic of the three. None of these surveys is ideal. They all suffer from small sample sizes, regional biases, and self-selected samples. However, at the time of writing, these decades-old surveys are the only data available. Although wage rates have gone up since the 1990s, we have no reason to believe that other characteristics of the labor force have changed significantly.

In general, the field workforce consists primarily of relatively young (age twenty-seven to thirty-three), middle-class college graduates. In the UAFT survey 70 percent of field technicians had college degrees, and 87 percent of Wilson's (2001b:37) respondents were college graduates. Of the twenty-one *Underground* survey respondents who classified themselves as technicians or crew chiefs and who listed their education, twenty were college graduates. The UAFT survey indicates that 75 percent of technicians leave archaeology after an average of three years. The *Underground* data do not disagree with this, although the sample size is too small to be definitive. Over 61 percent of Wilson's respondents (2001b:37) had worked in CRM three years or less. The pattern suggested by these data is that the average field technician has been in archaeology 2.8 years. Those who have been in the field longer tend to be crew chiefs, which increase the mean to five years in archaeology. Seventy percent of technicians and crew chiefs that responded to the *Underground* survey had been in the field for less than five years. These surveys confirm common knowledge that the CRM labor force turns over continually.

The job of field technician is still temporary, but it is no longer an apprenticeship position, traditionally a step on the way to master/principal investigator status. But instead of adhering to the tradition, technicians appear to be leaving the field of archaeology altogether. The CRM industry consumes workers, drawing on a pool of fresh college graduates, essentially a reserve army of labor. This reserve army of labor gives CRM the flexibility so crucial in fast capitalism. These workers toil in the trenches for three to five years, until, disgruntled and probably in debt, they leave the field altogether. Toward the end of their careers, they are expected to train the incoming replacement workers, workers who earn the same wage as the more experienced people training them.

In the late 1990s, field technician wages averaged from $8.00 per hour (UAFT 1996) to $9.10 (ACRA 1996) with a range of $7.00 to over $10.00 (Wilson 2001b:37). The mean annual income for field technicians ranged from $11,200 in the UAFT survey to $12,000 in the *Underground* survey. Assuming year-round employment, the annual income at even $8.00 per hour should be higher, $16,640. But we must also take into account their unreimbursed job expenses, which Wilson (2001b:37) reported as averaging $817 per year in 1997, and also the common knowledge that many field technicians have substantial periods during the year with no work. Field workers can serve as crew chiefs, who are paid on average $2.00 per hour more, but otherwise experience- and seniority-related pay raises do not become an option until one has a permanent staff position, generally director or principal investigator.

In addition to experiencing little job security, few field workers receive benefits, such as health insurance, but supervisory personnel usually do (Wilson 2001b:38). In general, the wage structure of CRM is bifurcated. The *Grapevine* survey suggests an incremental progression in wages from "crew member" (archaeological technician) through "archaeologist I" (equivalent to director) in roughly $2.00-per-hour "hops" and then a leap of $7.00 to $10.00 per hour when principal investigator status is achieved (ACRA 1996). The disparity in wages between field workers and management (directors and principal investigators) is, in fact, even greater than these figures suggest. Managers have staff positions and benefits and also do not pay hidden costs, such as travel time or depreciation of personal equipment, such as vehicles. Unsurprisingly, most field workers find the pay insufficient. Wilson (2001b:38) indicated that her respondents worked in CRM only half the year. They managed to survive by taking other jobs, by going on unemployment, by relying on per diem for housing, or by taking loans from parents, or any combination of these (UAFT 1996).

Another less quantifiable, but equally important, issue that field workers face is the alienation that comes from the devaluation of their labor (Wilson 2001b). In modern capitalism, mental or intellectual labor is separated from and valued over physical labor (Braverman 1989). Fast capitalism has only intensified this distinction as technical skills and wages have been progressively devalued (Agger 2004). Although this separation is less pervasive in archaeology than in other disciplines, the blue-collar workers of CRM, the field technicians, are still often made aware of their inferior or junior status. The appeal that we are all archaeologists and scholars stands in contradiction to the common representation of field technicians in stereotypical proletarian terms as alcoholic, childlike, and in need of firm discipline, the "field animal" (Kintz 1995). We have all heard the slang terms for field workers—*shovel bums, grunts,* and, in a revealing overlap with racial discourses, *digroes* (UAFT 1996; Brandon 2003; de Boer 2004; Hirst 2005). Indeed, one of the largest sources of dissatisfaction among field technicians is the alienation of their intellect and interpretive abilities (Wilson 2001b).

Deskilling also devalues archaeological fieldwork and leads to inferior archaeology (Paynter 1983; Berggren and Hodder 2003). In a pattern that has occurred repeatedly in the past two hundred years for many kinds of capitalist workers, the workers of archaeology, once considered skilled craftsmen, are now being redefined as unskilled laborers, essentially relegated to an "archaeological proletariat" (Paynter 1983). In fast capitalism, this deskilling has penetrated the professions, including archaeology. Deskilling flows from the economic pressure to routinize archaeological research, the pressure to produce more for less. Just as cookie-cutter research designs and reports increase production for principal investigators, cookie-cutter excavation methods, data recovery, and recording increase production for field technicians. The devaluing of archaeological field workers goes hand in hand with a devaluing of archaeological fieldwork (Lucas 2001:12; Berggren and Hodder 2003). Routinizing some aspects of recording and excavation to the point that anyone can do them may be possible, but we all know that good excavation requires experience and mastery of the craft of archaeology. Field techs must have knowledge of archaeological principles, such as stratigraphy, an understanding of what kinds of material can be sampled for what kinds of analysis, artifact identification, manual skills in the use of trowels and other tools to expose delicate features, and an awareness of how to use photographic and drawing to record what is found (Berggren and Hodder 2003). For all archaeologists a tension exists between standardization and creativity, but the alternative to deskilling is not chaos. We cannot do good archaeology without standards or tested techniques, but neither can we reduce good archaeology to a series of repetitive motions.

Whether archaeological fieldwork is skilled or unskilled labor is not an abstract issue or a distinction that is important only in regard to the quality of archaeological research. This issue is the terrain on which the struggle over wages has taken place. In the late 1990s, this debate erupted over the United States Department of Labor's (DOL) definition of archaeological technicians. Within archaeology, the main voices in this debate and those that had the greatest potential for effecting change were the UAFT on one side and ACRA on the other.

The UAFT arose from field technicians laboring beside organized workers on pipelines in the early 1990s. "Working alongside Union Pipefitters on countless jobs in countless states and watching them make six times our annual wage with no one to blame but ourselves for failing to stand together, we decided to do something" (UAFT 1997:1). The UAFT was a local (no. 141) of the Union of Operating Engineers. This affiliation with the pipeline workers union logically followed from the kind of work field technicians do. It allowed the UAFT to draw on the legal and organizational expertise of the AFL-CIO (UAFT 1997; West 1994). Even though the UAFT was the strongest effort to date to organize archaeological workers, it did not speak for all field technicians, although all field techs shared in the benefits the union achieved. Field technicians may be more resistant to organizing than workers in many other industries because of the middle-class background of most technicians and the dispersed and mobile nature of the workforce. In the end, the UAFT largely failed in its attempt to organize the CRM proletariat. As of this writing, the union has disappeared from the scene. Fast capitalism is hard on unions.

Founded in March 1995, ACRA functions as a trade association to advance the interests of the cultural resources industry in the national arena. As such it is comparable to other trade associations, including the American Egg Board, the Contact Lens Manufacturers Association, the Lead Industry Association, and the Valve Manufacturers Association. In 2005, ACRA represented 142 firms of the more than 500 it estimated in existence in the United States at that time. ACRA seeks to promote the business needs of cultural resource practitioners, professionalism in the industry, education, and public awareness of cultural resources (ACRA 2005). Although all CRM companies may share in the benefits of ACRA's work, not all CRM companies belong to ACRA or support its goals. A considerable diversity of opinion exists within ACRA (ACRA 1997).

Individual CRM companies reacted in different ways to the UAFT, engaging in various activities to stem unionization of archaeological field technicians. Some firms were scrupulously legal but proactive in their stance against unionization, contracting with firms from the union-busting industry of fast capitalism to instruct their middle management and supervisory personnel on how to act, and not act, if union organizers appeared at the workplace. The Labor Relations Committee of ACRA disseminated information to its members to assist them in dealing legally with union organizing efforts (Pape 1996b). Other firms engaged in actions that have been patently illegal under U.S. labor law, such as rejecting individuals for employment because of their union association (i.e., blackballing them).

Both the UAFT and ACRA participated in the legal debate over whether archaeological workers are skilled or unskilled labor. The UAFT justified a higher wage for field technicians on the basis that they are skilled workers who are entitled to a living wage comparable to that of skilled workers in other fields (UAFT 1996, 1997). As it stands, field technicians receive less than many unskilled workers in other fields. For example, in upstate New York, the 2005 prevailing federal wage for unskilled labor on highway projects was $18.64 an hour. Archaeologists on the same projects routinely received around $10.50 an hour. Unskilled labor is cheap labor, and unorganized labor, regardless of skill, is cheaper still.

In the mid-1990s the UAFT had considerable success using the existing U.S. Department of Labor classification of an archaeological technician to enforce prevailing wage laws on federal jobs. The prevailing wage of an archaeological technician (29020) in 1994 ranged from a low of

$8.49 for Fayetteville, North Carolina, to a high of $21.75 for Houston, Texas (Pape 1996a). If companies had paid all archaeological field techs the prevailing wage, the mid-1990s average wage would probably have doubled. An increase of this scale for field workers would have had severe ramifications for the CRM industry, by increasing labor costs, not just for crews, but at all levels of employment.

ACRA sought to maintain a field tech wage of around $8.00 to $10.00 an hour in the late 1990s. They established a special fund and hired a labor lawyer for an appeal to the Department of Labor (Pape 1996a, 1996c, 1997a). ACRA also met with several federal agencies (the U.S. Forest Service, the National Park Service, the Bureau of Land Management, and the U.S. Corps of Engineers), the objective being to "develop a unified strategy for presenting modified (Archaeological Technician) descriptions to the DOL" (Pape 1996c:6). With input and assistance from ACRA, the U.S. Forest Service led the effort to convince the DOL to revise the job descriptions (Pape 1997a). The DOL accepted the three-tiered classification proposed by the U.S. Forest Service in 1997, and it remains in effect at the time of this writing (DOL 2005). This classification made explicit the trend toward deskilling archaeological fieldwork (Paynter 1983). The archaeological technician I, the bottom tier of the classification, works under "the direct supervision of archaeological crew chiefs and under the general supervision of field director/project archaeologist performs unskilled and semi-skilled tasks at archaeological field sites" (Pape 1997b; see also UAFT 1997). Although it is not stated in the DOL classification, the stance taken by ACRA appears to be that the tier-I position is a crew member, and the other two positions (tiers II and III) are crew chief and field supervisor (Pape 1996c:6, 1997b). In contrast with this, UAFT argued that the archaeological technician I cannot be a field technician position (West, pers. comm.) but instead can be filled only by untrained laborers.

Many CRM managers express a pervasive fear that the UAFT, by seeking to increase labor costs, has threatened the existence of CRM. CRM companies are caught in the unfortunate contradiction of selling a product that is mandated by laws embodying nonmarket values to corporations embracing the market ethos of fast capitalism. Given fast capitalism's impetus to free business from the "burdens" of such laws, CRM companies worry that an increase in the expense of doing CRM could turn the tide against CRM legislation in the federal government (Duke 1991:11). Many apparently feel that the preservation of the archaeological record requires that field technicians work for low wages. In order to hold wages low, some managers, arguing that the archaeological record can be excavated by unskilled labor, would sacrifice the quality of the data and the archaeological record in order to avoid paying their workers a living wage.

CRM archaeology has come of age as a business, and it is caught up in the hypercompetitiveness and processes of fast capitalism. It has labor problems. Realistically, we can see that these labor problems are not going to go away. CRM companies are not going to be able to maintain a skilled, highly motivated, but low-paid workforce. The alternatives appear to be either dealing with a unionized workforce or resorting to assigning the most publicly visible aspect of archaeology largely to unskilled laborers. Neither of these alternatives is without consequences for the practice of CRM and for the preservation of the archaeological heritage of the United States.

The extreme bifurcation of the labor force that characterizes fast capitalism in the United States has had a profound effect on the profession of archaeology. In both the academy and CRM, we now have a growing archaeological proletariat that lacks a living wage, job security, benefits, and respect. Its members are exploited. The question before us, then, is, What is to be done?

CLASS PRAXIS IN ARCHAEOLOGY

Much of the evidence of class relations in archaeology is buried and often fragmentary, leaving our analysis incomplete in many ways. In addition to more conventional sources, we have found our data largely in photocopied newsletters that go out to select mailing lists, Internet Listservs, Web pages, and informal conversations at conferences and in our places of work. In formulating an abstract picture of class in archaeology, we speak in generalizations: "the middle-class is . . . ," "archaeologists are . . . ," "managers in CRM believe . . . ," "field techs are . . . ," and so forth. The complex and concrete ways class is experienced by individuals in different circumstances require finer scales of analysis. Our understanding of class in archaeology remains incomplete in large part because few researchers have studied archaeology in class terms. Numerous studies have been done of the gender composition of our field (Chester et al. 1994; Beaudry 1994; Association Research, Inc. 2005; Baxter 2005), and they have been very valuable in identifying inequities and the reasons for them. We know of no comparable studies of the class experience of archaeologists and the relationship of that experience to their success in the field.

Our analysis does, however, demonstrate that a complex web of class relations confronts archaeology and that class distinctions exist within archaeology. The discipline of archaeology retains a middle-class orientation and produces a product primarily for a middle-class audience. The class relationships involved in this production are complex. Producing archaeology requires the labor of working-class individuals, and not all middle-class consumers desire the product that we generate (e.g., Yamin 1997). The awareness of this, linked with a consciousness of race and gender, has implications for the praxis of archaeology.

Building class praxis that addresses the existing class struggle in archaeology is difficult. Before archaeologists can address the inequities that exist within the practice of archaeology, they must first recognize that many of these inequities rest in class structures. The increased employment of adjuncts in the universities and the legions of archaeological field technicians in the country represent class positions that exist outside the traditional guild model of archaeological training. In both cases, the ideology behind these employment practices has been used to marginalize, underpay, and withhold benefits from the individuals involved. The resulting class relations are not simply foibles of the discipline of archaeology or of its practice. They are, rather, manifestations of the restructuring of class relations in fast capitalism. We cannot simply wish away this restructuring or change it on a case-by-case basis. The academic department that refuses to use adjuncts will find its budget cut when enrollments drop relative to departments that do use adjuncts. Less scrupulous companies will underbid the contract firm that pays its workers a living wage and benefits. We must confront class exploitation in archaeology on both the global scale and local scales.

We can join our scholarly and political efforts with those forces that seek to transform the larger structures. Archaeologists might do well to enter into the developing dialogue between organized labor and historians. The election of John Sweeney as president of the AFL-CIO in 1995 led to a revitalization of the organization as a broad-based social interest movement. As part of this movement a joint labor-academic teach-in was held at Columbia University on October 3–4, 1996, with over twenty-five hundred people in attendance (Murolo 1996; Sugrue 1996; Tomasky 1997). At least ten other teach-ins followed on campuses across the country (Tomasky 1997). Our discussion of the Colorado Coalfield

War Project, in chapter 5, represents our effort to participate in this larger struggle. These efforts are important in the long term, but they do not necessarily address the immediate needs of archaeologists.

Ben Agger (2004:131–168) concludes his analysis of fast capitalism by arguing that social change must begin with changes in people. He contends that changing fast capitalism first requires the realization that people can do more than just struggle to keep up with it. They can change it. Changing fast capitalism requires distance and critique. Distance comes from stepping back from our own position to look at how we individually fit in the larger processes of fast capitalism. This allows critique, or the critical awareness of what needs to be changed. Distance and critique may not be possible for the poor, the desperate, and the marginalized, who must struggle just to survive, but they are possible for college-educated, middle-class archaeologists (Agger 2004:134). We experience fast capitalism as individuals, but our individual selves are fundamentally social. From distance and critique should come action that changes the social self and, through this change, the structure of fast capitalism.

On the local scale of archaeology we would propose a six-step program to a praxis that confront the inequities that exist in the field. The first step is to gain a better understanding of class in archaeology (distance) and to engage in a critique that raises the consciousness of archaeologists about the class position of the discipline and about the exploitative class relations that exist in the profession of archaeology. This chapter is our contribution to that first step. Second, those of us who have privilege in the existing class structure should question that privilege and the false consciousness that sustains it. Third, we need to recognize graduate teaching assistants, adjuncts, and field technicians as professionals and formulate standards for their employment. Fourth, all archaeologists deserve a day's pay for a day's work. Fifth, we need to change the priorities of both the academy and CRM. Sixth, members of the archaeological proletariat must recognize that they will never simply be given respect, living wages, benefits, and decent working conditions because it is right to do so. They must organize to win these rights.

Question Privilege and Fight False Consciousness

The class structures of our profession have changed. The guild model of apprenticeship no longer functions, if it ever did. It has become, instead, a false consciousness, a secret writing that allows those of us who occupy privileged positions in the class structure, such as tenured professors and project directors, to ignore the exploitation of others. The time has come to question our privilege and the ideology that justifies it (Nelson and Watt 2004:24–26; Jancius 2006).

It is difficult to get individuals who have achieved success in a social hierarchy to question that hierarchy, because success there validates the self-worth of the privileged. For these individuals to gain distance and critique, they must question their own achievement and self-worth. Part of the false consciousness involves the denigration of the new archaeological proletariat of adjuncts and field technicians. The privileged reflect on the experience of their own rise to mastery and conclude that those who have failed in this process are somehow inferior. They presume that the members of the proletariat have failed to achieve privileged positions because of personal faults such as laziness or want of intellect or ability.

But fast capitalism does not respect even the privilege of the successful. It corrodes all distinction and reduces all relations to the principles of the market place. It hounds even the masters of the guild. Using information technology, universities can outsource and deskill the teaching of the professor (Noble 2003; Nelson and Watt 2004:156–163). A faculty member can design a Web-based distance-learning course, and graduate students or adjuncts can deliver it. In such a system, the university needs far fewer tenured faculty members. Universities are increasingly profit driven and favor academic disciplines that pay their way (Nelson and Watt 2004). Archaeology can pay its way only through CRM. But CRM faces an explosive contradiction. The market principles that structure the enterprise of CRM corrode the values of the legal structure that makes CRM a profitable enterprise. All archaeologists, privileged or not, need to challenge fast capitalism's corrosion of our discipline.

All archaeologists deserve respect as professionals and members of our profession. We all suffer from the disrespect that those of us in positions of power give the archaeological proletariat and from the economic exploitation of these archaeologists. Those processes that lower the wages and degrade the labor of temporary and part-time workers also erode the prestige and earning potential of fully employed project directors and tenured professors (Nelson 1997b:6).

A Bill of Rights

The guild model of apprenticeship justifies the exploitation of graduate students, adjuncts, and field technicians by portraying these positions as temporary rites of passage that must be endured to achieve mastery. In reality they have become permanent career tracks that most individuals can escape only by leaving the discipline. Those who occupy these positions are professional archaeologists, and within our discipline we need to formulate standards for their treatment as professional employees, not as apprentices.

What we are calling for is a bill of rights for the existing archaeological proletariat that will recognize its members as professionals deserving of respect, living wages, benefits, and decent working conditions. In the academy, such rights should include provisions for teaching load, class size, professional benefits such as departmental support of travel and research activities, and professional respect for graduate students and adjuncts. In CRM, these rights should include decent living conditions in the field, working conditions that allow field technicians to build and refine their skills, and respect for their professionalism and craft.

Our call for a bill of rights for archaeological workers participates in a larger movement to confront fast capitalism in the academy. In June 2000, the American Association of University Professors adopted the Statement on Graduate Students, which addresses the rights of graduate students as professionals, workers, and teachers (AAUP 2000). In February 2001, a conference at the University of Massachusetts, Boston, proposed the Charter of University Workers' Rights (Nelson and Watt 2004:51), based on a charter adopted by Northeastern University, in Boston (Northeastern University 2001). This charter extends rights to all members of the university community including student workers, service workers, faculty (part- and full-time, tenured and untenured), library workers, research workers, administrative workers, and administrators. And it entitles contracted workers to the same rights as permanent workers.

A Day's Pay for a Day's Work

The most basic right of every worker is to make a living. At the very least, all archaeologists should receive a living wage, that is, a wage at least commensurate with the actual cost of living. In both the academy and CRM, the archaeological proletariat is routinely paid less than a living wage. Currently in the academy, graduate students and adjuncts are paid far less per course or per student than regular faculty. Per class payments for temporary teachers should be comparable to those paid to regular faculty, and temporary teachers, like regular faculty, should be rewarded commensurately with their experience and skill. Archaeological field technicians work for substantially lower wages than those paid to unskilled laborers working on the very same construction projects. In recognition of the skills that field techs must have to do archaeology, their compensation should be comparable to that of not just the unskilled workers but the other skilled workers on these projects. Finally, all temporary workers should receive benefits, such as health and retirement, comparable to those that permanent workers in our society rightfully receive.

Changing Priorities

The respect and compensation that the archaeological proletariat deserves cannot be achieved without changing priorities. This is equally true in the academy and CRM. Most graduate programs in the United States still train and treat students as apprentices working to become university professors. This practice is doubly pernicious in archaeology, because the vast majority of jobs in the discipline are outside the academy and the number of tenured university slots for archaeologists is shrinking (Fagan 2006). Every archaeology department has an obligation to educate students at the beginning of graduate training about the realities of the job market and then to provide these students with the skills they need for that market. By producing a large number of graduates at all levels, university archaeology departments also produce and replenish the reserve armies of labor that both the academy and CRM consume. Having this large number of students often serves the department's interests and those of the tenured faculty; furthermore, a seemingly unlimited supply of new fodder allows universities and CRM companies to use up people rather than reform exploitative practices. Larger student-to-teacher ratios also erode academic standards and worsen the training of graduates. The professoriat should resist this erosion. It may be time for fewer departments to produce fewer, but better trained, graduates.

CRM has been driven by two major goals, profit and research. Some firms have funneled profits into not-for-profit branches to support research, but in most cases the welfare of both managers and field technicians has been sacrificed to do research. We would argue that CRM companies should respect three goals: profit, research, and the welfare of their employees.

Organize

Archaeologists are largely paid less in comparison to those in other middle-class professions and those in working-class trades. In the middle class, doctors, lawyers, dentists, engineers, and many others generally earn more than archaeologists. In the field, archaeological field techs and even crew chiefs and supervisors routinely make less than the heavy equipment operators, welders, carpenters, and even laborers working on the same projects. What do these people have that we don't? In a word, organization.

Doctors and lawyers earn more than archaeologists chiefly because of the American Medical Association and the American Bar Association. Professional associations such as these license individuals as members of the profession, establish professional standards, and grant accreditation to the institutions that train these individuals. Archaeologists have formed the Register of Professional Archaeologists (RPA) to promote professionalism among archaeologists and to maintain a code of conduct and a standard of research performance (Altschul 2006). The RPA is a registry of archaeologists who meet certain standards, such as holding an advanced degree, and who agree to conform to the code of conduct and standards of the organization. The RPA does not, however, address the needs or interests of field techs, adjuncts, and graduate students.

Given the larger structures of fast capitalism, the archaeological proletariat of field techs, adjuncts, and graduate students would be naive to believe that they will receive respect, living wages, benefits, and decent working conditions simply because it is humane or right. They would be equally naive to think that they can achieve these rights and benefits though individual action. They must engage in collective agency. Labor in the United States has won these things only through organization and struggle. The reason that the people flagging traffic on a road project are paid higher wages than archaeologists is that they have engaged in collective bargaining and must be paid prevailing wages on federal contracts. Archaeologists have no reason to believe they can win equitable working conditions by any other means. At twenty-three universities in the United States and twenty universities in Canada, graduate student employees (including archaeologists) have unionized (CGEU 2006). At three U.S. campuses, adjuncts have gained union recognition. These unions have won their members higher compensation, benefits, grievance procedures, and respect. The failure of the UAFT shows that it is very difficult to organize the archaeological proletariat of field techs. Those of us who have stable employment need to assist the archaeological proletariat to organize and fight for respect, fair treatment, and security.

We offer our six steps not as a panacea but instead as a starting point to a dialogue to stop the deterioration of archaeological labor in fast capitalism. We feel archaeologists should give this dialogue a high prominence in our scholarly and professional associations, a prominence comparable to that given reburial and repatriation in the last decade and a half. This dialogue must start with the realization that archaeologists live class. We live it every day, and it structures the whole of our professional lives. It confronts us in our classrooms, on our excavations, in our offices, and in our audience. As Ollman points out, "One doesn't advocate class struggle or choose to participate in it" (2003:20); we are all part of it. Our only choice is which side we will be on.

CHAPTER 4

México

It seems to me that it is not difficult to find splendid formulas
for life, but it is difficult to live.

Antonio Gramsci (1994:13)

In the mid-1980s I initiated archaeological research in northern Sonora,
México, and threaded my way into the tangled skein of double colonialism along the border. I did so with a keen awareness of the imperialist
archaeology that U.S. scholars traditionally practiced in México. I also
had a developing sense of the colonialist nature of prehistoric archaeology in the United States. Since beginning this project, my Mexican collaborator Elisa Villalpando and I have tried to create a praxis of archaeology that challenges both the imperialism and the colonialism that we
encountered on the border. Creating emancipatory praxis will never be
an easy thing to do. The realities of social relations and ethics are never
so clear and distinctly defined as they are in abstract discussions.
Splendid formulas for life simplify the real politics, conflicting interests,
ambiguities, and contradictions of working with multiple communities.

In this chapter I will discuss a process for building emancipatory
praxis in archaeology. This process begins with a consideration of the different approaches that archaeologists may use to interact with communities. In order to interact with communities productively, archaeologists
need to be knowledgeable about those communities and their interrelationships. From this knowledge archaeologists may engage in critique to
decide which approach will guide our action. Our action should create
more knowledge and be subject to constant critique. There is no cookbook for praxis. Rather, it is a relational dialectical method that flows
from the questions we ask and the contexts that we ask them in.

The archaeology of the Trincheras Tradition Project shows how praxis has worked out, albeit imperfectly, in one case. The project has involved four communities from both sides of the international border: U.S. archaeologists, Mexican archaeologists, Norteños, and the Tohono O'odham (the Papago). The relationship between U.S. archaeology and both Mexican archaeology and the descendants of Spanish settlers in Sonora, the Norteños, has traditionally been an imperialist one. Archaeology has played a role in the United States' economic, political, and cultural domination of México. The relationship of all three of these communities to the Tohono O'odham has been colonialist. The traditional lands of the Tohono O'odham straddle the international frontier, and O'odham live on both sides. México and the United States have subjugated the Tohono O'odham, and in both Sonora and Arizona the descendants of the conquerors study the ancestors of the conquered.

Double colonialism exists in two senses here. In the simplest sense it lies in the colonial relationship of both the United States and México with the Tohono O'odham. U.S. archaeologists crossing the border into Sonora also enter into an additional colonial relationship. Here they encounter a tradition of U.S. imperialist archaeology in México and they study the ancestors of a people their ancestors subjugated. An emancipatory praxis should seek to confront and transform these unequal relationships in both of these colonial relationships. Our efforts to do this in the Trincheras Tradition Project have met with uneven success. We have built a collaborative approach between the two communities of Mexican and U.S. archaeologists that mitigates the traditional imperialist U.S. archaeology in México. We have also entered into an educational dialogue with the Norteños of Sonora. But our consultations with the Tohono O'odham remain problematic.

The border creates a distinctive context for our research. The frontier between the United States and México west of the Río Grande is an unnatural line defined only by the artificial grid of longitude and latitude. For the people who live and work along this line, including archaeologists, the international frontier is in one sense very artificial but at the same time a very compelling reality (Alonso 1995). A mix of Español and English, tortillas and white bread, Norteño and country-western tunes, and El Pollo Feliz and Kentucky Fried Chicken defines a zone that is culturally neither U.S. nor Mexican but simultaneously both. Yet, there is nothing fuzzy about the line slashed through aboriginal territories, dividing native nations and leaving the archaeological record of ancient pasts unnaturally sundered. This line is a rigid social institution made up of walls, fences, and checkpoints and patrolled by agents of the state with guns, dogs, jeeps, and planes.

This line both impacts and structures the social relationships that generate the four communities of the Trincheras Tradition Project. Europeans created the United States and México by conquering and subjugating aboriginal peoples. The elite of each nation developed a national ideology that legitimated this conquest and defined the place of Indian peoples in the heritage of the state. Archaeologists participated in the development of the national ideology in both countries, and archaeology was also defined by these ideologies. The respective ideologies delineate very different relationships among archaeology, Indian peoples, and the state. Furthermore, the two nations are not equal. The Treaty of Guadalupe del Hidalgo ended the U.S. war of conquest that took approximately half of the territory of México (Griswold del Castillo 1990). Within México a distinctive subculture known as Norteño arose along the frontier. The unnatural line defined the limits of two nations but split a third, that of the Tohono O'odham, in two. Even though both the Norteño and the Tohono O'odham communities share the common history and reality of the border, they experience that heritage and reality in different ways. From those experiences spring different relationships to and interests in the past of the region.

PROCESS AND PRAXIS

An emancipatory praxis based in the interrelationship of knowledge, critique, and action can exist only within real contexts of social relations, struggles, interests, institutions, and agents. The four border communities (U.S. archaeologists, Mexican archaeologists, Norteños, and Tohono O'odham) are an example of such a context. Each of these communities exists in relation to the others. Each has its own interests in past and present borderland issues. Each is a product of a shared history, but each also experienced that history differently. How can archaeologists undo this tangled skein to ethically establish useful relationships among these communities that lead to an emancipatory praxis? How do we decide which communities we will oppose, which we will educate about archaeology, which we will consult with, and which we will collaborate with?

A relational dialectical process is necessarily historical. As we decide how and why we interact with communities and what modes that interaction should take, archaeologists need to gain knowledge of the world and engage in a critique of it. The questions we need to ask are necessarily historical questions, seeking to learn about the historical processes that produced the relationships that created the communities we study. The relationships that create communities flow from historical processes. At the same time archaeologists should critically analyze those relationships to understand the power relations they entail. Finally, archaeologists need to take action in the world. This action may entail different modes of interaction with different communities. Action may require taking sides, since the interests of the communities involved may be in conflict.

Wherever archaeologists do research, we step into a historically created social context. Once we make that step, we are part of that context and the relationships that it entails. Each community has its own historical experience, culture, interests, relations to other communities, and ideologies. Archaeologists enter into social relationships as fully constituted social beings, with identities that include class, race, gender, profession, sexuality, and nationality. The communities that we encounter will initially evaluate and interact with us based on their perceptions of those identities, their historical experience with the communities the archaeologist represents, and their evaluation of the power relationships between themselves and the archaeologist. Archaeologists cannot assume that we will be judged by our intentions or personalities. We will be stereotyped. We need a historical understanding of the social contexts in order to counter stereotypes as we interact with the communities affected by our research.

Strategies for Interacting with Communities

Archaeologists may interact with diverse communities in different ways. Four approaches to interaction in archaeological research are opposition, education, consultation, and collaboration. Each of them implies a different level of investment by archaeologists in a community and a different power relationship between the archaeologists and the community. The four approaches are not necessarily mutually exclusive and may be fruitfully integrated. Each of them has an appropriate use in an emancipatory praxis of archaeology.

Arguing that archaeologists can engage communities in different ways takes as given that we need to form relationships with the communities that have interests in our work (Shanks and McGuire 1996). The alternative is to ignore them. Social engineers and members of the vanguard party may choose to ignore the interests of communities, because they believe that scientists possess "true" knowledge. As I have argued in pre-vious chapters, ignoring the interests of others can lead to totalitarian-ism. An emancipatory praxis of archaeology can ignore only those com-munities that do not have interests in our research.

Opposition Opposition entails confronting, hindering, obstructing, and resisting the interests of a community. Archaeologists should not simply let every community's interests go unchallenged; we need to oppose some voices on the past and make ethical judgments based in an explicit discussion of the morality of archaeology (Meskell and Pels 2005; Hamilakis and Duke 2006). Archaeologists have traditionally opposed those social groups and communities that would commodify the archaeological record for personal profit, such as looters, metal detector clubs, and collectors of antiquities. These groups interfere with the inter-ests of the archeological community by destroying the archaeological record. Some social groups wish to use the past in ways that are contrary to human emancipation. The nazi archaeology in Europe (Arnold 1990) and the Hindu nationalist archaeology at the Babri Mosque in Ajodhya, India (Romey 2004), provide examples of such malicious voices. Archae-ologists who accept an ethic of human emancipation must oppose these malicious voices.

Education Education is the act of imparting or acquiring knowledge, developing the powers of reasoning and judgment, and acquiring self-awareness. Education has received much attention in archaeology at the turn of the twenty-first century (Bender and Smith 2000; Smardz and Smith 2000). Often scholars have argued that through education we can reach the looters and collectors and convince them not to destroy archae-ological sites (Judge 1989). I have expressed two reservations with the general tone of these discussions (McGuire 1992b:257–261). The first is that archaeologists have tended to use a consumerist model for educa-tion. The second is that the audience or community to be educated is usu-ally identified as "the general public."

In a consumerist model, archaeologists produce a watered-down ver-sion of our scholarly research, which we then package and sell to the public. This model assumes that the archaeological community has the knowledge, the skill, the authority, and the right to determine what the correct knowledge or interpretation of the past should be. The issue be-comes how our interpretation of the past can be communicated or made relevant to the public (J. Jameson 1997; McManamon 2000; Smardz and

Smith 2000). Or, put another way, how do we educate the public to see the world our way and to protect our interests in the past (Lynott 1990)?

The implicit assumption in the consumerist model is that those communities who do not share our interests in the past lack that interest because of ignorance, which education can eliminate. What is not considered in this view is that other communities or social groups my simply have different interests in and ways of knowing the past. As I argued in the last chapter, archaeology is primarily a middle-class pursuit driven by middle-class interests. Other social groups, classes, and communities have interests in the past different from ours. Parker Potter (1994) argued over a decade ago that archaeologists should seek an ethnographic understanding of other communities' interests in the past.

This book's relational approach to education views this ethnographic understanding as a dialogue. Archaeologists possess authority invested in our craft. We can make observations about the past that people who have not mastered that craft cannot make. Such observations transmit as knowledge only within a social discourse. In approaching education, archaeologists must first recognize that societies are made up of varied social groups with distinct and even conflicting interests. An undifferentiated "general public" is an illusion, as Potter has demonstrated. In the United States, Native Americans have made this clear by challenging us with a very different concept of the North American past (Deloria 2002). Recognizing this diversity among communities means that education must become a process of discourse with them. Such a discourse considers our craft, the interests of both communities, and the ethics of emancipation. Such a discourse educates both the community and the archaeologists.

Consultation   Consultation involves a discussion between two or more parties to address a particular issue or question. It is an instrumentalist process that seeks a decision or resolution. It seeks to avoid or resolve conflicts related to particular goals by providing a structured way for groups or individuals with differing interests to compromise and come to an agreement. For this reason, consultation may be a very formalized or bureaucratized process. Consultation also implies a meeting of groups and individuals that have differential rights, authority, or power, or any combination of these. To consult with someone (or some group) is to recognize his or her (or their) rights, authority, or power.

Consultation as a mode of interaction in archaeology usually addresses issues of rights and responsibilities to artifacts, knowledge, money, and sites. Archaeologists consult with others who have rights or authority in relationship to those things in order to be able to do archaeological research. Examples of such others include landowners, funding sources, local communities, Native American nations, and governmental units. Usually the archaeologist has a predetermined goal, and the process of consultation relates to how the archaeologist may meet that goal. Establishing long-term relationships and conversations with individuals and groups promotes effective consultation. Such relationships may lead to greater understanding and transform the interests and practices of the individuals or social groups that consult with each other. If such relationships move beyond an instrumentalist concern, then they can be transformed into collaboration.

Collaboration   Collaboration implies the integration of goals, interests, and practices among the individuals or social groups that work together. It entails a dialogue that goes beyond an instrumentalist concern with resolving a conflict or respecting rights and responsibilities. It requires humility, patience, listening, careful consultation, equality, and respect (Clifford 2004:22; Zimmerman 2005). Collaboration should be transformative of the parties involved. Each party brings different resources, skills, knowledge, authority, and interests to a collaborative labor. Collaboration involves the melding of these unique qualities into common goals and practices. Effective collaboration begins before the definition of an objective or problem so that all parties can contribute to this definition. Collaboration becomes praxis when it gives subordinate groups a greater voice in the actions of dominant groups. In true collaboration, local communities need to be able to say no (Clifford 2004:6).

Archaeologists have most often discussed collaboration in terms of joint efforts among scientists from different disciplines. More recently, many archaeologists have turned their attention to collaboration with descendant communities, such as African American and Native American communities (e.g., Watkins 2000; Stapp and Burney 2002; Singleton and Orser 2003). Collaboration is the keystone of indigenous archaeology, and the most insightful discussions of collaboration are found there (Colwell-Chanthaphonh and Ferguson 2004, 2006; Smith and Wobst 2005). In all such cases, the archaeologists have entered into collaboration with an intention of giving subordinate communities a greater role in the archaeology of their ancestors. In each case, collaboration has involved knowledge, critique, and action and has been transformative of the archaeologists' practice. This is praxis.

Knowledge and Critique

The communities in a social context share a common history, but their experience of that history is different. The same history creates many pasts. For example, the Mexican, Anglo, and Tohono O'odham peoples who lived along the international frontier experienced the history of the border very differently. A historical understanding should ask, How were these experiences both different and similar? How did the interrelationships among the communities both shape and result from these experiences? How did this history of varied experiences mold the culture, interests, and ideologies of the communities involved?

Just as disparate communities have experienced a common history differently, so too do disparate communities experience modern realities differently. Although the international border is a modern reality shared by U.S. archaeologists, Mexican archaeologists, Norteños, and Tohono O'odham, the experience of crossing La Línea is very different for members of each group (McGuire 1997). U.S. archaeologists usually cross the line in comfort, with a minimum of hassle or delay on both sides. Mexican archaeologists, like most middle-class Mexican people, can cross the border in comfort. Before they can do so, however, they must first apply for and receive a visa from a U.S. consulate. This process is long, bureaucratic, and in many ways degrading. At the border, they are far more likely to be delayed and hassled than Anglos are. U.S. immigration officials require more paperwork of them and can arbitrarily decide not to admit them. Mexican customs agents are far more likely to press them, rather than U.S. citizens, for bribes. Working-class Norteños who enter the U.S. illegally do so in great discomfort and at risk of arrest, injury, or death. Even though Tohono O'odham do not recognize the border that splits their people as legitimate, their ambiguous physical appearance and status cause them problems on both sides when they attempt to cross. A relational historical analysis is necessary to understand why these differences exist, especially if the goal of the scholar is to eliminate such inequalities.

A critique of border history and modern reality must ask about power (Alonso 1995). What are the relationships of power? How are they justified, hidden, or challenged by different ideologies? How do inequities structure experience? More important, such critique should involve self-reflection. How does the community of archaeologists enter into power relationships? Can the goals of emancipation be better served by archaeologists giving up power and authority, or by wielding power and authority to confront inequalities? These questions have answers only in real social contexts.

The international border separating Sonora and Arizona is a very difficult social context in which to address these questions. This context involves two nation-states, three different languages, three distinct cultures, and four communities. The context is further complicated by the double colonialism that defines the relationship among these communities. Praxis in this context consists of confronting the power relations and inequalities of double colonialism. But the double colonialism creates contradictions that may require buttressing some inequalities to diminish others.

Archaeologists working on the U.S.–Mexican border enter a complex space where various histories converge to create ambiguous, paradoxical, and contradictory social, cultural, political, and economic relations (McGuire 1997). Each individual has multifaceted identities and relationships, and effective praxis is possible only if the archaeologist has knowledge of the tangled social and political skein of which he or she will become a thread. The double colonialism of the border springs from the national histories of the United States and México and the ambiguous histories that the meeting of these two chronicles creates for native peoples on the frontier.

Since 1985, in a joint project sponsored by Binghamton University and the Centro INAH de Sonora, Elisa Villalpando, of the latter institution, and I have been conducting archaeological field research on the Trincheras Tradition of northern Sonora, México (map 1). Before the 1980s it was rare for either Mexican or North American archaeologists to work in northwest México. It is only with the establishment of ongoing archaeological projects in the region, such as our project, that the challenge of double colonialism among the four communities has arisen.

I begin my relational historical analysis with a consideration of the two different communities of archaeologists—the U.S. and the Mexican— that meet at the border. I go on to consider how each of these archaeologies relates to the indigenous peoples of the nations involved and to the Norteños. Finally, I examine the implications of these relationships for the Norteño and Tohono O'odham communities on the border.

U.S. AND MEXICAN ARCHAEOLOGY

The double colonialism that characterizes the Trincheras Tradition Project is a complex product. U.S. archaeologists participate in an imperialist archaeology throughout Latin America; this is the first colonialism. Both U.S. and Mexican archaeologies entail members of the educated middle class studying indigenous peoples who are politically and culturally marginalized in the nation; this is the second colonialism. Both archaeologies developed in the process of their respective states, seeking to legitimate the establishment of a European nation on indigenous lands. Yet each nation and archaeology came to a very different ideology to legitimate themselves (Lorenzo 1998:99–101). These ideologies come into conflict on the border.

Imperialist Archaeology in México

By the end of the twentieth century, U.S. and Canadian archaeologists had worked in every part of México, with hundreds of projects on archeological sites, ranging from the impressive to the mundane. U.S. institutions have a long and well-established tradition of doing archaeology in México, with U.S. archaeologists first entering the country over a century ago. In stark contrast, I cannot identify a single archaeology project carried out solely by a Mexican institution in the United States or Canada during the last century.[1]

In general, U.S. archaeology in México differs in significant ways from México's own archaeology (McGuire 1997; Lorenzo 1998). Anglo researchers enter México with more money than their Mexican colleagues possess and material resources superior to theirs. Often, the U.S. projects do nothing to share these resources with the national archaeological community. Also, North Americans tend to ask different questions about the past. They focus more on theoretical issues and broad questions about the process of culture change on a global scale. Mexican archaeologists tend to emphasize the understanding of local developments within their nation-state. North American projects may include a few token Mexican students or archaeologists. By contrast, individuals associated with U.S. institutions rarely work on Mexican projects.[2] Even when North American projects include Mexicans, the language of the project tends to be English. In México, two overlapping but separate archaeologies exist. One is a local nationalist archaeology, and the other is a U.S. imperialist archaeology.

U.S. archaeologists began working in México in the late nineteenth century. From then to the middle of the twentieth century, U.S. scholars largely focused on the archaeology of the Maya lowlands, while Mexican archaeologists focused on the cultures of the highlands, especially the

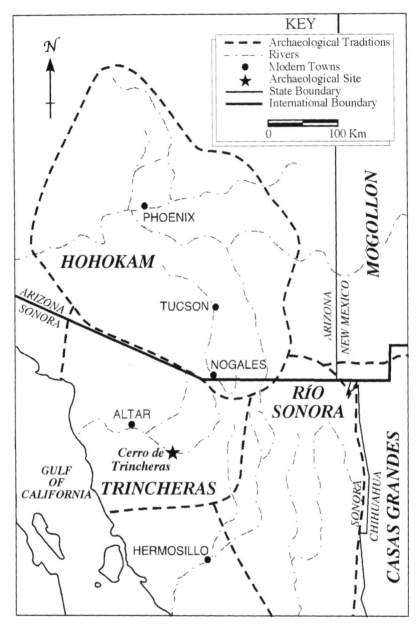

Map 1. Archaeological traditions in northern Sonora and southern Arizona.

Mesa Central (Patterson 1986:12). North Americans downplayed the achievements of the highland cultures, such as Teotihuacán and the Aztecs. Instead, they championed the ancient lowland Mayan civilization as the high point of cultural development in the Americas. In contrast, Mexican archaeologists focused on the highland civilizations as the most advanced and as the base for a national heritage in México (Bernal 1980:173–176; Lorenzo 1998:159). Following World War II, this regional distinction began to break down. In 1960, the Valley of México Project integrated cultural anthropologists, biological anthropologists, and archaeologists from México and the United States in a notable collaborative effort that transcended the divide between the two communities (Wolf 1976). More North Americans began working in the highlands, and more Mexican archaeologists began working in the lowlands, but two distinct practices of archaeology remain to this day.

In some exceptional instances, U.S. archaeologists in Latin America undertook an even more sinister imperialism when they worked as spies for the U.S. government (Price 2003). In 1917, the Mayanist Sylvanus Morley used his archaeological activities as a cloak for espionage in Central America. During World War II, Samuel Lathrop worked as a U.S. spy in Peru. In El Salvador during the 1980s, guerillas killed two CIA agents posing as archaeologists. In the mid-1960s, the U.S. Camelot Project became public knowledge. This project enlisted cultural anthropologists to gather information to assist, both knowingly and unknowingly, in CIA-backed counterinsurgency efforts in Latin America and Asia. Even though the project included no archaeologists, the scandal cast doubts in México on the actions of all North American anthropologists, archaeologists, and ethnographers, doubts that linger today (Palerm 1980:27). North American archaeologists are by and large unfamiliar with this history of active cooperation by anthropologists with U.S. political and military actions in Latin America. It is, however, a well-known history in México, where many scholars see it as one small aspect of a larger pattern of U.S. imperialism (Lorenzo 1976, 1982; Lorenzo et al. 1976).

Archaeology and Nationalism in the Americas

Throughout the modern era, "national movements" led by "national" intelligentsia have created, or failed to create, nation-states, as discussed in chapter 1 (Anderson 1983; Thomas 2004:97). National movements take cultural variation and history and construct a sense of nationalism, which they then use to justify possession of a territory. Sometimes this construction precedes the possession of the territory, and other times it follows. Archaeology participates in these national movements as a way to create heritage or mythic charters that legitimate the state (Trigger 1989a, 2006).

In the United States and México at the turn of the eighteenth to the nineteenth century, mostly native-born individuals of European descent established and led the national movements.[3] The struggle to define nation-states continued throughout the United States and México for a hundred years or more.[4] Both of these national movements faced the same two contradictions. First, they sought to establish their nations on lands that clearly had been taken from other peoples. Second, each state contained Indians, Africans, and mestizos, peoples different from the Euro-Americans who founded and led the movements.

The nationalist programs of the United State and México had different ways of ideologically resolving the contradictions that native peoples presented to their nationalisms (Lorenzo 1998:99–101). In the United States a debate raged throughout the nineteenth century about the country's ideological approaches to the resolution. The first ideology claimed that Indians were the "First Americans" and had passed on their legitimacy to the Europeans who followed. The second ideology, the Mound Builder myth, denied a significant Indian presence in the territory of the state. Scholars claimed the Indians had been few in number, recent, and had built little of consequence. The First American ideology triumphed by the turn of the twentieth century. In México, the twentieth-century nationalist ideology used the concept of *indigenismo* to deny the European origin of the nation and to identify the population of the state as indigenous.[5] *Indigenismo* glorifies mestizos (people of mixed Indian and European ancestry) as the people of the nation. In this ideology the mestizos inherited the heritage of both the Europeans and the native peoples of the state to form a new nation.

Archaeology has played a key role in the national struggles over heritage and in determining which resolution would dominate in a nation. The ideological resolution that triumphed in each country has also had a profound impact on the nature of the archaeology in each. Even though archaeology is largely a colonialist enterprise throughout the Americas (again, the study of the ancestors of the conquered by the descendants of the conquerors), the exact form this enterprise takes and its relationship to the state and nationalism vary greatly. Both U.S. archaeology and Mexican archaeology were born in these national struggles. Each took a very different form as a result of the different roles assigned to native peoples in nationalist programs. Each partici-pates in a different set of ideological, institutional, and political relation-ships with Indian people.

U.S. ARCHAEOLOGY AND NATIVE AMERICANS

Throughout the twentieth century, two types of histories existed for Native America. One was the official, public history of the First Ameri-cans taught in schools and universities, integral to the laws of the land, embodied in the interpretation at national parks, and presented in the halls of museums. The other was a history taught by native elders to the children in the home, in the kiva, and in the sweat lodge. The official his-tory empowered ethnographers, archaeologists, and historians as the keepers of the history of the First Americans (McGuire 1992b:240; Watkins 2000). In the last quarter of the twentieth century, however, Native American people questioned the privilege of archaeology and sought to regain control of their ancestor's remains, their sacred objects, and their past. This questioning resulted in a radically changed relation-ship between U.S. archaeologists and Native Americans at the end of the twentieth century. The Trincheras Tradition Project entered into consul-tation with the Tohono O'odham in the midst of this change.

The First Americans

The First American ideology originated at the end of the eighteenth cen-tury and dominated the official history by the beginning of the twentieth century. Thomas Jefferson excavated Indian mounds near his home to demonstrate that North America had previously produced a noble race; therefore, it could sustain the growth of a great European nation (Wal-lace 1999). He defined Indians as the First Americans. By calling Indians the First Americans, Jefferson gave Indian people a transient role in the U.S. national heritage, and he appropriated their ancient past for Euro-American scholars. Not everyone in the new nation wished to embrace Indians as part of the national heritage. They proposed that a lost race of Mound Builders had constructed the great earthworks that dot the Midwest. They argued that savage Indians had descended on this civi-lized race and destroyed it only decades before the European settlement of the continent (Silverberg 1968). In 1894 Cyrus Thomas published the results of the Bureau of American Ethnology's mound explorations, which proved Indians had built the mounds (Willey and Sabloff

1993:47). With this, the First American ideology came to dominate scholarly and government versions of the national heritage.

As the controversy over the mounds raged, archaeology established itself as part of four-field anthropology in the United States. Anthropology was institutionalized in the great museums of natural history, such as the American Museum of Natural History in New York, the Field Museum of Chicago, and the National Museum of Natural History in the Smithsonian Institution. The new discipline included Indians in natural history, their remains to be collected like so many fossils, insects, or rock specimens. By the end of the century, archaeology had become a professional career. Archaeologists began to argue that they should control Indian sites, ruins, and remains, because only they had the specialized skills and knowledge to study them (Willey and Sabloff 1993:34). The Antiquities Act of 1906 legalized the archaeological control of ancient Native pasts.

By the second half of the twentieth century, the general public took the archaeological control of Native American pasts for granted. In 1946 the U.S. Congress established the Indian Claims Commission, which met until 1978. This commission existed to legally resolve any outstanding claims by Native American tribes against the federal government in order to pave the way to the termination of those tribes (Indian Claims Commission 1978). Many ethnographers and archaeologists engaged in praxis by giving testimony in support of Indian claims (Ford 1973). Other anthropologists, including prominent figures such as Julian Steward, served as expert witnesses for the government to challenge these claims (Pinkoski and Asch 2004). The commission based its findings primarily on the testimony of Euro-American experts, historians, ethnographers, and archaeologists. The final report of the commission makes no mention of testimony by tribal elders (Indian Claims Commission 1978). Most archaeologists seem unaware that Native Americans commonly hold ambiguous feelings about the role of anthropologists in this process, seeing it not as justice but as proceedings to facilitate the theft of their reservations and sovereignty (Deloria and Lytle 1984:191).

Native Rights and Archaeology

In 1971, American Indian movement (AIM) activists made the native voice heard by disrupting an archaeological excavation near Minneapolis, Minnesota (Deloria 1993; Watkins 2000:4). The archaeologists involved were honestly surprised and shocked by the interference. As was already discussed in chapter 2, the group protested again that year by interrupting a physical anthropology class at Colorado State University and confiscating human bones from the teaching collection to negotiate their exchange for Indian remains the university's field school had excavated. Native peoples spoke loudly in the 1970s, and they proclaimed that archaeology was a tool of oppression.

By the 1980s, Indian activists had turned from the confrontational tactics of the previous decade to seek legal and institutional resolutions for their interests. A series of federal laws, beginning with the Indian Self-Determination Act of 1973, gave tribal governments greater authority and power (Deloria and Lytle 1984). Native activists came to archaeology meetings, including the Society for American Archaeology and the first World Archaeology Conference, to discuss reburial and repatriation of Indian remains with archaeologists. O'odham people, including Cecil Antone of the Gila River Indian Community, and Robert Cruz, a Tohono O'odham, were among the activists meeting archaeologists. By this point in time, the path of an emancipatory praxis of archaeology seemed clear. Feminist archaeology provided the model, and some feminist scholars took the lead (Spector 1993). If archaeology was part of the problem, then progressive scholars needed to transform archaeology (Sprague 1974; Trigger 1980a; Zimmerman 1989; McGuire 1992a). In 1990, the federal government passed the Native American Graves Protection and Repatriation Act (NAGPRA), which has transformed the practice of archaeology in the United States.

During the debates leading up to NAGPRA, the issues of reburial and repatriation became concrete in the San Xavier District of the Tohono O'odham Nation. In October 1983, a Santa Cruz River flood washed away the San Xavier Mission Bridge and exposed an ancient cemetery (Ravesloot 1990; Sheridan and Parezo 1996:129–133). The Arizona Department of Transportation contracted with the Arizona State Museum (ASM) to do archaeological work on the site before construction of a new bridge. The O'odham wanted a new bridge, but they were also very concerned about the well-being of their dead. The archaeologists from the ASM consulted with the San Xavier District Council and agreed to active supervision of their research by O'odham political leaders and an O'odham medicine woman. In response to O'odham requests, the archaeologists modified both their excavation methods and their analyses. In 1986, the ASM turned the human remains and mortuary artifacts over to the Tohono O'odham for reburial. This experience established a model for consultation and cooperation between archaeologists and

Indian people that would become a standard practice in Arizona after the passage of NAGPRA. The San Xavier Mission Bridge project also increased awareness of the reburial issue among Tohono O'odham people.

The Practice and Praxis of U.S. Archaeology after NAGPRA

NAGPRA transformed the practice of U.S. archaeology and redefined an emancipatory praxis of archaeology vis-à-vis Indian peoples. Interactions between non-Native archaeologists and Native Americans have increased dramatically, with consultation now a standard aspect of archaeological research in the United States. Collaboration between archaeologists and Indian communities is now common. Both archaeologists and Indian nations have put bureaucratic and institutional mechanisms in place to facilitate negotiation and compliance with the law. Thousands of human remains and sacred artifacts have been repatriated. Nonetheless, the struggle over who will control native pasts and the things from those pasts still continues, but with Indian people increasingly taking more control of the official and public histories of Native America.

The involvement of tribal governments in archaeology has dramatically increased in the twenty-first century. NAGPRA requires all museums receiving federal money to inventory their collections and provide these inventories to Indian nations. Indian nations have set up cultural affairs committees to deal with these inventories and with repatriation and reburial issues that arise as a result of contract archaeology. All five of the O'odham nations in southern Arizona set up such committees in the 1990s. Today, dozens of Indian nations have their own archaeology programs that employ both Native and non-Native archaeologists and have there own tribal historic preservation officers (Stapp and Burney 2002; NATHPO 2006).

Indian people are also gaining more direct control over how their histories are presented to the public and to their own people. This control flows from the development of an indigenous archaeology and the expansion of tribal museums. In virtually all cases, tribal museums have worked with non-Native archaeologists and ethnographers. In the early 1970s, the Gila River Indian Community opened a craft center, museum, and heritage park both for tourists on the interstate and for their own people. The most noteworthy of these efforts is the National Museum of the American Indian, which opened as part of the Smithsonian Institution in September 2004. This museum moved Native American exhibits out from behind the stuffed elephant in the National Museum of Natural

History and placed them under the control of a predominately Native American board of directors. In June 2007, the Tohono O'odham Nation opened a new museum and cultural center near Sells, Arizona.

Aboriginal archaeology in North America today presents a very complex field of praxis in contrast to the obvious path of the 1980s. Collaborations between archaeologists and Indian people in tribal archaeology programs, museums, research, and field schools introduce a very constructive transformative praxis. The development of an indigenous archaeology presents the opportunity to establish a permanent and effective rapport between archaeology and Native peoples. This situation is in marked contrast to México, where nationalist movements resolved the contradictions of heritage and indigenous peoples in a very different way.

ARCHAEOLOGY AND INDIGENISMO IN MÉXICO

México possesses a very well-developed tradition of academic archaeology with a long history of scholarship (Bernal 1980; Lorenzo 1998:45–64). This tradition developed with a usually ambiguous relationship with North American imperialist archaeology in the country. One of the first university-trained archaeologists in México was Manuel Gamio, who studied with Franz Boas at Columbia University in the first decade of the twentieth century (Bernal 1980:161, 164). Early in its history, Mexican archaeology became an instrument of the nationalist ideology of *indigenismo*, connecting itself to the ancient past of Mesoamerica through a national mestizo identity (Lorenzo 1982, 1998; Gandara 1992). According to this ideology, the mestizo sprang from the interbreeding of European and Indian peoples and thus can claim both heritages. Mexican archaeologists believe that they study their own ancestors, in contrast to the North Americans, who come to study the exotic. In part because Mexican archaeology exists in service to the Mexican state, it also developed in a far more consistent and centralized way than North American archaeology. In the twenty-first century, however, the role of archaeology in México and the ideology of *indigenismo* have been challenged by the global reach of fast capitalism. In México, market principles are currently contesting established ideals of heritage.

Indigenismo and La Raza

The Mexican Revolution, which raged from 1911 to 1918, devastated the country (Gonzales 2002). Violence and unrest continued into the

1920s, with political factions vying for supremacy until the Partido Revolutionario Institucional (PRI) consolidated its power in 1929. The PRI subsequently ruled México for more than seventy years.[6] The destruction wrought by the revolution was so great that a new nationalist movement was needed to unify the country under the political control of the PRI. The new nationalism was based in the concept of the mestizo, or La Raza (the race), melding indigenous and European heritage to create a new Mexican heritage of *indigenismo*.

A national intelligentsia, including historians, artists, ethnographers, and archaeologists, created *indigenismo* (Patterson 1995a). Gamio began excavations in Teotihuacán in 1917 to glorify the heritage of *indigenismo*, directing the reconstruction of Teotihuacán as a Mexican Williamsburg that embodied the identity of the Mexican people (Lorenzo 1982:199–200). In 1934, the left wing of the PRI triumphed, and Lázaro Cárdenas became the president of the Mexican Republic. Cárdenas invited the return of intellectuals and artists who had fled México during the revolution. They enshrined *indigenismo* as the nationalist ideology. The great Mexican muralists Diego Rivera, José Clemente Orozco, and David Alfaro Siqueiros emblazoned the walls of México with glorifications of La Raza, often using themes derived from archaeology.

Archaeology played a major role in the construction and maintenance of *indigenismo*. In 1939, the Cárdenas government created the Instituto Nacional de Antropología y Historia (INAH, the National Institute of Anthropology and History), with the archaeologist Alfonso Caso as its first director (Bernal 1980:186). The Mexican state granted the INAH sole responsibility for the direction of archaeological research and control of all national cultural heritage, including archaeological monuments and zones, historic sites, and museums in the nation (Lorenzo 1998). At the same time the Escuela Nacional de Antropología y Historia (ENAH, the National School of Anthropology and History) was created to train students to staff the INAH. In México, archaeology did not fall into the realm of natural history, as it had in the United States (Lorenzo 1998:173–185); rather, it was key to national heritage and identity. In INAH and ENAH, Gamio, Caso, and Ignacio Bernal developed a historical approach to archaeology that embodied anti-imperialist, socialist, and anarchist ideals. These trends differed from the intellectual developments in the Anglophone archaeology that guided North American archaeologists working in México and in the southwestern United States (Fowler 1987:234).

The ideology of *indigenismo* did not equally glorify all the indigenous pasts of México (Gandara 1992). Nationalist constructions of heritage tend to pick and choose from the history of a nation, and *indigenismo* is no exception, with its focus on the cultures and civilizations of the highlands. Although the scope of INAH's interests expanded gradually during the post–World War II era, INAH continued to expend the majority of its attention and funds on the central highlands of the country. Areas such as the West and North of México received only occasional and peripheral attention. This focus culminated in the late 1970s and the early 1980s with the excavation of the Aztec Templo Mayor in center of México City (Matos 1988). This nationalist Mexican archaeology developed alongside the imperialist foreign archaeology, which originated principally in the United States but also included German and French researchers. In the 1970s, advocates of *la archaeología social* confronted this imperialism.

La Arqueología Social

México became the center for a Latin American radical archaeology that opposed the hegemonic power of U.S. ideologies (Lorenzo et al. 1976; Patterson 1994; Bate 1998). In this radical climate, the INAH instituted structural changes in permitting archaeological research in the country, directly affecting U.S. scholars' access to Mexican archaeological sites.

In 1975 archaeologists from México, Peru, Chile, Venezuela, and Argentina came together at the Reunion de Teotihuacán in México to forge a common struggle (Lorenzo et al. 1976). During the 1970s, reactionary forces in Chile and Argentina violently established military dictatorships that sought to crush all leftist ideas and actions. This repression drove many intellectuals, including archaeologists, to more democratic countries, including México. In México these archaeologists came into contact with an already established progressive tradition of nationalism and *indigenismo* (Caso 1958; Bernal 1980). As a result of this process, México, especially the ENAH, became a hothouse for the intellectual development of *la arqueología social* in the 1970s and 1980s (McGuire and Navarrete 1999, 2004).

The political debates of the 1970s led the INAH to reevaluate the relationship between U.S. and Mexican archaeologists (Lorenzo et al. 1976). Many Mexican archaeologists felt that those from North American had exploited the national heritage of México and alienated it from Mexicans (Lorenzo 1982:201–202; 1998). They questioned the quality of work done by North American archaeologists and the use of Mexican sites to train U.S. students. They noted abuses, such as archaeologists leaving students at excavations without qualified supervisors and failing to publish the results of their research. U.S. excavations at sites with monumental architecture often left INAH with expensive problems of stabilization and restoration of the exposed architecture. More important, Mexican archaeologists were concerned that North American archaeologists came to México to address academic debates that had no relevance to Mexican concerns (Lorenzo 1982:202).

In 1972, INAH sought to redefine the practice of archaeology in México by establishing a new set of rules for permitting archaeological research in the country (McClung 1999). With some modifications, this permitting process is still in force today, and it applies to both Mexican and foreign projects (INAH 1994). These rules include strict guidelines for the supervision of archaeological excavations, a mandate to submit a final report in Spanish, and a provision that 15 percent of the project budget must be transferred to INAH for the purposes of stabilization, restoration, and curation of materials exposed by the project. Many North American archaeologists worried that the changes meant the end of U.S. fieldwork in México. This did not happen, but foreign archaeologists now had to enter into consultations with INAH to work in México. More recently the conservative, neoliberal trends of fast capitalism have begun to transform Mexican nationalism and the role of archaeology in the Mexican state yet again.

Fast Capitalism, Neoliberalism, and Archaeology in México

The last decades of the twentieth century found México in economic crisis and the established political and nationalist program of the century in question. In 1982, México was plunged into a massive economic depression, followed by a brief recovery and then another crash in late 1994 (Middlebrook and Zepeda 2003). The PRI reacted by moving away from a governmentally controlled economy with high tariffs on foreign goods. Instead, factions within the PRI turned to a fast capitalist neoliberal policy of open trade, privatization of industries and services, and decentralization of the government. In 1994, the government signed the North American Free Trade Agreement with the United States and Canada. These trends have generally opened México up to foreign interests and to the domination of market principles in all aspects of society, including heritage and archaeology. The strong nationalist ideology of *indigenismo* has been eroded, because it does not fit well with the globalization of fast capitalism. The decentralization of politics and the economy has also threatened the role of INAH in heritage management and archaeology within México.

These changes were met with resistance within México, both from within the PRI and among the populace. A group of PRI leaders, including the son of Lázaro Cárdenas, split from the party and formed the Partido de la Revolución Democrática (PRD, the Revolutionary Democratic Party). The 1994 election was fraudulent, and accusations of vote tampering left many in the country believing that the PDR really won the presidency, rather than the PRI.[7] Then, in the 2000 elections, the conservative Partido Acción Nacional (PAN, National Action Party) won the presidency of México, ending seventy years of PRI rule. These political shifts have left all Mexican federal agencies, such as the INAH, in peril.

The fast capitalist neoliberal trend toward decentralization has had a direct impact on INAH, eroding its domination of archaeology in the country. In the 1970s, INAH began a program to expand the number of regional centers throughout the country. By the early 1990s, virtually every Mexican state had a Centro de INAH. Also in the 1970s, programs of study leading to the *licenciatura* in anthropology were established in state universities in Veracruz and the Yucatán.[8] In 1983, an additional program began in Guadalajara, and in the 1990s such programs sprang up in many states across the country. In the last decades of the twentieth century, students no longer had to attend the ENAH to obtain certification to be an archaeologist. The state programs, along with the Universidad Autónoma de México's Instituto de Investigaciones Antropológicas, are research centers doing archaeology independent of the INAH. In the last decade of the twentieth century, private companies also began to appear to do contract archaeology.

In 1999, PAN legislators began introducing legislation to the Mexican Congress that would transform INAH, and the efforts to pass it have continued and gained strength since PAN won the presidency in 2000 and 2006. If passed, the legislation will result in the virtual abolition of the INAH and the ENAH. It will commodify and privatize archaeology and heritage in the country, replace research and education with market principles as the philosophy of heritage management, and transfer control of most heritage issues from the federal government to state-level governments (McClung 1999). The legislation also seeks to privatize the national monuments and museums of México by granting concessions in them to for-profit corporations. This law fits with the general PAN desire to renegotiate nationalist ideology in México away from the ideal of *indigenismo*, associated with the PRI. These efforts also reflect a larger worldwide trend to create heritage industries that serve not to advance nationalist ideologies but rather to generate profits (Rowan and Baram 2004).

In January 1994, Mayan Indians in the state of Chiapas, calling themselves the Zapatistas, rose up in revolution (Collier 1994). In a few days, they seized control of a portion of the state, which they still hold in their power today. The Zapatistas timed their revolution to correspond to the date for the implementation of NAFTA. Their revolution is a clear rejection of the conservative neoliberal agenda of turn-of-the-century México. Perhaps less obviously, the Zapatista revolution's *indigenista* ideology challenges the nationalist ideal of *indigenismo*. Contemporary *indigenista* movements in Latin America, such as the Zapatistas, seek greater economic, cultural, and political autonomy for indigenous peoples (Joyce 2003, 2005; Ren 2006). The Zapatistas have rejected the ideology that identifies all Mexicans with La Raza. They have instead argued for the recognition of the highland Maya as a distinct people with their own heritage.

The archaeological community of México stands in an ambiguous relationship to the goals of the Zapatista movement. On the one hand, most archaeologists in México today favor leftist political movements and goals. In the spring of 2002, when the leaders of the Zapatista movement arrived in México City for two weeks, the faculty and students of the ENAH opened the doors of the school to house and feed them. On the other hand, *indigenistas* claim that the ancient past of México is the heritage of specific indigenous peoples, such as the Maya, rather than the heritage of a mestizo Mexican nation. The INAH fears it will lose control of monuments, museums, and collections to native groups.

The archaeologists, U.S. and Mexican, of the Trincheras Tradition Project share a craft of archaeology. But this craft developed and was put to the service of very different nationalist programs in each country. Even though both U.S. and Mexican archaeologists work on the same sites, they are the products and keepers of different cultural traditions of archaeology. Building a praxis of archaeology that challenges both the imperialism and the colonialism of the frontier requires that both communities understand critically the history that created them. In northern Sonora, they also need to understand the history that created the resident communities of the border, Norteños and Tohono O'odham.

NORTEÑOS AND TOHONO O'ODHAM ON THE BORDER

The United States and México developed different ideologies to resolve the inherent contradiction in the justification of their existence as nations, since both were established through the conquest of indigenous peoples. So too were the archaeological communities of each country created differently, and they face different challenges today. The culturally ambiguous nature of an international frontier means that the ideologies, processes, and social relationships that characterize a nation's core will not be the same on the perimeter. The nationalist ideologies of the First Americans and of *indigenismo* do not work well along the U.S.–Mexican boundary. This line also has created unique relationships among the archaeological communities of both countries, the regional population of northern México, the Norteños, and the Indian nations, such as the Tohono O'odham.

Norteños

The Northwest of México stands apart from the country's other regions (León-Portilla 1972; Alonso 1995). Elsewhere in México, the Spanish conquerors encountered large aboriginal populations and existing institutions and relationships of control and governance. The conquistadores and their native allies quickly defeated the indigenous armies and then placed themselves at the top of the state structure. Epidemic diseases decimated the native populations but left enough people that the Spanish could enlist their labor to build haciendas, mines, and workshops. In northwest México, by contrast, the Spanish encountered fewer people, and they lived in smaller settlements without overarching state structures. Each village had to be individually subjugated. After the conquest and the ravages of epidemic diseases, the remaining populations in this area were even smaller and more isolated. The new form of subjugation was slow, with missions reducing the Indians to smaller areas of land and Spanish settlers moving in to establish mines, farms, and ranches, much as settlers did in North America. It was a violent process with nearly three hundred years of near constant warfare between Indians and Norteños (Alonso 1995). As in the United States, much less intermarriage occurred between European and Indian populations in this area of México; both remained biologically more distinct than in the rest of the country.

The result of this process was a distinctive cultural identity in the north, the Norteño (León-Portilla 1972; Nabhan 1998; Sheridan 1998).[9]

Norteños by and large do not accept the nationalist ideology of *indigenismo*, because it does not speak to their experience of history. The things that distinguish Norteños from other regional populations of México include obvious differences in food (flour tortillas and *carne asada*), music (with accordions and a polka beat), and dress (jeans, cowboy boots, and cowboy hats). The Norteños' "membership in the nation has always been contradictory and ambiguous" (Alonso 1988:55). This is most strongly seen in their relationship to two other communities on the border, Indians and gringos.

Norteños are taller, lighter, and more European in appearance than the mestizo populations to the south. They draw a strong distinction between themselves and the Indian cultures that survive in the region, speaking of Indian people in pejorative terms or referring to them in the diminutive, los Oaxaquitas or los Mayitos. The Indian cultures that survived in the Northwest did so in part by isolating themselves either socially or geographically from Spanish and later Mexican society. Today, much like Euro-Americans in the United States, Norteños speak of local Indians as people who once were on the land but now have vanished from it. They tend to regard Tohono O'odham people from the United States as gringos, with more wealth, power, and privilege than the Norteños have.

The reality of the international frontier is that, for the past 150 years, contact with the United States and Gringos has shaped Norteño culture. Virtually all Norteños have relatives who live in the United States, and many, if not most, have crossed the border legally or illegally. The power of the United States and the contrast between lives on either side of the border are an ever-present backdrop to Norteño life. Although Norteño attitudes about North Americans are at best ambiguous, these people are usually welcoming and friendly to North Americans. Those of us involved in the Trincheras Tradition Project have mainly encountered graciousness and hospitality in the villages of Atil, Oquitoa, and Trincheras, Sonora, where we have worked. But negative feelings also exist. Joaquín Murrieta, a mythologized Norteño "Robin Hood," who robbed his way through California during the gold rush era, is a cultural icon and hero throughout Sonora (Ridge 1955; Nabhan 1998:9–10). The town of Trincheras claims him as a native son.

Tohono O'odham

The O'odham populations of the international frontier area are composed of two peoples, the Akimel of the Phoenix Basin and the Tohono

O'odham of southern Arizona and northern Sonora; they are commonly known in English as the Pima and the Papago, respectively (Fontana 1981; Erikson 1994). They speak a common language, O'odham (Pima). Before the late seventeenth-century Spanish conquest of northern Sonora and what is now southern Arizona, these peoples occupied the area of the rivers of the Sonoran Desert, bordered by the Gila in the north and the Río San Miguel in the south and centering on the Río Magdalena, south of the modern international frontier, with concentrations of people in the Tucson Basin and along the San Pedro River in southern Arizona. The Tohono O'odham (the desert people, or the Papago) lived to the west of the Tucson Basin and between the Río Magdalena and the Gila River in an area that lacked flowing streams. The Akimel (the river people, or the Pima) lived along the Gila, San Pedro, and Santa Cruz rivers.

The Spanish established the first missions among the O'odham at the end of the seventeenth century, but the O'odham population declined there because of diseases and low fertility (Fontana 1981:48). At about this same time, the Apache of southern Arizona acquired horses and started raiding both the O'odham and the Spanish. As a result of these two pressures—Spanish from the south and Apache from the east—O'odham populations shifted north and west.

By the time of the Gadsden Purchase, in 1854, the O'odham had been greatly reduced in population and geographic extent (Fontana 1981:60). The international border split the O'odham territory in two and left about half of the O'odham living between the international border and the north side of the Río Magdalena in México. The Tohono O'odham still lived to the north of the Río Magdalena, in the Tucson Basin, and to the west of the Tucson Basin. The Spanish had labeled this area the Papaguería, or the land of the Papago. To the north, the Akimel O'odham (the river people) lived near modern Phoenix (Fontana 1981:60).

The O'odham allied themselves with the United States against the Apache. In the 1870s and 1880s the federal government established five reservations for these allies (Fontana 1981:64). In 1916, the president of the United States issued an executive order creating the Papago Indian Reservation, now known as the Tohono O'odham Nation. This reservation stretches from Tucson in the east, to Ajo, Arizona, in the west, and almost to the Gila Bend Reservation in the north. Sixty-four miles of the international border define the southernmost edge of the Tohono O'odham Nation.

Following the Gadsden Purchase, the Tohono O'odham in Sonora lacked any special status; they were simply Mexican citizens (Fontana

1981:68–83). México did not establish reservations for them, as was done in the United States, so they lived in isolated communities and along the edges of Mexican towns and villages. For nearly a century, the border was a line on the map with little meaning. It was not until the hoof-and-mouth epidemic of the 1940s that the U.S. government built a barbwire fence along the sixty-four miles of the reservation to prevent livestock from wandering between the two countries (Erikson 1994). Throughout this period before the fence was erected, the Tohono O'odham moved freely back and forth, but forces pushed them to leave Sonora, and other forces pulled them north.

The Tohono O'odham in Sonora have experienced continued and extensive encroachments by Mexican ranchers. The most dramatic incident occurred in 1898 in the small mining town of El Plomo (Fontana 1981:73–74). A party of about forty Sonoran and Arizona O'odham attacked the town to free a jailed headman, but the Mexicans drove them away in a bloody fight. For over a decade after this, Mexican *rurales* (rural police) attacked Tohono O'odham throughout northern Sonora. Hundreds of O'odham left Sonora to settle in what would become the southern district of the Tohono O'odham Nation. They continued to intermarry and regularly interact with their relatives who remained in Sonora. Throughout the twentieth century, residence in the United States generally offered Tohono O'odham better economic conditions and better access to social services than residence in México, so informal immigration has continued.

The status of the Tohono O'odham in Sonora today is ambiguous. On the one hand, the Mexican federal government has taken actions to recognize and protect O'odham property and rights, but, in general, state and local officials regard the O'odham as U.S., not Mexican, Indians. In 1928, the Mexican government chartered an *ejido* for the O'odham community of Pozo Verde in Sonora.[10] The Mexican Instituto Nacional Indigenista (INI, National Indian Institute, the Mexican equivalent of the U.S. Bureau of Indian Affairs) recognizes the Tohono O'odham as Mexican Indians (Fontana 1981:75), but despite these recognitions, the general opinion in Sonora, both of the populace and of local government officials, is that the El Plomo hostilities drove all of the O'odham to Arizona and that they are really U.S. Indians or just a different kind of gringo.

The sixty-four miles of the international border in the Tohono O'odham Nation is no longer simply a line on a map or a four-wire livestock fence. At the end of the twentieth century, in response to drug smuggling and illegal immigration, the U.S. government instituted extensive surveillance and frequent patrol of the line. The Tohono O'odham can no longer casually cross from one country to another but must pass through U.S. and Mexican customs and immigration checks. The official position of the Tohono O'odham Nation is that all Tohono O'odham are members of that nation and have the right to move freely across the sixty-four-mile line. Yet, the Mexican border agents treat the Tohono O'odham from the United States as U.S. citizens, and the U.S. Immigration Service regards Mexican Tohono O'odham as Mexican citizens.

Northern Sonora remains a sacred and important place for the Tohono O'odham. To the northwest of Caborca lies the desert oasis of Quitovac, where a spring-fed earthen tank provides a year-round water supply in the desert. Here, according to Tohono O'odham belief, a cultural hero known as either I'itoi or Montezuma killed a great water monster that had been slaughtering people in the region (Fontana 1981:79). Every summer, Tohono O'odham from Sonora and Arizona gather at Quitovac for the Wi:gita ceremony to pray for rain, good crops, lush desert growth, health, and long life.

THE TRINCHERAS TRADITION PROJECT — BUILDING PRAXIS

The international border arbitrarily cuts the Southwestern-Northwestern culture area in half.[11] It had no meaning for the aboriginal history of the culture area, but it has had a profound effect on the archaeology of the region (McGuire 2002a). The amount of archaeological research done north of the border greatly exceeds that undertaken in northwest México. Today the southwestern United States could be the most intensively researched archaeological region in the world. To the south of the culture area, Mesoamerica is also an intensively researched archaeological region. Sandwiched between these two areas, northern México may be, archaeologically, the least well-known region in North and Central America.

The paucity of archaeological research in Sonora provided an opportunity for our goals of creating a praxis of archaeology that challenged the traditionally imperialistic practice of archaeology by North Americans in Mesoamerica. When we began the Trincheras Tradition Project, there was no established imperialist tradition of North American archaeologists working in northwest México. Previous U.S. projects had been expeditions that entered and then left the region. The same was true of most Mexican projects before the founding of the INAH center in Hermosillo in 1973 (Braniff and Felger 1976). We had an opportunity to build a new praxis of archaeology without having to confront an existing local practice and well-established prejudice on either side.

The Project

I received my graduate education at the University of Arizona and worked in southern Arizona during the mid- to late 1970s. I found the *cerros de trincheras* there intriguing. The possible relationships in pre-Hispanic developments between the Hohokam Tradition of Arizona and the Trincheras Tradition of Sonora were an open question. At that time very little archaeological research had been done in northern Sonora. The Trincheras Tradition in Sonora was known only from travelers' reports, a few surface surveys, and a handful of test excavations at a few sites. In 1982, I went to my current academic job at Binghamton University with the goal of establishing a field project in Sonora. In the summer of 1985, I met with Elisa Villalpando at the INAH center in Hermosillo to plan the project, and we agreed to codirect it.

The Trincheras Tradition Project has been from its start a joint project of Binghamton University and the Centro INAH de Sonora. The project has gone through several stages and five seasons of fieldwork. The National Science Foundation, the National Geographic Society, and Binghamton University have funded the project.[12] As is customary for both foreign and national projects in México, our project employed local people as cooks, laborers, and artifact washers.

The Trincheras Tradition of northern Sonora stretched from approximately the international border on the north to Desemboque on the south and from the Río San Miguel on the east to the Gulf of California on the west (map 1). A distinctive purple-on-red pottery and the site type *cerros de trincheras* characterize this archaeological tradition. *Cerros de trincheras* sites consist of rock walls, terraces, and structures built on the isolated volcanic hills that dot the Sonoran Desert. Such sites occur in other archaeological traditions in southern Arizona, in northeastern Sonora, and in Chihuahua, but they appear the most common and elaborated in the Trincheras Tradition. The largest of these sites is Cerro de Trincheras itself, overlooking the town of Trincheras, Sonora. This site was a pre-Hispanic town on a hill with over nine hundred terraces and a population of one thousand or more (O'Donovan 2002). The beginning date for the Trincheras Tradition is not well established but probably falls between 300 and 500 C.E. The site of Cerro de Trincheras was abandoned by 1450 C.E. The first Spanish missionaries

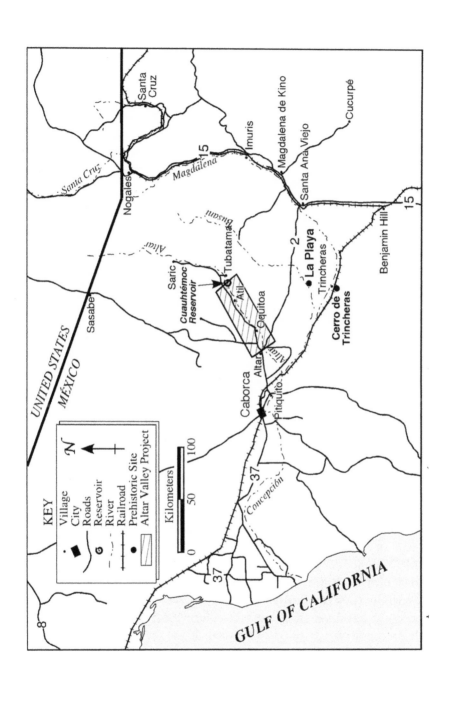

Figure 1. Cerro de Trincheras. Photo by Randall McGuire.

found this area occupied by the O'odham in the late seventeenth century, and the Tohono O'odham claim the archaeological sites of the region as the handiwork of their ancestors.

Elisa Villalpando and I initially selected the Río Altar valley from the Cuauhtémoc Dam to the town of Altar for an intensive pedestrian survey (map 2), executing a systematic total area survey of this region in 1988 (McGuire and Villalpando 1993).[13] We rented two field houses in the town of Atil, Sonora, and lived there for four months. We hired a local woman to cook for us. An archaeological team of six Binghamton University archaeologists and four archaeologists from the Escuela Nacional de Antropología y Historia in México City did the fieldwork.

In 1991, we shifted our research to the site of Cerro de Trincheras, at Trincheras, Sonora (figure 1). In that year we made a map of the site and surface collected it (O'Donovan 2002).[14] The crew then consisted of Elisa Villalpando, three Binghamton University archaeologists, one archaeologist from the Escuela Nacional de Antropología y Historia, and myself. We rented a house in Trincheras and spent two months there. We hired a local woman to cook for us and a teenager to wash artifacts. In 1995 and

Figure 2. Archaeologists at Valle de Altar, Sonora, 2006. From left to right: Elisa Villalpando, Adrián López, Stephanie Bowers, Randall McGuire, Alex Button, and César Villalobos. Photo by Génesis Ruiz.

1996 we returned to Cerro de Trincheras to excavate (McGuire and Villalpando, forthcoming). This was a large project with over fifty people employed at its peak. We rented two houses in Trincheras each year, and we lived in the community for four months during each field season. The archaeology team consisted of Elisa and me with five or six U.S. archaeologists and four or five Mexican archaeologists. We employed up to forty local people as laborers, cooks, and artifact washers.

In 2006, we returned to the Altar Valley to map and make systematic surface collections of two *cerros de trincheras,* Tío Benino and La Hormiga. Our field crew included two Binghamton University archaeologists and two archaeologists from the Centro INAH de Sonora (figure 2). We rented two houses in Oquitoa and hired a local woman as a cook.

One of our goals from the beginning of the Trincheras Tradition Project has been to build an archaeology that recognizes, confronts, and attempts to alter the power relations of double colonialism on the border. To do so we have used different modes of interaction in attempts to engage Mexican archaeologists, U.S. archaeologists, Norteños, and Tohono O'odham communities. We have tried to transform the imperialist relationship that normally characterizes North American archaeology in México by creating a binational and collaborative archaeology. Also, we have tried to involve the local Norteño community in our research through a program of education that began with an ethnographic understanding of their interests in the past. Finally, we have tried to address the colonialist relationship between Mexican and U.S. archaeology and the Tohono O'odham through a process of consultation.

Building a Binational and Collaborative Archaeology

We see binational collaboration as the alternative to the traditional imperialism of North American archaeology in México. This collaboration recognizes the power relations and inequalities between the two archaeological communities, eliminating the inequalities whenever possible and mitigating them when not. Collaboration requires the establishment of long-term personal, social, and professional relationships that allow the parties involved to identify, create, and build on common interests. Such a process best precedes and transcends a specific project or set of goals.

I began planning my research in Sonora at a time when *la arqueología social* was flourishing, anti-imperialist sentiments were strong, and the INAH had recently revised the permitting process for archaeological research in México. Many of my colleagues and even some of my professors questioned my interest in Sonora. They expressed the fear that it would not be possible for U.S. researchers to work in México. As it turned out, however, this was a very opportune time to initiate archaeological research in Sonora.

The new INAH center in Hermosillo established for the first time a community of Mexican professional archaeologists, including Beatriz Braniff, Arturo Oliveros, and later Julio Montané, whose primary interests were the archaeology of northwest México (Villalobos 2004:64–66). Montané (1980) had been one of the founders of *la arqueología social* in South America. He had fled Chile to avoid persecution by the military dictatorship that overthrew the government of Salvadore Allende in 1971. Braniff sponsored students from the ENAH to do their theses on the archaeology of Sonora. She brought them to southern Arizona to visit collections and to meet with archaeologists there. In 1979, I met Braniff and two of her students, Elisa Villalpando and Ana María Álvarez, in southern Arizona. Because they were trained in *la arqueología social* and because of my own interest in Marx, we had much in common to discuss beyond the archaeology of the Northwest-Southwest.

I began traveling to Sonora to visit the center, to assist on INAH projects, and to build social and professional relationships. Braniff left Hermosillo in 1984, but Villalpando stayed at the center as a research archaeologist, and Álvarez joined the faculty of the ENAH in 1985. Throughout this period I studied and practiced Spanish to attain a level of competency that would allow me to use the language in Sonora.

In 1985, Ben Brown and I did a windshield survey of the Río Magdalena and met with Elisa Villalpando at the INAH center in Hermosillo. We began discussing the collaborative approach to research that we would develop in our subsequent projects together. Key to this was shared responsibility for the direction of the project. Binghamton University and the Centro INAH de Sonora have jointly sponsored each stage of the project, with Elisa and myself as codirectors. We have identified five issues that we needed to address to build a collaborative, binational archaeology: research goals, resources, participation, language, and publication.

Research Goals   One of the things that most clearly define the two distinct archaeologies of North Americans and of Mexicans in Mesoamerica is the difference in their research goals. In part this reflects the difference between the global, imperialist interests of North American archaeology and the local, nationalistic interest of Mexican archaeology. In the 1980s and 1990s, these distinctions also sprang from the profound theoretical differences between the processual archaeology of North America and *la arqueología social* of Latin America. Mexican researchers from the regional centers in Sonora and Chihuahua have tended to focus on issues of culture history in order to establish basic understandings of time-space dynamics in the regions. They have also tended to interpret northwestern archaeological sequences in terms of local events and processes rather than in terms of those in the southwestern United States or Mesoamerica. Along these lines, in 1981 the Centro INAH de Sonora established the Management Plan for the Cultural Heritage of the State of Sonora.[15] This plan called for all archaeological projects in the state of Sonora to contribute in some way to the priorities that the plan lays out for researching the archaeology of the state at the local, regional, and global levels. The plan formed a baseline for defining our collaborative research efforts.

Resources   One basic problem facing a collaborative North American and Mexican project is the striking difference in the economies of the two countries. Archaeologists can address power relations on projects, but we cannot change the basic economic relationship between the United States and México. North American projects in México generally have access to greater resources than Mexican projects. These resources include both equipment and money. We have not been able to transform the economic inequity that separates the United States and México through archaeology, so we have had to consider how to mitigate it.

We have used part of our grants to try to mitigate this economic inequity by balancing the logistical support of the Centro INAH de Sonora with long-term infrastructural benefits to it. The center has provided logistical support for the project through the use of its facilities, computers, tools, support staff, curatorial services, and vehicles. It has also facilitated the project by helping us to obtain INAH permits for our work. The 15 percent charge that the INAH collects on all foreign research grants in México was designed to fund the stabilization and preservation of exposed monumental architecture. The local center has been able to convince the INAH that since no such architecture exists in Sonora, the funds should be used in Hermosillo to maintain the infrastructure of the center.

Archaeologists are paid more in the United States than in México. In such a situation, fairness in the compensation of archaeologists from both countries is difficult to achieve. In the field, we have always paid Mexican and American archaeologists on the same scale, slightly higher than INAH has defined pay rates. For the Mexican students, this is a good rate of pay, but for the North Americans it is a token amount that allows them to break even on their participation in the project. The North Americans have accepted this situation, in part because of the ideologies of archaeological work discussed in chapter 3. For them the project work was an opportunity to gain data for their theses and dissertations and to do archaeology in a foreign locale. When we employ Mexican archaeologists in the laboratory in Hermosillo, we again pay slightly higher than INAH scale. Graduate students employed at Binghamton are paid as university research assistants at the going rate for the university.

Participation   At each stage of the project we have endeavored, usually successfully, to employ archaeologists in equal shares from each side of the border. We have drawn North American archaeologists from Binghamton University, the University of Arizona, Arizona State University, and the University of New Mexico, and Mexican archaeologists have come from the ENAH. Generally, these archaeologists have worked in binational teams of two, either as surveyors or as supervisors of local laborers in excavation. This organization has provided useful training for the students in working together across cultural differences and has been very successful. When we have employed archaeologists to do laboratory work outside the field season, we have always employed one archaeologist at Binghamton and one in Hermosillo.

Transcending cultural differences and differences in training in the binational teams of archaeologists has presented us with numerous challenges and opportunities in our research. The most obvious challenge has involved North Americans' adaptation to living in the isolated Norteño villages where we base our projects. Less obvious has been the issue of the Mexican archaeologists adapting to these villages. Most of the Mexican archaeologists who have worked with us have been from the central and southern parts of the country, steeped in the mestizo culture of México. The Norteño culture of Sonora is almost as different for these students as it is for the gringos. We hire local women to cook for us, and this entails a cuisine that does not fit either group's conceptions of Mexican food.[16] A few times cultural frictions have arisen in the project, both within the crew and between the crew and the local population, but they have always been resolvable through discussion and compromise.

We have found that the Mexican archaeologists come to the field with training and sets of skills different from those of the U.S. students, reflecting in large part the differences in how archaeologists are trained in the two countries (Newell 1999).[17] In the United States, students generally receive a broad undergraduate education that is intended to teach them basic analytical skills, raise their awareness of world issues, and prepare them to enter the world as educated individuals. At the ENAH, the students receive a rigorous training in archaeological theory and practice to prepare them to take professional positions in the INAH. As a result of this particular training and its domination by a single school of archaeology in México, the Mexican ENAH students have invariably been more proficient at the practice of archaeology, arriving on the project with a much more consistent set of methods, conventions, and skills as well as a wider range of technical skills than the U.S. archaeologists possess. These conventions and methods, which distinctively reflect the practice of Mesoamerican archaeology, often vary from the conventions and methods of the southwestern United States. Working out these variations has involved a long erratic process.

Language   The most basic problem we have faced in building a collaborative archaeology is language. North American projects in México usually use English. All archaeologists trained in México are expected to read English. The actual competence of individual archaeologists in English varies greatly, but almost all of the Mexican archaeologists and all of the students with whom we have worked can read articles and books in English. Although most U.S. graduate programs in anthropology require that their students read a second language, these requirements are rarely rigorously enforced. Archaeology professors in the United States do not routinely assign readings in Spanish to classes and seminars. Most of our U.S. archaeologists do not speak Spanish.

Publication   The commitment to a bilingual project extends to publication. A number of article-length reports on the project have been published in both Spanish and English. We have published project results in both the United States and México. Although we have not attempted to publish every page we write in both languages, which would simply cost too much in money and effort, we have consciously sought to publish comparable summaries and reviews of the project's findings and results in both English and Spanish, so that they are accessible to speakers of either language. Technical analyses and reports have been done in the principal language of the individuals doing the work. At each stage of the project, a detailed descriptive report in Spanish has been submitted to the INAH. Project personnel have also presented multiple papers at professional meetings in both México and the United States. The project has resulted in one *tesis de licenciatura* at the ENAH written in Spanish, and students at Binghamton University have produced undergraduate honors theses, master's theses, and a dissertation, all written in English. A full report of the 1995–1996 excavation project has been prepared in Spanish, and an English version is currently in progress.

In many ways, our attempt to build a collaborative, binational archaeology in Sonora has been successful. The project has trained a group of archaeologists—Mexican and North American—who continue to work in Sonora using collaborative approaches. Indeed, in Sonora today, all projects that involve North Americans are collaborative and binational. In October 2003, the Centro INAH de Sonora celebrated its thirtieth anniversary with scholarly and public events in Hermosillo. These events included U.S. and Mexican researchers, and behind them was a history of collaborative research under the leadership of the center. We did not achieve our success by ignoring or erasing the differences in wealth, purpose, and training that characterize Mexican and U.S. archaeology. Rather, we attempted to confront these differences and build a praxis of archaeology that would benefit from the dissimilarities and in turn benefit both archaeologies. This praxis does not eliminate the basic imperialist nature of U.S. archaeology in México. It does, however, mitigate this imperialism to create something new.

Our research results have reflected the international collaboration of the project. Previous research focused on the Trincheras Tradition as an extension or a by-product of processes in other regions. Mexican archeologists had interpreted it as the far northern reaches of developments emanating from the Valley of México and as a pale reflection of Mesoamerican cultures. U.S. archaeologists had interpreted the tradition as the southern extension of the Hohokam Tradition in southern Arizona, altered as a result of the ebb and flow of changes north of the border. Our research has shown that the tradition had its own history, developmental trajectory, and processes of change. The major site of Cerro de Trincheras was a town and regional center in its own right. Our research has helped to transform the archaeology of the Southwest-Northwest into an international field of study that seriously considers processes occurring in northern México as important to understanding the whole cultural area. In Sonora, our research has addressed issues laid out in the Management Plan for the Cultural Heritage of the State of Sonora. Our demonstration that the Trincheras Tradition was a development in its own right, not simply the extension of processes from the north or south, calls into question the nationalistic programs of both the United States and México. The Trincheras Tradition is not understandable as the ancient history of La Raza, because it was not simply an extension of Mesoamerica. Neither was it the prehistory of the First Americans, because it shows the irrelevance of the border to aboriginal history. The limitations of these nationalist traditions were also made apparent in our interactions with the Norteño and Tohono O'odham communities that live in the region.

Norteños and Heritage

Our research affects the Norteño people of rural northern Sonora in two ways (Villalobos 2004:124–128). We have an economic impact on the communities in which we work, because we rent houses, employ people, and purchase local goods and services. We also seek to educate the people in these communities and build their appreciation for the aboriginal heritage of the region. In both of these endeavors we enter into social relations with the community inhabitants and become objects of their curiosity. All of this occurs in the preestablished social and historical context of the border.

Rural Sonoran communities like Atil, Oquitoa, and Trincheras are filled with old people and children. These villages offer few employment opportunities. The majority of the younger people leave for cities such as Hermosillo, the *maquiladora* (export assembly) factories along the border, or the United States to find work, or they *burrean* (that is, backpack marijuana illegally through the desert and across the border into the United States). They often leave their children with relatives and send remittances to help support them until they return. Many individuals, however, do not return to the village but, instead, become permanent residents of Hermosillo, Tucson, or Southern California. A few families support themselves with privately owned farms, but most people in the communities seek irregular day work to live.

Our projects have fitted into this economic situation as other sources of day work. Over the last decade we have employed members of numerous families on a regular basis as cooks and day laborers (figure 3). These opportunities have allowed those families a few more comforts, but they have not appreciably changed their economic position in the village. In 1995 and 1996, when we employed up to forty local people, we were the largest private employer in the village. Some individuals came home to work for us during each of these seasons, then returned to itinerant labor. We have had a real, but not profound or transformative, impact on the local economy.

While in the field our workers and friends have often asked us to take on the role of *padrinos*—that is, to serve as supporters and sponsors for important social celebrations and events. Routinely in México aspects of a celebration, such as food, beverage, music, and photography, will be parceled out to different *padrinos*. For example, we have supplied photography and transportation for wedding celebrations.

The Norteño people of Sonora tend to view the pre-Hispanic archaeology of the region as something left over from vanished Indians. They do not necessarily see it as their own heritage. Individuals routinely loot pots from the cremation cemetery of Cerro de Trincheras and collect skulls from burials eroding in the nearby archaeological site of La Playa. Nevertheless, they do have some pride in the aboriginal site of Cerro de Trincheras, which looms over them, recognizing that it gives the town

Figure 3. Norteño workmen at Cerro de Trincheras, 1996.
From left to right: Eugenio Bejarano, Ramón Alejandro
Yescas, Raúl Murrieta, and Medardo Salazar. Photo by
Júpiter Martínez.

distinction. During the 1940s, those who built the current railroad line to
Tijuana stripped many volcanic hills along the line of stone to construct
bridges. Locals told us that the mayor of Trincheras at the time stopped
the builders when they started to bulldoze Cerro de Trincheras for stone.
Our excavations uncovered tracks of the bulldozer in one of the most
important features in the site, La Cancha.

This ambiguous interest in the archaeological site does not mean,
however, that the people of Trincheras have no interest in heritage. The
town claims to be the birthplace of the California "Robin Hood"

Joaquín Murrieta. For most local residents, this is the most important aspect of the community's heritage. A small statue erected to the bandit sits at the entrance to the town.

The INAH is an institution that serves the Mexican nation, the people of México, and the discipline of anthropology. Consistent with this service, our project has included an effort toward public education, which Elisa Villalpando has led. All members of the project have participated in public presentations, site tours, and television programming of the archaeological work. Much of our public education has been directed toward building local awareness of this archaeology and of the continued presence of the Indians, whom many presume to have vanished. We have also aided local efforts to build a small museum in an attempt to use the site of Cerro de Trincheras to draw U.S. tourists to the community. Recently three students in the architecture program at the Universidad de Sonora developed plans for a restaurant, the museum along with visitor's center, and a hotel in Trincheras, which they presented to the director of the state tourism office, where they were received with great interest.

Indians and Archaeology on the Border

The Indians who lived along the Río Magdalena have not vanished. A handful of the Tohono O'odham still live in Sonora, and many thousands live in Arizona. They form the other half of the double colonialism that confronts the archaeologist on this frontier. We tried to confront colonialism through consultation with Tohono O'odham people. These efforts occurred in a context of shifting political interests.

When we started our work in Sonora, a French archaeological project was already ensnarled in a double colonialism. From 1984 till 1987, the French Center for Studies of Mexico and Central America conducted an ethno-archaeological project at Quitovac, Sonora (Villalobos 2004:77–109). The French researchers obtained permits from INAH's Consejo de Arqueología in México City, but they did not contact the traditional authorities of the local native communities in Sonora or Arizona. The project ultimately ended in bitter conflict with the Tohono O'odham.

Tohono O'odham from Sonora and Arizona gather at Quitovac each year to celebrate the Wi:gita ceremony, but in the late 1980s, the only O'odham actually living there were one elderly couple. With no Indians nearby who could witness their work and object to it, the French researchers excavated graves from the cemetery, and they collected materials from the blessed cave where the Tohono O'odham keep the sacred eagle feathers for the Wi:gita ceremony (Villalobos 2004:80–85). In 1987, the French also found a skeleton of a mammoth, which they uncovered and removed to Hermosillo for stabilization (Villalobos 2004: 85–87). The skeleton was eventually returned to the community, but then the local Norteños took charge of it, constructing a case to display it. Also in 1987, after the Wi:gita ceremony, the French systematically mapped and collected the ceremonial ground without permission of the Tohono O'odham.

In 1988, we began our first field project in Sonora. The institutional and bureaucratic mechanisms that NAGPRA would inspire to facilitate cooperation between Native Americans and archaeologists did not yet exist. Confrontation was still the norm for such relationships. Nevertheless, Elisa and I felt that a radical praxis of archaeology in the region required that we involve Indian communities, so we sent copies of our grant proposals to the O'odham communities of southern Arizona (the Tohono O'odham Nation, the Gila River Indian Community, the Salt River Indian Community, and the Ak Chin Indian Community). We asked for comments and offered to host representatives of these communities if they wished to visit our project in the field. Only one community replied. I visited and talked to the leadership of the San Xavier District, of the Tohono O'odham Nation, before we went to the field. These individuals were sensitive to the archaeological issues because of their involvement with the Arizona State Museum during the San Xavier Bridge Project (Ravesloot 1990). Later, a delegation from San Xavier visited our survey project in the Altar Valley of Sonora. After all was done, we sent each of the communities copies of our reports.

In 1991, when we began our mapping and surface collection of Cerro de Trincheras, we followed the same procedure. This time, none of the communities responded. During this field season, all our research involved survey and surface collection. We had little chance of encountering human remains or sacred objects, and we did not. Following the 1991 field season, as we planned our excavations at Cerro de Trincheras, we realized that the situation had changed, both in the United States and in México. We did not plan to excavate in the cremation cemetery we had found at the site. We knew, however, that we might nevertheless encounter human remains.

After the passing of NAGPRA, archaeologists and Native Americans in southern Arizona developed institutionalized means and procedures for consultation on archaeological research. All of the Native American nations and communities of southern Arizona established either a committee or a designated individual within their governmental structure to handle this consultation. At this time, relations between archaeologists and Tohono O'odham people in southern Arizona ranged from bitter conflict to cordial cooperation. The Tohono O'odham had generally allowed the nondestructive analysis of skeletons and mortuary goods before their return and reburial (Ravesloot 1990).

In México, all archaeological materials are legally the heritage of the Mexican people. The national government owns all archaeological sites and artifacts, regardless of the ownership of the land they are found on. Any negotiations concerning the disposition of burials and sacred goods must be made with INAH, and only INAH has the authority to repatriate these things to Native American nations or communities. INAH had never done such a thing before the French project at Quitovac.

In designing the excavation project for the spring of 1995, we felt that we had to make a greater effort at consultation with the O'odham than we had in the past. We came to this position both because we would be excavating and because of the changing relations between archaeologists and Native Americans in the region. We thought that the repatriation and reburial at Quitovac gave us precedent for future repatriation and reburial in Sonora.

We were optimistic. The experience of the French was foremost in our minds, because we wanted to avoid the misunderstandings and abuses that had happened at Quitovac (Villalobos 2004). The Centro INAH de Sonora had played a leading role in returning the burials and sacred objects to the Tohono O'odham. The center was also involved in negotiations with the Tohono O'odham Cultural Affairs Committee about plans to develop the Sierra Pinacate as a Mexican national park. Because of the changes wrought by NAGPRA, we felt that it might be easier than in the past to initiate and maintain a process of consultation. The cultural affairs committees and offices of the Native American nations and communities of southern Arizona made it more convenient for us to contact key individuals in those communities. Once initiated, we also thought less effort would be required to maintain the process with standing committees or offices that would survive changes in tribal governments.

We made initial contact with the Tohono O'odham Cultural Affairs Committee by sending them a copy of our grant proposal for the project. We then arranged to meet with representative of the committee in Trincheras during September 1994. One member of the committee and an Anglo lawyer who represented the committee came to this meeting, along with representatives of the Comunidad de Trincheras and INAH. The meeting was very cordial, and the Tohono O'odham were quite appreciative that we had sought to consult them about a project in México. We agreed at the meeting that if we encountered any burials in our excavations, we would excavate them so they would not be looted and then contact the Cultural Affairs Committee.

The Tohono O'odham recommended that we should contact other indigenous nations and communities in Arizona in addition to the O'odham governments we had contacted in the past. They suggested we also inform the Pasqua Yaqui Indian Community and the Hopi Nation of our project. We subsequently sent all of the O'odham groups, the Yaqui, and the Hopi copies of our proposal. Only the Ak Chin community and the Hopi Nation responded to our query. Both indicated that we should deal directly with the Tohono O'odham Nation.

We started fieldwork at the beginning of February 1995. Within the first few weeks we had located several possible cremations, one definite cremation, and two inhumations. We left the cremations in place. They did not contain ceramic vessels, and we thought they were not obvious enough to attract looters. Our workers, however, immediately recognized the bones in the inhumations as human. Even though none of the inhumations contained extensive grave offerings, we excavated them on discovery to prevent them from being looted.

We notified the Tohono O'odham about our finds, then met with two members of the Cultural Affairs Committee and their attorney in Caborca, Sonora, on March 4. There, they agreed that we would be allowed to do nondestructive analysis of the inhumations and that afterward they would be reburied. The only point of contention was how long we would keep the bones before reburial. Since we had not yet talked to a physical anthropologist about doing the analysis, we wanted a year to get the work done. The Tohono O'odham wanted the work done more quickly.

On March 13, 1995, a delegation of four from the Cultural Affairs Committee and their attorney visited us in the field. The visit was quite cordial, except for one of the Tohono O'odham, who adopted a confrontational attitude. The Mexican archaeologists on the project had no experience with Indian criticism of archaeology, and the confrontational Tohono O'odham offended them greatly. They were, however, pleased with the cordiality and obvious sincerity of the other Tohono O'odham people who visited the site. Conversations at this meeting led to the decision to backfill the known cremations without excavating them.

After our 1996 field season, we had excavated a total of ten burials containing twelve inhumations from scattered locations in the site. We had made arrangements with biological anthropologists to analyze the remains. We anticipated that with the completion of this analysis, the remains and the few artifacts we had found with them would be repatriated to the Tohono O'odham and reburied at Quitovac.

In 1997, the Centro INAH de Sonora sought permission from the governing council of INAH, the Consejo de Arqueología, to repatriate and rebury the inhumations from Cerro de Trincheras (Villalobos 2004:112–121). To our surprise, the *consejo* refused this permission. Despite a formal request from the Tohono O'odham Nation and further pleadings on the part of the center, the *consejo* would not change its position, expressing two basic reservations about the repatriation. Officials there felt that the requests represented an attempt to import U.S. problems into México, and they feared losing control over Mexican heritage. The *coordinador nacional de arqueología* also raised legal issues. Under national law the skeletons and artifacts from Trincheras were part of the national heritage of México. The law vested responsibility for the analysis, interpretation, display, and curation of this heritage in INAH, and a local community could not co-opt this responsibility. The regulations of INAH also required that such materials be kept in a recognized museum.

The *consejo* did not want a U.S. dilemma in México, and it took an anti-imperialist stance, withholding recognition of the Tohono O'odham Nation as having the legal or moral standing to request repatriation. INAH regarded the nation as U.S. Indians and U.S. citizens. Needless to say, this infuriated the O'odham, who see both México and the United States as invaders. The *consejo* accused the archaeologists at the Centro INAH de Sonora of being unduly influenced by North American archaeologists and of not representing the interests of the Mexican people and nation. They expressed concern that the North American archaeologists on the projects wanted to dictate policy to the INAH. Archaeologists from the Sonora center tried to explain that things were different on the border. Issues of heritage and legitimacy were much more complicated than they seemed in México City. But, for the *consejo,* issues of heritage and legitimacy were much broader than a few inhumations from the far end of the nation.

The national politics of heritage and legitimacy had shifted in México. Much had changed since the reburials at Quitovac in 1993. On the right, the Partido Acción Nacional agitated for the decentralization and privatization of heritage. This included the INAH, the ENAH, the museums, and the national monuments of the country. The right wanted a profit-making heritage industry, not nationalist lessons and scientific study. On the left stood the Zapatista revolution in Chiapas. The Zapatista program included an *indigenista* plank that refuted a pan-Mexican identity of La Raza. Zapatistas called for greater autonomy for indigenous groups. INAH feared that this call could come to include control of national monuments, such as Palenque, Bonampak, and Yaxchilán, in Chiapas. These fears raised the specter of other indigenous groups in the country demanding return of their heritage, the most important archaeological sites in the nation. Too much was at stake to risk any of it for a few inhumations in far-off Sonora. The situation remains much the same today.

In the end, our attempts to repatriate the inhumations from Cerro de Trincheras failed. Not surprisingly, the Tohono O'odham felt betrayed by the turn of events. In retrospect, we should have included the Consejo de Arqueología in our consultations with the Tohono O'odham from the beginning. The incident strained relations between archaeologists in northern Sonora (both Mexican and North American) and the O'odham, although dialogue continues. In addition to creating a situation in which we could not repatriate inhumations, the history, paradoxes, and ambiguities of three nations on the border also created a loss of trust.

Three causes lie at the heart of this lack of success. The first was our failure to establish a long-term and involved collaborative relationship with the Tohono O'odham as a community. Consultation was just not enough. The consultation model that we followed is typical of contemporary relations between archaeologists and native communities. Such a model may permit compliance with NAGPRA, but it does not build the trust and dialogue with native peoples that lead to true collaboration. The second was our failure to understand the shifting context of Mexican nationalism and the place of archaeology in it. Finally, the compelling realities of the border worked against us. In the absence of true collaboration and trust, there was no way to escape the snare of double colonialism.

Building an emancipatory praxis of archaeology requires more than splendid formulas for life; it requires that archaeologists confront the political, cultural, and economic difficulties of living communities. We have struggled to do this on the border with the Trincheras Tradition Project. We continue to build on the foundation of a collaborative binational praxis of archaeology involving U.S. and Mexican archaeologists. We persist in our dialogue with the Norteño people of northern Sonora and our programs of education. And we struggle to move beyond consultation to a true collaboration with the Tohono O'odham. Not all contexts, however, are as difficult and complex as the border. In southern Colorado, the historical archaeology of the 1913–1914 Colorado Coalfield War offers a less conflicted stage for an emancipatory praxis of archaeology.

NOTES

1. I do not consider field projects carried out by Latin American students or faculty in U.S. or Canadian universities as Latin American projects.

2. In México and to a lesser extent other Latin American countries, U.S., Canadian, and other foreign nationals are employed by local institutions. I would consider these individuals to be local, not North American, archaeologists.

3. The major exception to this was in Haiti, where enslaved Africans overthrew their French masters and established the second American nation-state after the United States.

4. This is obvious for the countries of Latin America, most of which did not take their modern form until very late in the nineteenth century. It is, however, also the case for the United States, as evidenced by the Civil War and the conquest of the West.

5. *Indigenismo* should not be confused with the contemporary *indigenista* movements of Latin America (Sieder 2002). These are nationalist movements that seek to empower native groups with a sovereign status within or independent of the nation-state.

6. Originally the party was called the Partido Nacional Revolucionario (National Revolutionary Party). In 1938 it changed its name to the Partido de la Revolución Mexicana (Party of the Mexican Revolution), and finally in 1949 it took its modern name, the Partido Revolucionario Institucional (Institutional Revolutionary Party). The reader should note that the final name of this party is an oxymoron.

7. My Mexican friends like to compare the 1994 Mexican election to the 2000 presidential election in the United States. I, too, find it an apt comparison.

8. The *licenciatura* is the initial university degree in the Mexican education system (Newell 1999:29–30). It requires a thesis and more course work than a U.S. bachelor's degree, but it is not a master's degree. It is a specialized professional degree that prepares the archaeology student, for example, to practice in his or her field.

9. Indigenismo is a nationalist ideological concept that is institutionalized in Mexican society. "Norteño" is a popular cultural category that has not been institutionalized.

10. Under the Mexican constitution adopted in 1917, *ejidos* grant peasant communities inalienable rights to land.

11. By traditional definition, the Southwestern cultural area includes the American states of Arizona and New Mexico with small portions of Utah, Colorado, and Texas and the Mexican states of Chihuahua and Sonora. This is the Southwest of the United States but the Northwest of Mexico. The hybrid

term Southwest-Northwest reflects the accurate geopolitical position of the region.

12. The project is ongoing. In 2004 we received National Science Foundation money (NSF no. BCS 0419353) to map and surface collect several cerros de trincheras in the Río Altar and the Río Magdalena valleys. Subsequently we received an additional grant from the National Geographic Society (no. 7845 – 05) in support of this research. Fieldwork for this project occurred in the winter of 2006.

13. The National Science Foundation funded this survey with grant no. BNS-8703515. Our 1995 – 1996 excavation project was funded by NSF grant no. SBR9320224.

14. The National Geographic Society funded this mapping with grant no. 4454 – 91.

15. Plan de Manejo del Patrimonio Cultural del Estado de Sonora.

16. The North Americans come expecting to find the type of Mexican restaurant food that is served in the United States. The Mexican students encounter few of the fruits and vegetables they are accustomed to and a cuisine based in beef and flour tortillas instead of corn.

17. Both sets of students usually join the project after taking a course in the archaeology of the Southwest-Northwest, so they all share a basic understanding of the cultural developments of the region. The differences lie in their theoretical and practical training.

CHAPTER 5

Ludlow

WITH THE LUDLOW COLLECTIVE

The man who possesses no other property than his labour
power must, in all conditions of society and culture, be the
slave of other men who have made themselves the owners
of the material conditions of labour. He can only work with
their permission, and hence only live with their permission.

Karl Marx (1938:3)

Then came Ludlow and the nation heard. Little children
roasted alive make a front-page story. Dying by inches of
starvation and exposure does not.

Mary Harris (Mother) Jones (2004:126)

In June 1999, I stepped up to a podium in Pueblo, Colorado, to address
a gathering of striking steelworkers and their families. Oregon Steel had
locked them out of the Rocky Mountain Steel mill after the workers had
gone on strike to challenge forced overtime. I had come to the gathering
to talk about our archaeological research at the site of the Ludlow
Massacre. My first words were, "I greet you as a brother in the AFL-
CIO."[1] The applause that followed my declaration told me they had
been the right words.

The Ludlow Massacre was the most violent and significant event of
the Colorado Coalfield War of 1913–1914. On the morning of April 20,
1914, Colorado National Guard troops and armed strikers engaged in a
pitched battle at a tent colony of twelve hundred striking families, at
Ludlow, Colorado. The battle continued through the day. As dusk gathered, the Guard finally drove off the armed strikers, and the troops swept
through the camp looting it and setting it aflame. The next dawn saw the

camp a smoking ruin and nineteen of its inhabitants dead, including two women and twelve children. What followed is one of the few true examples of class warfare in the history of the United States. Armed strikers took control of southern Colorado, burning company towns and killing company employees. Ten days later federal troops restored order to the region. The significance of the Ludlow Massacre goes far beyond the struggle of the 1913–1914 Colorado Coalfield War. The American public was shocked and outraged by the killing of women and children at Ludlow, and popular opinion soon turned against violent confrontations with strikers. Progressive reformers used the massacre as a focal point in their attempts to change labor relations in the United States. At this pivot point of U.S. history, labor relations began to move from class warfare to corporate and government policies of negotiation, co-option, and regulated strikes. Since 1918, the United Mine Workers of America (UMWA) has maintained the massacre site as a shrine, and descendants of the strikers and union members make an annual pilgrimage to the site.

Dean Saitta of Denver University, Philip Duke of Fort Lewis College, and I began the Archaeology of the 1913–1914 Colorado Coalfield War Project in 1996.[2] Our joint effort soon grew into something we have called the Ludlow Collective. The collective consists primarily of faculty and students from the University of Denver in Colorado, Fort Lewis College in Colorado, and Binghamton University in New York, but has also included students from other U.S., Spanish, and British institutions.[3] Even though this chapter mainly reflects my personnel reflections, it is very much a product of the collective and not me alone. In 1996, Binghamton University gave me a faculty development grant to begin the project. The Colorado Historical Society generously funded our research from 1997 to 2004 using public monies generated from taxes on casino gambling (the Colorado State Historical Fund).

The project has sought to fulfill multiple goals and address diverse audiences. Our scholarly goal was to exhume the class struggle of the strike. We have joined the national discourse about labor rights, unions, and the role of working-class people in U.S. history in order to raise academic and popular consciousness about the contemporary struggles of working families. The project also has confronted two major ambiguities in the practice of United States archaeology. We designed the project to escape the colonial practice of archaeology in North America and to transcend the tradition of archaeology primarily serving middle-class interests. We began our project with the assumption that our work should and does serve multiple communities (Shanks and McGuire

1996). These communities include the scholarly community of archaeologists and historians as well as the traditional, middle-class, public audience for archaeology. But the primary community that we wish to address is unionized labor in the United States. We have joined with them in the battle against fast capitalism's erosion of organized labor. We are building an archaeology of the American working class that speaks to a working-class audience about working-class history and experience. We are doing this through an ongoing dialogue with both the descendants of the participants in the Colorado Coalfield War and unionized workers in southern Colorado.

COMMUNITIES AND PRAXIS

The three of us who began the Coalfield War Project all built our careers by studying the heritage of Native Americans, and we are well aware of the colonialism of that practice. In the 1980s, we joined other progressive scholars supporting the efforts by Native Americans for repatriation and for the passage of the Native American Graves Protection and Repatriation Act of 1990. The struggle over repatriation required a real commitment to political action, and it entailed a degree of risk that was largely absent from then contemporary abstract discussions of ideology and hegemonic discourses. Many in the discipline regarded the handful of archaeologists in the United States who supported the Native American position and called for the reform of archaeology as traitors (Zimmerman 1989). Individuals were denied jobs, cut off from publication opportunities, not allowed to present papers at national meetings, and denied promotion because they were "too political," or, to put it more simply, because they opposed the political stance of the majority of the profession. This distrust did not evaporate in 1990, when federal legislation forced archaeologists to concede the Native American position. After 1990, some mainstream U.S. archaeologists sought to rewrite the history of the repatriation struggle to deny that archaeologists, as represented by the Society of American Archaeology, ever opposed the Native American position. The radicals who did support repatriation are an inconvenient fact that disputes this revisionist history (Zimmerman 1992).

The accommodation that existed between Native Americans and archaeologists in the mid-1990s was an uneasy one (D. Thomas 2000; Watkins 2000). On the positive side, NAGPRA forced archaeologists to consult and work with Native Americans. It also addressed deeply felt

Native American desires to protect the sanctity of their ancestors' graves and to recover sacred objects. The accommodation did not, however, go deep enough in the 1990s to resolve the fundamental contradiction of U.S. archaeology, that is, its rootedness in colonialism. NAGPRA gave Native Americans ultimate control over the bodies and some of the objects that archaeologists recover. However, it left archaeologists to write aboriginal histories and overlooked the essential difference between the way Native Americans think of their own history and the way we think of it. Accommodation and consultation allow archaeologists to avoid the troubling questions that Native American people continue to haunt us with: Why do we as archaeologists seek to study pasts that are not our own? Can we, in fact, study this stolen heritage in a way that is liberating for Native Americans and not oppressive? These are questions that we still struggle with, but the development of an indigenous archaeology since the turn of the twenty-first century has provided us some guide to answering them.

Our discomfort with the colonialism of our profession in the mid-1990s led Dean Saitta, Philip Duke, and me to consider our own heritage and a history that has meaning for working people. The Colorado Coalfield War of 1913–1914 is not exotic or ancient history. It is familiar, close to home, relevant, and about ourselves. It is also part of my own heritage. In the 1890s, my great-grandfather worked in the southern Colorado coalfield, although above ground as a blacksmith, and married my great-grandmother there. Her sister's family participated in the 1913–1914 strike. In 1901, however, my great-grandparents moved to the mines at Hannah, Wyoming. When I was a child, my grandmother told me the story of the 1903 mine explosion at Hannah that killed over two hundred men, including four of her male relatives. My great-grandfather survived the 1903 explosion and a second one in the Hannah mine in 1907. After that, he had had enough of coal mining. He moved his family to Fort Collins, Colorado, where he resumed working as a blacksmith and also became a machinist and a union leader. Driving from our home in Texas to visit my grandparents in Fort Collins, my mother would stop at the Ludlow Monument and explain to my sister and me what had happened there.

The radical reorientation of the class position of archaeology that is necessary to develop a working-class archaeology began in our case with the assumption that archaeology is a craft that can be used to serve the interests of multiple communities (Shanks and McGuire 1996). We have entered into a dialogue with the academic community of archaeology through published works like this one and through papers presented at meetings. We have sought to educate archaeology's traditional middle-class public audience about labor's struggles for a decent living, benefits, and dignity. However, the primary community that the Colorado Coalfield War Project seeks to serve is unionized labor in Colorado and beyond. To accomplish this goal, we have sustained collaboration with the United Mine Workers of America in union halls and at community meetings, picnics, and rallies. We have confronted the public with the realities of labor's past, realities that the processes of fast capitalism are re-creating to make labor's future.

Because archaeology lives in the middle class, attracting primarily a middle-class following, we have imbued our scholarly labor with working-class interests to broaden its appeal (Sennett and Cobb 1972; Frykman 1990; Potter 1994:148–149; McGuire and Walker 1999). Our project participates in the dialogue between organized labor and scholars that began with the election of John Sweeny as president of the AFL-CIO in 1995. Seeking to unite labor and the academy to confront the fast cap-italism that threatens us both, the labor movement has attempted since the mid-1990s to reforge connections with the academy, which were sun-dered by disputes over the Vietnam War in the 1960s. This alliance has more recently manifested itself in broad-based globalization actions led by anti-corporate interests, such as the protests against the World Trade Organization in Seattle in 1999 and in statements opposing U.S. military action against Iraq, recently adopted by many labor unions. We are con-tributing to these efforts by studying a history that has meaning for working people and by addressing their interests in this history.

A praxis based in collective agency has guided our work. In our research at Ludlow we have attempted to examine collective agency and consciousness in the formation, execution, and ultimate failure of the 1913–1914 strike, as well as the role of Ludlow in the formation and maintenance of a modern working-class consciousness (Saitta 2005, 2007). This examination begins with us asking a series of questions.

What was the social reality of interests, identities, and communities that existed in 1913? In southern Colorado we are dealing with an eth-nically diverse working class of miners. The owners of the mines were uniformly white and Anglo and lived in Denver or other urban areas out-side the state. A white, Anglo, middle class of managers, administrators, and professionals represented them in southern Colorado. This industrial society of the mines was embedded in a rural society ethnically differen-tiated between Anglos and Chicanos, with a rural working class of cowboys and field hands, smallholder herders and farmers, and a rural bourgeoisie of large ranchers and merchants.

How did the interests of these identities and communities relate to one another, with special attention to the conflicts and contradictions that have existed among them? The most obvious distinction in interests was among the working-class miners who worked the mines, the bourgeoisie who owned the mines, and the middle class who ran the mines. This is the classic capitalist contradiction between the bourgeoisie and the proletariat. The members of the working class, however, did not uniformly experience day-to-day life in the southern Colorado mining community. Gender, ethnicity, race, and workplace differentiated their experiences.

In this social reality, how is a shared consciousness created to form a community of struggle? Here we examine the identities (ethnic, gender, and racial) that crosscut the miners and that worked against the formation of class consciousness. We look at how conditions before, during, and after the strike were differentially experienced by individuals as a result of these identities and the social relations that created them. Our goal here is to see how differences were maintained, redefined, and even created within the working class of miners through the struggle of the strike.

Finally, we have asked, How does our study fit with and participate in contemporary social struggles in southern Colorado and in the United States in general? Or in other words, what communities does our research serve, and how does it do so? The most obvious of these communities is the scholarly community of archaeologists, whom we address in scholarly meetings, articles, and books. We have addressed the middle-class community of Colorado through newspaper articles, teachers workshops, and public presentations, especially in conjunction with the Colorado Historical Society and the Colorado Endowment for the Humanities. Our active engagement with these two traditional communities of archaeological research demonstrates that we accept them as valid, but we would argue that a truly radical praxis of archaeology requires that we involve ourselves with other communities, those that are locked in struggle against inequality and exploitation. Yet if we were to concentrate only on the middle class, we would surely be guilty of reproducing the same sort of bourgeois ideologies that theories of individual agency tend to reproduce. Thus, we designed our study in collaboration with the United Mine Workers of America.

The people who died at Ludlow—men, women, and children—engaged in collective agency (Saitta 2005, 2007). They struggled in solidarity to transform the world, and their deaths had a significant effect on the course of labor history in the United States. Their sacrifice helped working people in the United States to win the rights that they enjoy today. Had they been individual agents, had their sacrifice been solely personal, it would not have been transformative. Only their families would remember it, and we would not be doing archaeology at Ludlow.

THE 1913–1914 COLORADO COALFIELD WAR

At the beginning of the twentieth century, the United States had a rapidly growing industrial economy. Two things powered this expansion: cheap immigrant labor and coal. The third wave of immigration, from eastern and southern Europe, crested in the second decade of the century. Immigrants filled the burgeoning slums of the cities and the mines and mills of the West. Progressive reformers sought to Americanize these immigrants and improve their lot in the United States. The reformers challenged the laissez-faire capitalism of the end of the nineteenth century, struggling to break up monopolies and make the political system more democratic. Unions also fought to improve the lot of workers through violent strike after violent strike. Many in the United States feared class warfare. All of this occurred under a pall of smoke from the coal fires that drove the mills, factories, mines, and trains.

In 1913, Colorado was the eighth largest coal-producing state in the United States, with most of its production coming from the southern part of the state (McGovern and Guttridge 1972). The bituminous coalfields in Huerfano and Las Animas counties, north of Trinidad, Colorado, primarily produced coke for the steel mills farther north at Pueblo (map 3). The largest company mining coal in this region was the Rockefeller-controlled Colorado Fuel and Iron Company (CF&I). This company employed approximately fourteen thousand miners in 1913, 70 percent of whom were immigrants, most of them having come from southern Europe (principally Italy and Greece) and eastern Europe (primarily Austria-Hungary, Poland, and Russia), along with Welsh, Irish, and Japanese. The remaining 30 percent included mostly Euro-Americans, along with some African Americans and Chicanos. Union organizers bemoaned the problem of organizing workers who spoke at least twenty-four different languages.

Although most families shared a working-class life in the isolated mining communities of early twentieth-century southern Colorado, their day-to-day experience varied. Ethnic differences were evident in each

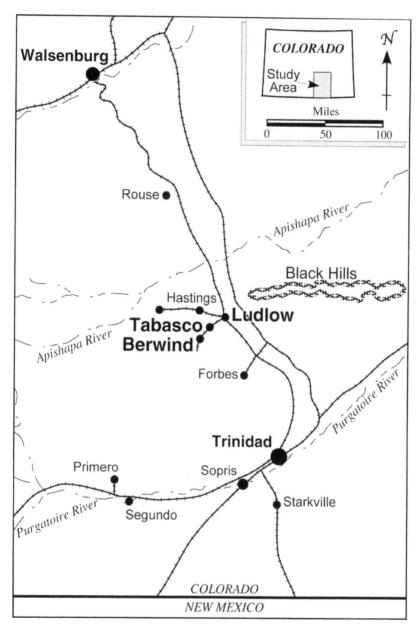

Map 3. Trinidad coalfields area.

group's formation of its own subcommunity, both in patterns of residence and through social institutions such as churches, ethnic associations, and fraternal organizations. Also, gender differences occurred within these households, creating power relations and exploitation (Long 1985). Women had few if any opportunities for wage employment. They worked in the household to maintain the miners, who went down in the pit. They also contributed to household income by taking in boarders and laundry and by canning and sewing. Racial discrimination existed as well, with Euro-American workers discriminating against African American and Chicano workers, and with the union largely excluding the handful of Japanese in the camps from its activities. The Anglo-Americans who lived in local, rural, agricultural communities regarded the miners as inferior foreigners, and the mining companies hired many of their private guards from the ranks of the rural working class. The rural bourgeoisie by and large sided with management against the strikers. A small, primarily ethnic-based, petty bourgeoisie of shop owners and trade people identified with the miners, who were their customers.

Working conditions in the mines were unfair at best and dreadful at worst (Beshoar 1957; McGovern and Guttridge 1972; Papanikolas 1982). The miners loaded their cars with coal, which occurred in seams in the mountains, and sent them to the tipple, where check weighmen weighed the cars and credited the miners for their tonnage. The miners, paid by the ton by the companies, all agreed that the company's check weighmen routinely shorted their weight. Reports of the Colorado mine inspectors confirmed short weights on several occasions. The companies did not pay miners for deadwork, that is, the work that was necessary to maintain the mines but did not involve loading any coal. Such work included removing rock, timbering mine shafts, and removing roof falls. Deadwork kept the mines safe, but lack of pay for it discouraged miners from doing it. In 1912, Colorado mines had an accident rate three times the national average (Whiteside 1990). The companies operated the mines in southern Colorado in flagrant violation of numerous state laws that regulated safety and the fair compensation of miners. Sometimes death came in a dramatic explosion and collapse of the shaft, killing dozens or hundreds of men. More commonly it came from a rock falling from the roof, a run away coal car, or the kick of a mine mule. Early twentieth-century miners in southern Colorado did not worry about black lung disease, because most of them died or left the mines crippled before they could die from the black choking filth that filled their lungs.

In addition to owning the mines, the companies owned all the land around them. They built unadorned, isolated towns near the mines to house their workers. When workers did put up their own rude shacks, they did so on company land. The company usually owned the only store in each community and often they paid the miners in script usable only at that store. The miner and his family went to a company doctor, drank in a company-approved saloon, studied under company-hired teachers, and played baseball on a company-owned field. The companies surrounded the towns with fences, and the enclosures were policed by company guards, who also guarded the gates to the towns, regulating who could enter and leave. For instance, during the 1913–1914 strike, company guards turned the governor of Colorado away from the company town of Hastings. The companies instructed their employees on how to vote. They arranged the election of the sheriff of Huerfano County and the county corner. In 1914, the journalist Edwin Seligman (1914) described the situation in the southern coalfields as feudal.

The UMWA had first tried to organize southern Colorado coal miners in a 1907 strike, but in the end the companies won that labor action. When the UMWA launched a new, massive organizing campaign in southern Colorado in 1913, the companies fought back by expelling miners suspected of union sympathies, and company guards harassed and brutally assaulted union organizers. The newly unionized miners called for a strike in the fall of 1913 (Beshoar 1957; McGovern and Guttridge 1972; Papanikolas 1982). The strikers had seven demands:

1. recognition of the UMWA as their bargaining agent
2. a 10 percent increase in the tonnage rate
3. an eight-hour day, as already required by Colorado law
4. pay for deadwork
5. the right to elect their own check weighmen, as already required by Colorado law
6. the right to trade, seek medical care, and board in any facility of their choosing, as already required by Colorado law
7. the enforcement of existing Colorado mining laws and the removal of mine guards

Simultaneously the companies brought in the Baldwin-Felts Detective Agency to violently suppress the organizing efforts and later the strike. The agency, which specialized in breaking coal strikes, sent dozens of agents and two machine guns fresh from strikes in West Virginia. The companies also recruited members of the southern Colorado rural working class to work as mine guards. The Colorado Fuel and Iron Company built a homemade armored car called "the death special," which the Baldwin-Felts agents equipped with a machine gun and a spotlight.

Figure 4. Ludlow tent colony before the massacre. Photo by Lou Dold, courtesy of the Denver Public Library, Western History Collection, Z-193.

On September 23, 1913, the strike began with over 90 percent of the miners leaving the shafts. The companies evicted people from company-owned housing. Several thousand people moved into tent camps that the UMWA had set up on the plains below the mines. Ludlow was the largest of these camps, with approximately 150 tents and about 1,200 residents (figure 4). The UMWA made Ludlow the strike headquarters for Las Animas County. The miners at Ludlow elected Louis Tikas, a Greek, as the camp leader. Each of these camps contained a mix of nationalities, including Italians, Greeks, various eastern Europeans, Chicanos, and Welsh, along with African Americans.

The strike began violently, with both sides committing assaults, shootings, and murders (Beshoar 1957; McGovern and Guttridge 1972; Papanikolas 1982). Shortly before the strike, mine guards gunned down a union organizer on the streets of Trinidad. The day after the strike began, strikers ambushed and killed a particularly hated mine guard. On numerous occasions the Baldwin-Felts agents used the machine gun on the death special to fire over the camps. The violence escalated until late October, when pitched gun battles between strikers and mine guards in Walsenberg and Berwind left two deputies and three strikers dead and a company building in flames. At the urging of the coal companies, the governor of Colorado called out the National Guard on October 24, 1913. Over the winter of 1913–1914, relations between the strikers and the Guard deteriorated. On January 22, 1914, mounted guardsmen rode down a peaceful demonstration of miners' wives and children on the streets of Trinidad. By April, the state of Colorado could no longer afford the cost of having the militia in the field. The governor removed the regular guardsmen from the region, and the mining companies filled the two remaining National Guard units with their own employees and Baldwin-Felts agents, under the command of Colorado National Guard officers.

On April 20, 1914, a battle broke out at the Ludlow tent camp. At about 9:00 A.M., the Guard commander ordered Louis Tikas to meet him at Ludlow Station. On a hill overlooking the tent camp, a dozen guardsmen with rifles and a machine gun loaded their weapons. Fearing that this might be a pretext for an attack, a contingent of strikers armed themselves and moved into a railroad cut overlooking the station and flanking the position of the guardsmen. This movement unnerved the guardsmen. In the midst of this tension, a rifle discharged, and the guardsmen began firing the machine gun into the tent camp. By noon, up to two hundred guardsmen had joined the fight, and company guards added a Baldwin-Felts machine gun to the first. Mary Thomas (1971) later remembered that, after a few hours of firing, the tents were so full of holes that they looked like lace. Although the strikers had dug cellars under many of their tents to shield their families from bullets, they tried to draw the machine gun fire away from the camp by shifting their position across the plains, and the pitched battle shifted with them.

Chaos reigned in the camp. Women and children huddled in a large walk-in well that the railroad company used to fill steam engines. Many families took shelter in the cellars under their tents. The camp's leaders, Louis Tikas, Pearl Jolly, and Mary Thomas, ran from tent to tent all day, telling people to flee up a dry creek bed north of the camp. In the early afternoon, a twelve-year-old named William Snyder came up out of a cellar to get some food and was shot dead. His distraught father then went from tent to tent, countering the instruction to flee, telling people their children would be killed.

As dusk gathered, a railroad crew stopped their train in front of the machine guns, blocking their line of fire. Guardsmen threatened to shoot the train crew if they did not move the train, but the crew stayed, providing the miners a respite from the machine gun fire. By the time the shooting stopped, the armed strikers were out of ammunition. Tikas ordered them to withdraw because they could do no more good, so the majority of working families who had been pinned down in the colony fled up the dry creek bed. In the fading light, the guardsmen charged into the camp, looting tents, and the train's brakeman saw them setting tents aflame.

In a cellar below tent 58, Mrs. Alcarita Pedragon and the pregnant Mrs. Cadilano Costa and Mrs. Patria Valdez huddled with their eight children. Mrs. Costa did not know that her husband, Charles Costa, had been shot dead in the battle. Flames drove Mary Petrucci and her three children from the cellar below tent 1. She then sought refuge in the hole beneath tent 58, huddling with her three children on the steps into that cellar. The women and children cried, cringing in fear as the flames consumed the tent above them. One by one they passed out. Outside, the guardsmen seized Louis Tikas and two other of the camp's male leaders and summarily executed them. The next day, the early morning light showed the camp to be a smoldering ruin (figure 5). Mary Petrucci woke up in the dark hole below tent 58 to find her children, Cadilano Costa, Patria Valdez, and the other eight children dead. Alcarita Pedragon climbed out of the pit and staggered to Ludlow Station. There, the station master put her on a train, and she later left the region. In addition to the thirteen deceased in the "death pit" and eleven-year-old William Snyder, five strikers, at least one militiaman, and a hitchhiker on the highway, a mile away, died.

Following the attack, enraged strikers took up arms and seized control of the southern Colorado mining district. They attacked and destroyed several company towns. Finally, after ten days of open war, President Wilson sent federal troops to Trinidad to restore order. During the ten-day war, at least twenty-one company employees and militia perished in the fighting, and a handful of strikers died. That summer, the strikers returned to Ludlow and built a new camp. The UMWA sent three female survivors of the massacre on a national tour to raise money for the strike. The funds they raised prolonged the strike but were not enough to win it. In December 1914, a bankrupt UMWA ended the action. At least seventy-five people died violently during the eighteen months of the strike, and at least two hundred others were wounded.[4] In the first eighteen months after the strike, over one hundred miners died in accidents in the pits. The National Guard hastily convened a court martial that cleared the guardsmen who had attacked the Ludlow colony of any crimes. No person was ever convicted for any of the murders committed during the strike. In 1918, the UMWA erected a monument at the massacre site to the men, women, and children who died there. John D. Rockefeller Jr. showed up uninvited at the dedication ceremony and asked to speak, but the union officers turned him away (Gitelman 1988).

Figure 5. Ludlow after the massacre. Photo by Lou Dold, courtesy of the Denver Public Library, Western History Collection, Z-199.

Violence in coal strikes and adult male deaths were commonplace in the early twentieth century, but the killing of women and children at Ludlow stunned the nation (Gitelman 1988). Progressive reformers such as Upton Sinclair and John Reed used the massacre to demonize John D. Rockefeller Jr. The United States Commission on Industrial Relations investigated the events of the strike and issued a twelve-hundred-page report condemning the companies and National Guard (U.S. Congress, Senate 1916). In response to this bad press, Rockefeller hired the first corporate public relations firm and embarked on a campaign of charity that included the founding of Colonial Williamsburg. He also employed the Canadian socialist Mackenzie King to set up a series of reforms in the mines of southern Colorado. The Rockefeller Plan established YMCAs in the camps, improved camp services, and set up a company union. It is not clear what practical impacts these reforms had on the lives of miners and their families, but they did not bring labor peace. From the end of World War I, until the Depression of 1929, the miners went out on strike three times. The United Mine Workers of America finally organized the southern coalfields in 1934 following the passage of New Deal legislation that guaranteed the legal right of workers to join a union (McGovern and Guttridge 1972).

HOW CAN ARCHAEOLOGY ENHANCE UNDERSTANDINGS OF THE COLORADO COALFIELD WAR?

Thousands of pages of primary text, hundreds of photographs, and scores of oral histories constitute the incredibly robust documentary record of the Colorado Coalfield War. Very little of this documentary record, however, addresses in any systematic way the mundane realities of day-to-day life in the mines, the company towns, and the strike camps. The craft of archaeology allows us to systematically examine the material conditions of daily life in the coal camps and in the strike colonies of southern Colorado. These mundane conditions shaped the experience and consciousness of miners and their families. This shared experience and shared class consciousness are what prompted the miners to go out on strike, but their day-to-day life is obscured in the documentary record.

Historians have dug in the rich archival record of documents and photos related to the Colorado Coalfield War to produce several key histories of the strike (Beshoar 1957; McGovern and Guttridge 1972; Papanikolas 1982). These studies focus on the events, the politics, the companies, the strike leaders, and the organizational work of the UMWA. They highlight the male miner and the common experience of working in the mines as the source of the class consciousness that united ethnically and racially diverse men to strike. The histories often assume, and sometimes state, that men shared a common lived experience at work but that they returned home each night to ethnically different domestic lives. These historians have accepted a traditional theory of labor action that accentuates the actions of men in the workplace and overlooks the agency of women in the home. Their theory tends to link class and class struggle with active men in the workplace, and ethnicity and tradition with passive women in the home.

The striking steelworkers I have spoken to in Pueblo, Colorado, and the UMWA members we have worked with have a very different perspective on class consciousness, solidarity, and strikes from that of the historians. They tell us that it is families, not male workers, who go out on strike. They emphasize that families make the decision to strike at the kitchen table before miners affirm it in the union hall. We, and many other academics, doubt the traditional theory of solidarity (Long 1985, 1991; Beaudry and Mrozowski 1988; McGaw 1989; Cameron 1993; Shackel 1994, 1996; Sider 1996; Mrozowski et al. 1996). We see the ethnic identities that crosscut class in southern Colorado, and we agree that they hindered the formation of class consciousness. But we have misgivings about the formulas of class = workplace = solidarity = male, and ethnicity = home = alienation = female. We find that class and ethnicity crosscut both mine and home, male and female. We hypothesize that working-class men in the mines and working-class women in the homes both shared a common, mundane, lived class experience and that ethnic differences alienated them in both contexts.

The existing histories clearly show that ethnic divisions existed in the mines. The companies hired miners as independent contractors, and the workers organized their own work crews. The miners chose to work with family members and friends, usually all of the same ethnicity (Beshoar 1957; McGovern and Guttridge 1972; Papanikolas 1982; Long 1991). Historical and industrial archaeologists have also demonstrated in many other cases that nineteenth- and early twentieth-century workplaces were ethnically structured (Hardesty 1988; Bassett 1994; Wegars 1991). The traditional theory holds that the male camaraderie of the work experience sweeps away these ethnic divisions in the mine and that it prevails over a passive domestic ethnicity to create class consciousness.

We cannot demonstrate from the existing histories and analyses that a class-based commonality of lived experience in the home also aided in the formation of class consciousness and solidarity. The primary histories all concur that the mundane lives of miners' families were difficult, but they offer only anecdotal evidence of the reality of those lives. Anecdotes and assertions of hardship pepper the oral histories, but they lack systematic information and detail on that lived experience. The research of the historian Priscilla Long (1985) helped inspire our position. She has demonstrated that women in the early twentieth-century Colorado coalfields shared an experience of sexual and gender exploitation, but her work also lacks detailed data on the realities of day-to-day lived experience in the home.

Scholars can use historical archaeology to analyze the relationship among social consciousness, lived experience, material conditions, human agency, and transformative change (Orser 1996; Shackel 1996). Historical archaeologists can interweave documents and the archaeological record to understand both the consciousness and material conditions that form lived experience (Beaudry 1988; Leone and Potter 1988; Little 1992; Leone 1995; De Cunzo and Herman 1996; Wylie 1999; Delle et al. 2000). People speak in texts and oral histories about their consciousness, their interests, and their struggles, but not all people have the same presence, power, or voice in the documents. Also, they rarely tell us in detail about their mundane lives. They tend instead to speak about the unusual, the significant, the momentous, and the exotic. People, however, unintentionally produce the archaeological record with the residues of the small actions that make up their day-to-day experience. The archaeological record consists primarily of these mundane residues, which all people leave behind.

Archaeological research gives us one means to gain a richer, more in-depth, and more methodical knowledge of the everyday domestic experience of Colorado mining families. These families unwittingly left evidence of their day-to-day lives in the earth. We have recaptured lived experience from the charred remains of their tents, from the plans of camps, from the contents of their privies, and by from the trash that they abandoned. Interweaving these data with information from documentary and photographic sources allows us to infer domestic life. In order to understand the dynamic relationship of lived experience, solidarity, struggle, and change, we apply these methods to company towns occupied before the strike, to the strikers' tent camps, and to the company towns rebuilt under the Rockefeller Plan.

Our position stresses the importance of domestic life in the formation of class consciousness and solidarity. We can archaeologically demonstrate that a class-based, everyday, lived experience of the home transcended ethnic divisions before, during, and after the strike. Our analysis demonstrates that women and children were active agents, with male miners, in creating class consciousness in solidarity for the strike.

ARCHAEOLOGICAL FIELDWORK

With the help of our field school students, we did five years of excavations both at Ludlow and in the ruins of the CF&I-owned company town of Berwind. The massacre site is a near perfect archaeological context, a very short-term occupation destroyed by fire. The construction of a memorial with a fenced-in area, the lining of the death pit with concrete, and a building disturbed one small portion of the former colony. Outside this area, cattle grazing and other activities have had little impact on the remains of the colony. We initiated our research in Berwind right after the area had been subdivided for sale, but the streets, foundations, latrines, and trash pits of the old company town remained visible on the surface. As the lots were sold, many of the new owners bulldozed and built over these remains.

Ludlow

The Ludlow Massacre site covers forty acres of gently sloping plains swathed in short grass. We conducted controlled surface collections over the site. The distribution of surface material corresponded quite closely with the plan of the strike camp as it is revealed in photographs taken in 1914 and assisted us in locating numerous features associated with the camp. We also systematically dug soil cores to find cellars and pits. There has been very little deposition on the site, and the majority of its features occurred at shallow depths of ten to twenty centimeters. We located and excavated one complete and several partial tent platforms, as well as several shallow pit features. We have also located a number of deep features, among them a possible privy and seven holes that were subterranean shelter or storage cellars constructed by the colony's residents (figure 6).

Photographs have been a valuable source of information, greatly aiding our excavations. Several hundred photographs exist of the strike, including dozens of the Ludlow tent colony. A few days before the massacre, the independent photographer Lou Dold took a panoramic photo that shows the camp (figure 4). Gene Prince (1988) and James Deetz (1993) pioneered a photo overlay technique to locate features that appear in old photographs but no longer exist in a modern landscape. In the summer of 1999, we used this technique to define the positions of the tents and other features in the colony. We had 35-mm negatives made of Dold's premassacre photo,[5] and we mounted each negative in turn on the ground glass in the viewfinder of a Nikon single-reflex camera with a 50-mm lens. Dold took his photograph from atop a water tower on the railroad line near the colony. We were able to locate the position of this water tower by using other photos and physical remains on the ground; then we elevated the camera with a hydraulic lift placed over that location. By superimposing the negative image on stable landscape features, such as hills, mountains, and the section line road, we were able to position the camera where Dold had stood to take his picture. With the camera in position, we sighted through the viewfinder to see the image of the camp superimposed over the existing landscape, then directed crew members to move within the image and place pin flags marking the locations of tents and other features. In this way, we were able to locate over a quarter of the tents in the colony.[6] In the summer of 2002, we located additional features by using the same technique with other photos taken at ground level within the camp (Jacobson 2006).

The various photographs from Ludlow and the Forbes tent camp show

Figure 6. Excavating a tent cellar at Ludlow, 2001. Photo by Randall McGuire.

how the miners set up the tents. They first dug a shallow basin, then laid wooden joists directly on the ground to support a wooden tent platform and frame, usually with a wooden door. After covering the frame with canvas, the miners piled a ridge of dirt around the base of the tent. In numerous cases, they dug a cellar or pit under the wooden platform.

In 1998, we excavated one tent platform. We were able to define it on the basis of soil stains and shallow trenches (probably drainage ditches to carry water away from the structure) and rows of nails that followed the joists. A large number of small artifacts, likely to have been lost by residents through the slats in the floor or with the burning of the tent, lay on the bottom of the shallow basin. These included a suspender part bearing an Italian inscription, "Society of Tyrolean Alpinists," and a collection of Catholic religious medals, suggesting that the occupants of the tent were Italian Catholics. Our excavation of other tent locations revealed extensive soil oxidation resulting from the intense heat of the burning tent, and we recovered metal tent and furniture hardware that survived the fire.

Work on a possible privy on the southern edge of the colony revealed evidence for early acts of memorialization at the site. We recovered a metal tripod and wire wreath frame from atop a series of artifact-rich deposits. Material from the lower strata of the feature consists of hundreds of steel cans, including a multitude of Pet brand condensed milk cans, medicinal and sauce bottles, tobacco tins, fragments of furniture, and a miner's lamp.

We located and tested seven other deep features that we believe to be earthen cellars the strikers dug below tents for storage and refuge. We fully excavated two of these. The stratigraphy and contents of each clearly tell the story of the attack on the colony. Fire-damaged family possessions sit on the floors of the cellars. To reach them, crews dug through the burned remains of the tent, a level of blackened wood, charred canvas, and rusted grommets. A layer of charcoal, coal clinker, rusted metal, and charred possessions, trash that the miners used to fill in the holes after the massacre, overlays the tent remains.

Berwind

The CF&I built Berwind in Berwind Canyon, near Ludlow, in 1892 and abandoned it in 1931. Miners occupied the town before and after the strike. Many of the strikers at Ludlow originated from Berwind. In 1998, we made a detailed map of the community based on remains visible on the surface of the ground. Using this map, old photos, and early twentieth-century plat maps, we were able to define numerous discrete residential neighborhoods and date them relative to the strike. Test excavations revealed stratified deposits as much as fifty centimeters deep in the yards associated with houses. At Berwind, we excavated in trash dumps, latrines, and yards. We divided these deposits into ones dating before, during, and after the strike. Our analysis of artifacts from the tests confirmed the dating of some neighborhoods to before the strike and others to construction after the strike as part of the Rockefeller Plan. We also contacted and started collecting oral histories from former Berwind residents, who recounted life in Berwind in the 1920s and 1930s.

Locus K dated to before the strike. Our excavations at a dump in this locus unearthed a stunning array of objects, from household furnishings to domestic rubbish to fragments of footwear, clothing, and other personal effects. Through fine-grained stratigraphic analysis, we also learned more about how families transported trash to the dumpsite and how the dump itself was operated. Our crews located and sampled a large privy associated with the residential area in the locus. The various filling episodes and the artifacts within it reflect the regular use and maintenance of the privy. The artifacts also date the capping of the pit and the destruction of the neighborhood to make room for a new junior high school in 1916. Combined with oral histories and census data, the material from this prestrike section of Berwind provides a window into the material conditions of life that in part motivated the collective struggle of 1912–1913.

Locus B dated to after the strike. Here, as part of the Rockefeller Plan, the company built a cluster of concrete-walled houses for the workers. Improving beyond Locus K, they built cement-lined privies, which the company cleaned on a routine basis. We mapped the houses, privies, and the outdoor beehive bread ovens behind the houses. Our excavations concentrated in the yards of the houses and in trash deposits thrown into the creek bed below the houses.

ARCHAEOLOGICAL CONCLUSIONS

In their dissertation research, several archaeologists with the project have elaborated on the themes of everyday domestic life and the construction of class consciousness. Margaret Wood has examined how women's contributions to household survival and reproduction changed before and after the strike. Michael Jacobson has analyzed how owners, working families, and the union manipulated the landscape in the struggle over class consciousness. Sarah Chicone has asked how working-class poverty in southern Colorado changed because of the strike and the Rockefeller Plan.

Margaret Wood's study of the Berwind remains (2002a) shows how working-class women in the company towns struggled to raise families on miners' wages that would not cover enough food for even two people. In trash dating before the strike, she found many tin cans, large cooking pots, and big serving vessels. Families took in single male miners as boarders to make extra income, and women used canned foods to make stews and soups to feed them. Wood calculates that through this activity women accounted for a third to half of the household's income. After the strike, the Rockefeller Plan forbade the taking in of boarders, but miners' wages remained too low to support a family. The tin cans and big pots disappeared from the trash, replaced by canning jars and lids and the bones of rabbits and chickens. Also, women now used the outdoor beehive ovens to bake bread in quantity. Wives and children, who could no longer earn money from boarders, instead produced and processed food at home to feed the family.

Michael Jacobson (2006) has looked at the landscapes of Berwind and the Ludlow tent colony as loci of class struggle. In Berwind before the strike, the struggle revolved around worker-built versus company-built housing. Company industrial buildings, such as coal tipples and coke ovens, dominated the landscape of the company towns, and the company-built houses for the workers were interspaced within this industrial landscape. Workers could escape company domination by building their own homes up the side canyons away from the company buildings, thus removing themselves from the constant gaze of the company and gaining some control over their landscape. During the strike, the company and the National Guard represented the strikers as dirty, anarchistic foreigners who could not function without the control and supervision of the companies; however, the UMWA and the miners laid Ludlow out in ordered rows of tents, with a central meeting tent and areas for team sports, realizing in the landscape the ordered democratic society they created in the camp. After the strike, the Rockefeller Plan provided company-built housing for all workers, which improved the material conditions of home life but left working families with less control over their lives and the landscape.

Sarah Chicone (2006) has asked about poverty and the lives of southern Colorado coal mining families. She looks at poverty not as a thing but as a process. She examines how middle-class ideologies of poverty affected the lives of working-class families and those families' lived day-to-day experience of poverty. Middle-class ideologies constructed the poverty of the mining families in one of two ways. A conservative point of view held that working families were poor because they were unclean, lazy, and drank too much. Progressive reformers argued that the impoverishment of working families sprang from company exploitation. Needless to say, the companies took the first position to justify the lot of the workers, and the union took the second to raise public sympathy for the strike. The workers saw their impoverishment in neither of these ways but rather as a struggle that affirmed family and community. The Rockefeller Plan only slightly improved the materiality of working-class poverty in southern Colorado, and it did little to alter the lived experience of poverty.

For almost ninety years, the United Mine Workers have maintained the site of Ludlow as a shrine to the workers who died there (Walker 2000). When we began our project in 1997, a monument was located at the site but little or no interpretative information existed there. In this context our archaeological work became a powerful form of memory and political action.

ARCHAEOLOGY AS MEMORY

The death of women and children in class warfare clashes with most accepted narratives of class relations in the United States, particularly in the West (McGuire and Reckner 2002). We argue that the painful reality of Ludlow represents a watershed in American history that needs to be retrieved for a broad range of constituencies. By doing so we raise popular awareness of labor's struggle and help to generate political support for the rights of workers. Many middle-class visitors to the memorial site arrive unaware of what happened there and become uncomfortable when they learn the story. Others see the story of Ludlow as a reminder of an unfortunate past that is best forgotten. They believe that we are all middle-class in the United States today and that class conflict has been banished to history. They do not see how fast capitalism has eroded workers' rights and dignity. I need not reexamine the ideological power of this line of thought. On the other hand, after we presented our proposal for archaeological fieldwork at the Ludlow Memorial to the UMWA's local in Trinidad, one coal miner suggested, "All you need to know about Ludlow can be summed up in three words: they got fucked" (Duke and Saitta 1998). The deep alienation and even hostility apparent in this statement was a wake-up call concerning the realities of working-class life and thought and the class differences that separate us from the miners. It also threw into question the wider social value of a pursuit like archaeology.

Outside union circles, few remember the story of the 1913–1914 Colorado Coalfield War and the Ludlow Massacre. The UMWA regards Ludlow as a place of pilgrimage, and it uses the site as a powerful symbol to raise class consciousness and build solidarity (Walker 2000). In 1997, Dean Saitta and I presented our proposal for the project to a union professional at the regional office of the UMWA in Denver, Colorado. At the end of our presentation, he indicated that what we wanted to do sounded okay but that we had to realize that Ludlow is sacred ground for the union. He had one question for us: "Are you Republicans?" I looked at Dean for a moment and then I replied, "No, we are not Republicans, we are socialists." He said that was okay as long as we were not Republicans. Memory leads to action when working people see their contemporary struggles against fast capitalism as a continuation of the struggle at Ludlow.

In 1997, the Colorado Department of Transportation erected a point-of-interest sign to mark the exit for the Ludlow Monument off Interstate

25. The sign draws a small but steady stream of summer tourists to the site, most of whom arrive expecting to find a monument to an Indian massacre (Walker 2003). In this context, our excavations have become a form of memory, recalling for these visitors the details of what happened at Ludlow, the sacrifices of the strikers, and the terrible struggle that won working people their rights. The story of Ludlow, made compelling by the violence and the death of women and children, has great popular appeal. Also, it is not a tale of a distant or exotic past. Descendants of the strikers still regularly visit the site, and the United Mine Workers hold an annual memorial service at the monument.

Our focus on mundane life humanizes the strikers, because it emphasizes relations and activities that our modern audiences also experience: relations between husbands and wives, between parents and children, and approaches to family food preparation and laundry. The parallel and contrast between the modern realities of these experiences and those of the miners' lives enable our modern audience to understand the harshness of the strikers' experience.

Archaeological excavations often make the news. Each season of our excavations in Colorado resulted in articles in major newspapers in the state. Farther afield, Eric Zorn, a columnist with the *Chicago Tribune,* picked up on our excavations for his Labor Day column in 1997. He titled that day's column "Workers Rights Were Won with Blood" and pointed out how fast capitalism has corroded many of the rights that were so hard won. Through our excavations, the events of 1913–1914 became newsworthy again and took on a modern reality.

An important part of the project was developing an interpretive program at the massacre site. We do not have to interpret the site for the members of the United Mine Workers, because the union has made Ludlow and the massacre a symbol of their ongoing struggle. But the tourists who regularly pull off the highway, presumably to visit the site of an Indian massacre, need background information in order to understand Ludlow's significance in the present. During each summer's excavation we greeted people, gave them a tour, and told them about what happened at Ludlow. During the summer of 1998, over five hundred people visited our excavations. At the Ludlow Memorial Service in June 1999, we unveiled an interpretive kiosk, which includes three panels: one on the history of the strike and massacre, a second on our archaeological research, and a third on the relationship of Ludlow to current labor struggles. Over seven hundred working people viewed the kiosk during that year's memorial service. We have also created two traveling exhibits of artifacts that we have displayed at each annual memorial service and have sent to union halls around the country. And in the spring of 2006, we installed a more detailed interpretive trail at the site.

The struggle for dignity and basic rights among working people in southern Colorado continues today. Between 1997 and 2004, several hundred striking steelworkers from United Steelworkers locals 2102 and 3267 in Pueblo, Colorado, joined the Ludlow Memorial Service. They went out on strike against CF&I to stop forced overtime, struggling against fast capitalism's pressures to erase the boundaries of work and home at the expense of their families. They also sought to regain one of the basic rights that the Ludlow strikers died for, the eight-hour day. The Ludlow Massacre became a powerful symbol in their struggle, powerful enough that the parent company (Oregon Steel) sought to distance itself from the killings of 1914 by altering the name of its Pueblo subsidiary from CF&I to Rocky Mountain Steel. The company wanted to break the union and thereby deprive the steelworkers of another of the basic rights that people died for at Ludlow, the right to collective bargaining. In June 1999, the steelworkers invited us to speak to them in Pueblo. In the spring of 2004, the United Steelworkers won the strike.

The struggle of labor for dignity and basic rights also continues to engender opposition in southern Colorado. In May 2003, vandals attacked the memorial to the Ludlow dead with a sledgehammer. They decapitated both the male and the female statues at the base of the monument (Saitta 2004). To repair the monument, the local union of the UMWA embarked on a national fund-raising campaign. Money poured in from individuals and union locals, and within a few months the local had raised the eighty thousand dollars necessary. The union rededicated the restored monument at the annual memorial service on June 5, 2005. Dean Saitta of our project joined union leaders at the podium to help celebrate the restoration and commemorate the events of 1914 (figure 7).

DESCENDANTS AND DESCENDANT COMMUNITIES

Many historical archaeologists have argued that scholars have an obligation to work with the descendant communities of the sites that we study (Spector 1993; Blakey and LaRoche 1997; Wilkie and Bartoy 2000; Singleton and Orser 2003). Because many of these researchers do not distinguish between individual agency and collective agency, they confuse the individual descendants of historical communities with a descendant community. In the case of Ludlow, we have tried to serve both individual

Figure 7. Dean Saitta addressing the 2005 Ludlow Memorial Service with UMWA leaders behind him and a portrait of John Lewis to his left. Photo by Randall McGuire.

descendants and the descendant community, but we recognize that in this case only the descendant community is a community of struggle.

Many descendants of the miners in the 1913–1914 strike (children, grandchildren, nieces, and nephews) come to the memorial each year. Few of them are miners or even working-class; they are principally middle-class Anglos. Their parents or they or both participated in the great social mobility of the 1950s and 1960s. Today they live scattered across the United States as teachers, lawyers, businesspeople, managers, and administrators. They share an identity as descendants of the massacre, but they do not form a community, either in living near one another or in forming any type of interacting group, organization, or club. The descendants desire a familial and personal memorialization of the strike and massacre. They come to the memorial to establish a connection to this familial heritage and to see to it that their family's role in these events is properly honored.

We have aided descendants in various ways. We helped the niece of Cadilano Costa locate the graves of her aunt, her uncle, and her cousins so that she could raise a stone on the unmarked plots. Irene Dotson was one of the last survivors of the strike.[7] A frequently published picture of strikers and their families in front of a tent in the Forbes camp includes her at age two (figure 8). The archives of the Colorado Historical Society and of the Denver Public Library listed the wrong family name for the individuals in the picture, and the photo has been published numerous times with this misinformation. Mrs. Dotson supplied us with the correct names, and we contacted the archives. They corrected the identification of the photo to "the Oberosler family and friends" and labeled it with the names of the individuals.

The unionized working people of southern Colorado make up the descendant community of the 1913–1914 coal strike. A few of them are descendants of people who participated in the strike, but the vast majority of them have no ancestral connection to it. Some of them are ethnic whites (Italians and eastern Europeans); the majority are Chicano. They maintain the monument, organize the memorial, and make the events of 1913–1914 part of their active union struggle.

When we conceived the project in the mid-1990s, an active, unionized coal mine, the Allen Mine, was still operating west of Trinidad. When we entered the field in the summer of 1997, we were very disappointed to learn that the mine had closed just before Christmas in 1996. We feared this closing would transform the project from an active engagement with a union community to a postindustrial memory project, but it did not work out that way. Ludlow remains a sacred place for all of the UMWA, and the District 22 office in Price, Utah, took over responsibility for the monument. The memorial service remains a national event for the union, with representatives from the national executive council attending each service. Since our project began, both the government workers in Las Animas County and the hospital workers at the Mount San Rafael Hospital, in Trinidad, have unionized. Both groups of workers have chosen the union of their fathers and uncles, the United Mine Workers of America. Both also identify with the 1913–1914 strike.

We did sometimes find our knowledge at odds with beliefs of the union community in southern Colorado. We encountered numerous pervasive myths about the massacre that our research proved false. These myths tended to brutalize the National Guard.

Contemporary reports sympathetic to the UMWA maintained that the National Guard had used explosive bullets (Seligman 1914). We have found spent bullets in our excavation, and we can identify their caliber and type. Ammunition boxes with readable labels also appear in numerous photos of the Guard. None of the spent bullets that we have found or the labels on the ammunition boxes shown in the photographs were

Figure 8. Oberosler family and friends. Irene Dotson is in the center, in a white dress. Photo by Lou Dold, Denver Public Library, Western History Collection, X-60448.

from explosive ammunition. Most of the Guard used standard military issue, steel-jacketed, ball ammunition. The one National Guard unit equipped by the companies fired civilian, lead, hunting rounds.

Many local people in southern Colorado told us that following the massacre guardsmen had ripped open Cadilano Costas belly and torn out her unborn child on the tip of a bayonet. We do not believe this happened, and the documentary evidence provides no support for it . None of the contemporary accounts of the massacre mentioned this story, and none of the hundreds of photos of the Guard show soldiers with bayonets. The coroner's report indicates no wounds on Cadilano Costas's body. The Red Cross party that recovered the body made no mention of mutilation. A UMWA representative accompanied the Red Cross party and observed the autopsy, but the UMWA never reported the bayonet story either. In 1914, British propaganda published in U.S. newspapers accused the "beastly Huns" who invaded Belgium of exactly this atrocity. We believe that this tale was picked up in the popular imagination of southern Colorado, and people transferred it to the Ludlow Massacre.

A few descendants of strikers told us that the number killed in the massacre had been far higher than the twenty-four recorded deaths. They believed that the National Guard had killed hundreds of people. They asserted that the Guard had dug a great trench in the middle of the camp and buried the uncounted bodies there to hide them. Our testing and excavations were extensive enough to have found such a pit in the camp, but our work revealed no evidence for such a trench. A photo of the second UMWA camp built on the site after the massacre clearly shows the remains of the burned tents from the massacre but no evidence of a freshly dug mass grave. We did, however, hear stories from descendants of relatives who had died days or weeks after the massacre. In some cases, these relations died of wounds. In other cases, they died from ailments or physical conditions that were worsened by the trauma and stress of the massacre or by exposure to the elements when they fled the carnage. We conclude that there were unrecorded deaths from the massacre, but they do not number in the hundreds, and the Guard did not bury bodies in the area of the camp.

We always listened to these stories respectfully, even when we had heard them many times. They were useful ethnographic information that demonstrated to us the depth of alienation that developed after the strike and massacre. In each case, we explained why we thought the story was not true. I do not know if we changed any minds, but people always respectfully listened to our explanations.

Attitudes about the environment presented another potential source of tension between archaeologists and UMWA members. As coal miners, the UMWA would like to see more coal dug in the United States. The union and most of its membership blame environmentalists and environmental concerns for decreasing and limiting the amount of coal currently mined. The UMWA consistently supports programs and legislation that would increase coal usage, principally in energy production. Archaeologists tend to be avid environmentalists. The interests of the archaeological community have long been linked with environmental interests. The goals and research of the project did not broach environmental issues, and as a whole we avoided such issues. Individual archaeologists and individual union members often discussed environmental issues, but these conversations were always respectful and measured on both sides.

We remember Ludlow by using our knowledge of the world to critique the world and to teach other communities how labor's rights were won with blood. They were not freely given but bought with the lives of working people like those who died at Ludlow. We also use Ludlow to reveal how fast capitalism has eroded many of those rights to the point of their endangerment today.

TEACHING LABOR AND THE LABOR OF TEACHING

The powerful ideology of a classless U.S. society typically silences the record of class struggle in popular narratives of American history. Ending this silence makes education an extraordinarily vital part of our project (Walker and Saitta 2002; Wood 2002b). We have extended our collaboration with the UMWA in building the interpretive program at the memorial site and in our traveling exhibits to teach our own field school students about American labor, past and present, and to help public school teachers incorporate labor issues into their curricula.

Fitting the predominant pattern in archaeology, the majority of students who attended our field school from 1997 to 2004 came from middle-class backgrounds. Most of these students grew up in North America. They had learned about labor unions from mainstream educational institutions and corporate media outlets. While a limited number had been exposed to U.S. labor history and been taught about class structures in U.S. society, the majority had had few experiences that made them aware of class in general or, more specifically, of their own class positions. The field school also included students from England, Spain, and Bulgaria. These foreign students had a much higher awareness of class and class relations than the U.S. students. The foreign students generally found the American students to be apolitical and apathetic in comparison to their peers at home.

The nature of the Ludlow Massacre site brings the reality of class and class conflict in American history into stark relief for students. Many of our students were shocked that such events could have happened in the United States. However, the awareness of labor history in no way guarantees the realization of class relations in the present. To challenge this situation, we always scheduled fieldwork to overlap with the annual June UMWA memorial service at the Ludlow Monument, a gathering that confronted students with the realities of labor unionism and working-class solidarity in a powerful way. Every summer, staff and students of the Archaeology of the 1913–1914 Colorado Coalfield War Project participated in the memorial service along with three hundred to one thousand union people from all over the United States and from many different occupations. Contact with striking steelworkers from Pueblo, Colorado, was particularly insightful for the students. Several times we traveled with our students to the union hall in Pueblo to have

Figure 9. At the National Endowment for the Humanities' 1999 teachers' institute, educators listen to a retired miner and his wife (standing second and third from left) at the Ludlow Memorial. Photo by Randall McGuire.

dinner with strikers and their families. At these and other events, students presented their work on the archaeology of Ludlow and discussed the significance of the massacre with working people.

The Colorado Coalfield War Project developed a relationship with the Denver-area AFL-CIO Union Summer Program. This program brings interns (often, though not exclusively, college-aged activists) together to support the organizing efforts of workers in the Denver metropolitan area. Union Summer groups made several visits to the Ludlow Memorial, which allowed our field school students to share their emerging perspectives on labor history with people their own age who had committed their summer to labor activism. We believe that these social interactions were some of the most important experiences the field school provided.

We also structured our field school to challenge the guild ideology that permeates the training of archaeology students. An aspect of traditional archaeological apprenticeship, the expectation that field school students will work long hours on weekends and into the night, trains students to self-exploit when they go to work for profit-making contract archaeology firms. In our field schools, we always kept eight-hour days. Students were occasionally asked to attend lectures in the evenings and to go on field trips on weekends, but work stopped at the end of the eighth hour. Any activities after that time were for the education or recreation of the students. Also in our profession, many archaeologists have a macho (macha) contempt for safety on excavation projects, commonly deriding safety concerns and OSHA regulations. A 1997 survey of field technicians showed that 33 percent had been injured on the job (Wilson 2001b). For this reason, we made instruction on safe practices in excavation and OSHA requirements part of our program, in addition to teaching the craft of archaeology. Throughout the field school we pursued a theme of teaching students their rights as workers. The union workers we collaborated with readily reinforced this theme.

We have worked with Colorado public school teachers to prepare school programs and educational packets, including a curriculum for middle school students on the history of labor in Colorado, with the 1913–1914 strike as its central focus. During the summers of 1999 and 2000 at Trinidad State Junior College, the Colorado Endowment for the Humanities used our project as the focus of training institutes for teachers (figure 9). These institutes strove to educate the teachers on labor history and to develop classroom materials to use in the teaching of Colorado labor history. We organized these institutes and did much of the instruction in them. We have also prepared a "history trunk" that circulates in the Denver, Colorado, School District. The trunk is a box filled with artifacts, photos, and text material that teachers can bring to their schools and use with their classes.

CLASS AND PRAXIS

The Archaeology of the Colorado Coalfield War Project continues to be a very productive scholarly endeavor. Our six summers of field school trained nearly one hundred students in the craft of archaeology and in their rights as workers. Members of the Ludlow Collective have presented more than fifty papers in professional meetings and published nineteen scholarly articles or book chapters. We have posted a Web atlas of the strike. Students in the project have produced eight master's theses and three Ph.D. dissertations, with three additional Ph.D. dissertations in process. A monograph describing our excavations is on file at the Colorado Historical Society. We have an edited volume of interpretive articles by members of the collective under review, and Dean Saitta (2007) recently published a book summarizing the project.

The real measure of the project, however, does not lie in this scholarly production or in how well the project has incorporated arcane aspects of academic theory. The real measure of the project lies in our praxis with our brothers and sisters in the labor movement. In order to initiate the project, we had to overcome suspicions (Are you Republicans?) and misconceptions (I thought archaeologists study dinosaurs) on the part of the leaders and members of the UMWA. Once we passed these hurdles, however, collaboration with the union and its members has been relatively easy. Occasionally class differences have been manifest (They got fucked), but we have all shared a common goal of telling labor's story and honoring the sacrifices of Ludlow. We have brought archaeology to union halls, and our efforts have been met with applause. Our students and we have learned about the labor experience from union people, and they have learned about archaeology and history from us.

We have made the Archaeology of the 1913–1914 Colorado Coalfield War Project something that working people can relate to, both emotionally and intellectually. It is one of the few archaeological projects in the United States that has spoken to the experience and struggles of working-class people, past and present, in a language they can understand, about events that interest them and to which they feel directly connected. While we feel that our work has won considerable interest and approval from the people closest to the history of Ludlow, we have no illusions that we have overcome all boundaries; we believe that a degree of continued unease and distrust on their part has been healthy. We have also worked to reach a broader audience that has never heard of the Ludlow Massacre and has missed, or misunderstood, the history of U.S. labor conflict and the legacy it represents. In so doing, we have engaged in praxis—seeking to know the world, critique the world, and most important to take action in the world.

NOTES

1. I am a member of the United University Professionals. This union represents faculty in the State University of New York system. My union is affiliated with the American Federation of Teachers and the AFL-CIO.

2. There has been a persistent rumor that we concocted the project while drinking martinis and soaking in Phil Duke's hot tub in Durango, Colorado. This is false. We were not drinking martinis. We were drinking gin and tonics.

3. The Ludlow Collective has included, among others, Philip Duke, Dean Saitta, Mark Walker, Margaret Wood, Karin Larkin, Amie Gray, Bonnie J. Clark, Paul Reckner, Michael Jacobson, Sarah Chicone, Summer Moore, Clare Horn, Donna Bryant, Jason Lapham, Stacy Tchorzynski, and me.

4. Calculating the number of people who were killed or wounded in the 1913–1914 Colorado Coalfield War is very difficult. Primary and secondary

sources report different counts. This is especially true for the number of armed strikers killed in the ten-day war. The count for the Ludlow Massacre itself is consistently presented as nineteen Ludlow residents (McGovern and Guttridge 1972).

5. Dold's panoramic print, which is frequently reproduced in histories of the massacre, is made from three overlapping original prints.

6. Several things prevented us from locating more than a quarter of the tents. Trees and the building in the monument area blocked our view of about a third of the colony area. Parallax made it difficult to locate tents with any accuracy in the eastern third of the camp area.

7. Irene Dotson died on November 13, 2003, in Colorado Springs, Colorado, at the age of ninety-one.

Conclusion

The mode of being of the new intellectual can no longer
consist in eloquence, which is an exterior and momentary
mover of feelings and passions, but in active participation
in practical life, as constructor, organizer, "permanent
persuader" and not just a simple orator.

Antonio Gramsci (1971:10)

Over seventy-five years ago, from his cell in a Fascist jail, Antonio
Gramsci charged intellectuals to abandon esoteric pursuits and academic
cheerleading and to enter into the practical life of political struggle. Near
the dawn of the twenty-first century, few intellectual pursuits seem more
esoteric than archaeology. As Vine Deloria has commented: "When we
stop and think about it, we live in a society so rich and so structured that
we have the luxury of paying six-figure salaries to individuals who know
a little bit about the pottery patterns of a small group of ancient people"
(1997:211). Yet, it is exactly this exoticism and seeming irrelevance to
practical life that give archaeology political power. Indeed, Deloria
(1997:215) challenges archaeologists and anthropologists not because he
had a grossly inflated notion of what we are paid but because he recognized that we have a key role in the modern U.S. political debate over
who defines what an Indian is. In the arenas of struggle over economics,
ideologies, politics, and identities, archaeology has traditionally been
used to support the powers that be. It has been mobilized to create
mythic charters for bourgeois nationalism, sometimes with horrifying
consequences as in Nazi Germany and the Babri Mosque in Ajodhya,
India. At other places, such as the former Gestapo headquarters in Berlin
and at the Club Atlético in Buenos Aires, archaeologists have used their
craft to challenge the status quo. My purpose has been to consider how
archaeology might be a form of praxis to help create a more humane
world. How can archaeologists be more than simple orators?

In this book I have reflected on how to adapt the modern practice of archaeology to those who do it, are interested in it, and are affected by it. I have considered praxis in concrete contexts of class relations in archaeology, binational archaeology along the U.S.–Mexican border, and an archaeology for the working class at the Ludlow Massacre site. In this final chapter I will return to these cases in order to reflect on how our concrete efforts inform a theory and method of praxis.

•   •   •

A spider conducts operations that resemble those of a
weaver, and a bee puts to shame many an architect in
the construction of her cells. But what distinguishes the
worst architect from the best of bees is this, that the
architect raises his structure in imagination before he
erects it in reality.

Karl Marx (1906:198)

Human action is conscious action that must first exist in people's minds before it can be realized. People often engage in the practice of reproducing and maintaining their social world with a minimum of awareness, imagination, or critical consciousness of what they are doing. Human consciousness may also entail free, creative, and critical contemplation, and through such thought people may engage in action that seeks to change their social world. People can embrace concepts of possibility and change. They may come to realize that they can subvert and transform the world that they make in their everyday lives. Such theoretically informed, goal-oriented, and potentially transformative action is praxis.

The whole of the practice of archaeology—that is, all of what archaeologists do—is necessary for praxis, but very few archaeologists engage in praxis. The vast majority of archaeologists practice their craft to gain knowledge of the world. Various archaeologists have sought to critique the world and the place of archaeology in it. Fewer have fully entered into the dialectic of praxis and built an archaeology of political action to transform the world. The test of praxis is collective action. The critiques, arguments, cases, knowledge, and theory of this book seek to build praxis, but that praxis is realized only through collective action. In Sonora, México, this realization comes with the establishment of a collaborative, binational archaeology that presents an alternative to the traditionally disconnected practices of Mexican and North American archaeologies. In southern Colorado, our praxis has been realized through our contributions to

solidarity building in the United Mine Workers and in educating a general
public that workers won their rights with blood. The praxis of this book
will be made real if other archaeologists also mobilize their practice to
confront alienation, strive for emancipation, and transform archaeology.

My arguments for a praxis of archaeology do not seek to dissuade the
vast majority of my colleagues from their fascination with learning about
the past. Archaeologists cannot, however, step outside the dialectic of
praxis. The question, Is archaeology political? has only one answer: it is.
Thus, we need to ask, How is archaeology political? and How does our
practice of archaeology fit into a praxis of archaeology? I do argue that
all archaeologists need to reflect on the coherence, context, correspondence, and consequences of the knowledge that we make. I hope this
book aids in that reflection. I have, however, written this book primarily
for those archaeologists who wish to fully enter into the dialectic that
will build archaeologies of political action to confront alienation and aid
emancipation.

FAST CAPITALISM

The pace of fast capitalism is dizzying. Like children on a merry-go-
round gone mad, we spin around until we succumb to vertigo and then
stagger about. We are disoriented, and we do not know how to do anything except hang on and try to keep up with the pace. Fast capitalism
has seeped into every corner of our society, eroding socially derived
moral frameworks, values, and political programs. It replaces the
humane with the ethos of the market. It reduces all social relations to the
cold calculus of cost and benefit and weighs all things in terms of profit.

Praxis begins when we realize that we can do more than just whirl
around in fast capitalism (Agger 2004:131–168). We can make social
change, beginning with changes in people. We can step back from the
pace and critically examine how our lives fit into the larger processes of
fast capitalism. From such critique we, can engage in a praxis that challenges fast capitalism's penetration of all areas of social and personal life,
both in the field of archaeology and in the world we practice it in.

Fast Capitalism and Archaeology

Fast capitalism attacks the values that drew us to archaeology and have
sustained us in our craft. It denigrates the life of the mind, because such
a life does not maximize gain. It transfigures heritage and education to

make profits from multinational cultural tourism. It leaves slight space for a craft of archaeology that unifies heart, hand, and intellect, and it exploits the camaraderie and shared purpose of fieldwork to boost speed and efficiency. Fast capitalism grinds down the community of scholarship that drew most of us to the craft of archaeology.

The hypercompetition of fast capitalism drives universities and cultural resource management firms to replace the traditional craft relationships of archaeology with market principles of flexibility, competition, and profit. These principles seek to proletarianize the academy and turn universities into diploma factories. Advocates of fast capitalism emphasize rote learning, skill acquisition, and value-added accountability while they attack liberal arts education, tenure, theory, philosophy, personal fulfillment, and humanism (Agger 2004:98; Siegel 2006). These advocates have actively interfered with governmental funding agencies and have challenged the privilege of the professoriat (Bloom 1987; Sykes 1988). Cultural resource legislation springs from values of heritage and community, but these run afoul of the market ethos of fast capitalism, because they interfere with the generation of profit. Thus, CRM faces an explosive contradiction. It must adapt to demands for flexibility, hypercompetition, and accelerated production to survive as a business in fast capitalism. Yet, fast capitalism wears away the values that validate CRM while fast capitalism's advocates seek to eliminate the laws that created CRM as an economic enterprise.

Fast Capitalism on the Border

A major transition facing the global politics of archaeology over the last twenty years has been the shift from archaeology primarily serving nationalist agendas to archaeology as a servant of heritage or cultural tourism. In the 1980s, my Mexican collaborator Elisa Villalpando and I began the Trincheras Tradition Project in northern Sonora, to create a radical praxis of archaeology that challenges double colonialism on the border. A confrontation with the nationalist agendas of archaeology in both countries lay at the heart of our project.

Even as we strove to confront nationalist programs, the processes of fast capitalism eroded and transformed the terrain that we stood on. At the turn of the twenty-first century, economic crisis, NAFTA, and the triumph of the conservative Partido Acción Nacional accelerated fast capitalism in México. The Instituto Nacional de Antropología y Historia now finds itself under siege. National heritage and scholarly research do not create profit, but cultural tourism does. PAN has sought to privatize archaeological sites and transfer control of México's heritage from the INAH to state governments. In Chiapas, fast capitalism finds its opposite in the Zapatista movement, which advances an *indigenista* program and seeks to wrest control of archaeological sites from the Mexican state. NAFTA has increased U.S. investment in and access to Mexican resources, and México is for sale. This is especially the case in Sonora, where the government strives to make the state a tourist playground for the inhabitants of Phoenix and Tucson. In a few cases, local governments and private individuals are seeking to exploit sites such as Cerro de Trincheras as tourist destinations. Construction of the tourist bubble buffering visitors from the social and economic realities of Sonora is destroying archaeological sites.

In this changing terrain, we have to rethink what a binational emancipatory praxis of archaeology might look like in México. Mexican law, like that of the United States, protects archaeological sites and requires mitigation of economic impacts on those sites. Erratic efforts to comply with these laws have led to more contract archaeology being done in Sonora. Presently, the INAH manages these efforts, and individual archaeologists move back and forth from grant-funded projects to contract jobs. The problem for the future will be how to maintain this integration and also how to develop a more consistent, regularized compliance with preservation laws. Heritage tourism in Sonora has traditionally been minimal, focusing on Spanish missions, but it is increasing and incorporating more archaeological sites, especially highly visible ones, such as Cerro de Trincheras. At the same time, multinational corporations are developing beachfront destinations that destroy less visible heritage sites. The Centro de INAH is charged with mitigating the impacts of this beachfront development on heritage sites. In general, the Centro de INAH works with communities to create tourism at heritage sites that will be educational and benefit the local people. The challenge for foreign researchers like myself is how to make our work complementary and supportive of these efforts.

Fast Capitalism and Organized Labor

Workers in the United States are increasingly losing control over their work and family lives because of the effects of fast capitalism. The hypercompetitiveness of fast capitalism compels employers to drive down wages and demand total commitment from their workers. This has meant a declining quality of life for many working families as a result of reduced real wages, increased levels of stress, less time spent with friends and families, and an overall dissatisfaction with their lives. Fast capitalism encourages union busting, because the struggle of unions to uphold respect, a living wage, the eight-hour day, and safe working conditions for working families slows capitalism. On October 3, 1997, United Steelworkers Locals 2102 and 3267 walked out on strike from Oregon Steel's Colorado Fuel and Iron Company steel mill in Pueblo, Colorado. They left the mill to contest forced overtime, which was stealing their control over their family lives and blurring the line between work and home. Oregon Steel welcomed a prolonged strike as a way to break the union. That same year, the Archaeology of the 1913–1914 Colorado Coalfield War Project, in collaboration with the United Mine Workers of America, launched full-scale excavations at the sites of the 1913–1914 strike by coal miners against Colorado Fuel and Iron. The steelworkers embraced the labor conflict of eighty years earlier as a symbol of their contemporary strike and made our project part of their struggle.

Unionized labor remembers the history of Ludlow and mobilized this remembrance in the steelworkers' strike. Through our research, archaeology became part of this memory. The project's message is simple: working families shed blood to win labor's contemporary rights to a safe workplace, benefits, reasonable wages, a forty-hour week, and dignity. Capitalists did not freely give these rights; rather, working people, such as those who died at Ludlow, bought them with their lives. We collaborated with the UMWA and the striking steelworkers to develop our education campaign. Our goal was to help them build solidarity among working families and to educate a broader public in support of labor's struggle. The realization of this praxis is ongoing, and the effectiveness of our efforts is hard to measure. Following Ollman (2003:20), however, we have decided which side we are on in the class struggle of fast capitalism and have joined the fray.

ENGAGING PRAXIS

The idea of praxis begins with theory and the realization of praxis in concrete experience and struggle should prompt the reconsideration and revision of that theory. Praxis can be built in archaeology in multiple ways. Processualists, postmodernists, and feminists have mixed up praxis in various hues and shades. The primary color of this book has been red, a relational, dialectical Marxism. This shade of red is compatible and complementary with many other hues. Where appropriate, I have drawn on compatible and complementary theory in the intersectionalities of dialectical Marxist, feminist, and indigenous theories to mix the most pleasing shade of red.

Not all theoretical approaches in contemporary archaeology help us build praxis. Agency has become a common buzzword. Archaeological discussions of agency have tended to focus on the actions of individuals as a remedy to a materialistic determinism (Hodder 1982; Meskell 1999; Dobres and Robb 2000). This emphasis on agency is well founded, because, in the absence of agency, praxis is impossible. At the same time, the reduction of agency to the actions of individuals is problematic. Individuals do not just live in society; they must make society to live. A dialectical view assumes that neither society nor the individual exists as an essential or autonomous "thing," but rather that the terms *society* and *individual* summarize complex webs of social relations that bring the two into being. Therefore, a focus on collective agency recognizes the importance of human action and the embeddedness of that action in social relationships.

Transformative social action occurs when people struggle communally to advance their common interests. A shared consciousness of group identity and interest makes collective agency possible. This consciousness may be based in class, gender, ethnicity, race, sexuality, or some combination thereof. A dialectical approach to collective agency defines the study of the reproduction and production of everyday life as the focal point of our research. The ability of human communities to engage in collective agency depends, in part, on their members' subjective evaluations of their identities and interests (that is, on consciousness) and on the historical processes and relations they enter into with other groups and communities. Individuals realize this social consciousness through the experience of everyday life. The ability of a social community to form social consciousness is not predetermined or given. Lived experience, cooperation, dialogue, and struggle produce consciousness. Struggle springs from the inevitability that the praxis of one group will be opposed by the praxis of other groups. For this reason, both consciousness raising and praxis often fail, generally resulting in unforeseen consequences.

For example, in the Colorado Coalfield War of 1913–1914, miners and their families created the class consciousness necessary for the solidarity of a strike. The shared experiences of men, women, and children in the workplace and in the home raised this consciousness. In the end, their collective agency failed when they lost the strike. However, the massacre of women and children stirred more Americans to support progressive causes that ultimately led to more rights, better benefits, and dignity for working people.

Many of the archaeologists who advocate individual agency also argue for a multivocal archaeology that requires archaeologists to surrender their authority as scholars and any claims of privileged knowledge. My colleagues and I have not done that. In México and at Ludlow we have surrendered the authority to unilaterally define research questions, but we have strived to use our craft as a tool to advance community interests. In México, the craft of archaeology has been the focus point of collaboration between Mexican and U.S. archaeologists. At Ludlow, we have used our craft to make the massacre news again, to connect modern observers to the events through artifacts and features, to understand the class-, gender-, and ethnic-based lived experience from which the strikers built consciousness, and to develop education programs.

A dialectical epistemology that stresses critique and knowledge has been our alternative to a relativistic multivocality. As Ollman comments, "What we understand about the world is determined by what the world is, who we are, and how we conduct our study" (2003:12). Ollman's observation accepts that a real past exists, but he also acknowledges that we cannot know that past apart from its making of the present. Thus, knowledge is a complex product of the observations that we can make of the archaeological record and the social context that we make them in. A dialectical epistemology seeks to weigh equally the subjectivities of knowing and the realities of the world but does not reduce knowledge to either. This is an intentionally uneasy epistemology. It rejects the security of true knowledge as well as the complacency of subjectivity. It is this discomfort and tension that provide the means to avoid the dangers of either extreme. In a dialectical approach, the evaluation of knowledge involves a four-part dialectic among the four Cs: coherence, correspondence, context, and consequences.

Feminist, indigenous, post-processual, and Marxist archaeologists have demonstrated that all knowledge is ultimately political. Empirical observations become significant, turn into knowledge, only by means of social discourses about the world. These discourses occur in the present and entail social and political interests. Accepting that knowledge is social and political, however, does not mean that empirical observations can not correspond or fail to correspond with reality (Eagleton 2002:103–109). Saying that the U.S. Declaration of Independence was signed on July 4, 1776, entails, among other things, a Western notion of time, the use of the Gregorian calendar, and prejudgments about the importance of this event and its date. The observation necessitates a culturally constructed awareness of how to make sense of the world, but it does correspond with reality, whereas the observation that the Declaration of Independence was signed December 23, 1951, does not.

Archaeologists need to retain some authority over the production of knowledge in order to assess correspondence. We undergo special training to master the perspectives and skills of our craft. People must be educated to think archaeologically, to acquire the background knowledge needed for archaeological research, and to learn the technical skills to do archaeology. Archaeologists make interpretations at all levels, from the first transect of a survey to the choice of illustrations for the final report (Hodder 1999). Realizing that the craft of archaeology entails interpretation does not, however, mean that it is simply subjective or that just anyone can do it.

Archaeologists need to retain the authority of our craft when the interests of communities spring from conceptions of the world that lack correspondence to our empirical observations or conflict with our existing knowledge. Cultural anthropologists have challenged our discipline to "speak truth to power." But what should scholars do when fictions support the subordinate and challenge the dominant? If we wield politically convenient falsehoods to support the cause, we lose any authority in the struggle. We cannot "speak truth" with deceit (Conklin 2003). Archaeological knowledge claims need to have some independence from the interests of social groups. This independence springs from our craft and is realized within the community of archaeologists.

The knowledge claims of archaeologists may come into conflict with the claims of the communities we work with. We encountered such conflicting claims during our work on the Colorado Coalfield War in the unfounded story that union members told of the National Guardsman ripping the fetus from its mother's womb with a bayonet. The story clearly demonized the guardsmen, and it spoke to the extent of animosity between the Guard and the strikers. Such contradictions can create beneficial tensions that force archaeologists and social groups to critically examine our dialogue. This critique may modify the perceptions and interests of the archeologists or the community or both, or it may reveal previously unrealized social relations and ideologies to any of them. In Colorado, our disbelief about the bayoneted fetus served to humanize the mine guards and state militia, which led archaeologists and union men and women to discuss why some working people would betray class solidarity and others would not. These discussions gained contemporary significance when they moved from individuals now dead to the scabs that crossed the steelworkers' picket lines at the Pueblo steel mill.

Archaeologists should practice their craft in the service of multiple communities. The craft of archaeology, however, lives in the community of archaeologists, and in order to develop, critique, modify, and enhance that craft, archaeologists must always interact within the community of archaeology. The community of archaeologists is who reviews, validates, and critiques the craft of archaeology and, through this critical process, lends authority to our craft. The internal dialogue of archaeology is indispensable, but it is not all that the discipline should engage in. Knowledge entails ideology, and for this reason archaeology has a political role in society, and it has the potential be used as a tool of oppression. The knowledge that we create also serves the social and political interests of other communities, and some of us should engage in praxis with those communities.

For archaeologists to work effectively with other communities, especially those outside the traditional middle class, we need to surrender some of our privilege. This privilege should not be the privilege and the authority that come from our craft. Rather, it should be the programmatic privilege to determine the questions, substance, and aspects of the archaeological record that we will study. In a praxis of archaeology, these factors should flow from a dialogue with the communities with whom we work. We can do research that is relevant to the interests of those communities if we collaborate with them in defining the research objectives, questions, and methods of our studies. By continuing the process of negotiation throughout the research process, we have the chance to engage in a praxis that will transform archaeology, communities, and knowledge.

WORKING WITH COMMUNITIES

An emancipatory praxis can exist only within real contexts of social relations, struggles, interests, institutions, and agents. Praxis has no importance or value in the abstract; it becomes significant only in its application. Thus, one of the most important questions of theory and method should be, How do we work with communities?

When archaeologists enter an area to do research, they step into a historically created social context. Taking that step inserts archaeologists into that context and into the social relationships that compose it. Specific historical experiences, cultures, interests, relations to other communities, and ideologies define each community. Archaeologists enter this social context as fully constituted social beings, with their own identities based on class, race, ethnicity, gender, profession, sexuality, and nationality. Communities will initially evaluate and interact with archaeologists on the basis of their perceptions of those identities, their historical experience with the social groups that the archaeologists represent, and their evaluation of the power relationships between themselves and the archaeologists. Archaeologists cannot assume that we will be judged by our intentions or by our personalities. Communities will stereotype archaeology and individual archaeologists. A historical understanding of social contexts provides archaeologists with the opportunity to counter stereotypes and to interact more effectively with the social groups affected by our research.

A historical understanding helps archaeologists structure their interaction with communities. With such understandings we can decide which communities we should oppose, educate, consult, collaborate with, or do any combination of these things. Voices can use the past to advance interests that archaeologists should oppose and resist. We have already considered examples of such malicious voices—the Nazi archaeology in Europe (Arnold 1990) and the Hindu nationalist archaeology at the Babri Mosque in Ajodhya, India (Romey 2004). Archaeologists who embrace an ethic of human emancipation must contest voices like these. The question of how to act is more difficult to answer when relations within subordinate communities alienate certain of their people from the others. Opposing the inequalities within the communities we work with could alienate their members or put the scholar in a paternalistic stance in relation to them or both. Here the archaeologist must weigh what the cost of larger emancipatory goals will be in terms of alienation within the community. If emancipation for the community means greater alienation for some subset of its members, then we need to question the larger effort.

As an indigenous archaeology has shown us, the key to praxis lies in collaboration. Collaboration occurs when individuals or social groups work together with integrated goals, interests, and practices. The dialogue of collaboration should go beyond an instrumentalist concern with resolving a conflict or respecting rights and responsibilities; it should be transformative of the parties involved. Each social group contributes different resources, skills, knowledge, authority, and interests to a collaborative effort. Collaboration entails combining these distinctive qualities to establish shared goals and practices. Effective collaboration usually starts with the definition of an objective or problem, so that all involved can have a say in this definition. In an emancipatory praxis, collaboration gives subordinate groups a greater voice in the practice of dominant groups. With true collaboration and the trust that comes with it, scholars can also engage a community with discussions of how to transform internal inequalities. As praxis, collaboration unifies knowledge, critique, and action to transform archaeologists' practice and the communities we work with.

The successes and failures in the Trincheras Tradition Project and the Archaeology of the 1913–1914 Colorado Coalfield War Project illustrate the intricacies of working with real communities. In each, archaeologists have stepped into historically created social contexts of which we have become a part. Each community has had its own historical experience, culture, interests, relations to other communities, and ideologies. These relationships have stereotyped and linked the participating communities and archaeologists in different ways. Each of these projects has involved archaeologists in education, consultation, and collaboration. In both cases, the most successful praxis has come from collaboration as opposed to education or consultation.

The Sonora project has presented a much more complex field of social relations and histories than the Colorado project. In Sonora, the archaeologists have engaged four communities divided by race, nationality, class, and language. In Colorado, class relations have separated working families and middle-class archaeologists. The histories of relationships between the communities have also varied. In Sonora, we entered into preexisting imperialistic relationships between Mexican and North American archaeologists. We brought with us a colonial history of conflict between archaeology and indigenous peoples, specifically the Tohono O'odham. These two parameters have created the bind of double colonialism on the border. At Ludlow, a class division has existed, but the relationship between archaeology and working families has been a new and unique one. As evident from the comment "they got fucked," different class perceptions of knowledge and action have distanced archaeologists and union members. We have had to overcome the popular stereotype of archaeologists as Indiana Jones and misunderstandings such as the idea that archaeologists study dinosaurs. We have not, however, had to transcend a history of conflict and bad feelings between the archaeological community and unionized workers in southern Colorado.

In both cases, praxis has followed from establishing linkages between the communities. Mexican and U.S. archaeologists share the craft of archaeology. We also share basic concepts about history and how to know the world that are different from those held by the Tohono O'odham. The project has revealed differences in the understanding that each group has of the craft of archaeology, but far more is shared than dissimilar. At Ludlow, the archaeologists from Binghamton University (both myself and the graduate students) have all been members of AFL-CIO affiliated unions. And the archaeologists from the University of Denver and Fort Lewis College have shared political positions and goals with the unionized workers of southern Colorado. We could honestly answer the pointed question, "Are you Republicans?" in the negative. In the halls of academia, in the steel mills, in the coal mines, in the corridors of hospitals, and working on county roads, we can all feel fast capitalism weathering away the control that we have over our work and family lives. In México and Colorado, these linkages and shared interests have become the basis for collaborative efforts between Mexican and U.S. archaeologists and between archaeologists and union families. In Sonora, we have not achieved collaboration with the Tohono O'odham, only consultation. Changes in the political position of Mexican archaeology and the challenges of fast capitalism to Mexican interests have prevented us from fulfilling the agreements we made with the Tohono O'odham.

FINAL THOUGHTS

It is obvious; it is painfully obvious that you are not
going to stop racism and fascism by writing songs about
it. I am surprised people ask me, still ask me that question: "Do you think that you are going to stop these
things by writing songs about it?" Of course you are
not going to stop it, but that doesn't stop you from
trying now, does it?

                                        Billy Bragg (1995)

The observation of English protest singer Billy Bragg about the efficacy of song writing for an emancipatory praxis could just as easily be applied to archaeology. It should also be obvious, painfully obvious, that doing archaeology will not stop racism and fascism, nor will it alone slow the wheels of fast capitalism. But this should not stop archaeologists from trying. I have argued that the power of archaeology to engage in a political praxis lies in its apparent irrelevance to political life and action. The political consequences of archaeology do not usually have direct costs for people's lives or for political issues. Inflation does not increase if we overestimate the volume of obsidian trade in the Neolithic of the Levant, and we cannot bring down a British government by exposing social inequalities in the Wessex culture. But it is archaeology's seeming irrelevance and uselessness as a political tool that have made it an effective instrument of ideology.

Political struggles over the past are first and foremost ideological, because their political nature is usually hidden or obscured. Archaeology produces symbols, knowledge, and heritage, which give rise to awareness and consciousness of group identity and are invoked to inspire and justify collective agency. Groups wage powerful struggles over what is remembered and what is forgotten about the past (Van Dyke and Alcock 2003). Archaeologists and the knowledge that we produce are part of those struggles, whether we like it or not. What we choose to remember, what we choose to study, what questions we ask, and how we frame the answers all have political importance for identity, heritage, social agency, and fast capitalism. What I have argued here is that we should make these decisions in a conscious praxis of archaeology.

In November 1938, Francisco Franco's Fascist army broke the back of the Spanish Republic at the battle of the Ebro River, and Barcelona fell in February 1939. Madrid would fall in March of the same year. Throughout the newly conquered areas, Fascist political officers hunted down officials of the Republican government, officers in the Republican army, intellectuals, teachers, and others for execution.

When the Fascists came to the Catalán town of Oleso de Monserrat, they rounded up ten men and two women and took them to a cemetery for execution. The army unit sent to perform the deed apparently had little stomach left for killing now that the war was over. The officer in charge of the execution squad stood the men and women up against the wall and instructed them to fall to the ground when the squad fired over their heads. The Fascist political officer on the scene, however, had no such qualms; she walked over to the prostrate men and women, drew her pistol, and shot each of them in the head. Her coup de grâce was badly aimed at one man, and the bullet passed through his cheeks. Wounded and bleeding, he stumbled back to his home in Oleso, where his family took him in and hid him. Three hours later the Fascists followed the trail of blood to his house. When they found him, they arrested two people who had hidden him. They took the wounded man and the two others to the cemetery at Oleso, shot them to death against the back wall, and buried them there.

In the fall of 2004, archaeologists from the Universitat Autònoma de Barcelona and bio-archaeologists from Binghamton University laid out excavations in the cemetery at Oleso (Gassiot 2005). The Associació per la Recuperació de la Memòria Històrica de Catalunya (the Catalán Association for the Recovery of Historic Memory) had asked them to come and locate the remains of the people shot to death in February 1939. After several weeks of work, they had not located any of the individuals (Gassiot et al. 2005). As I finish this book, they are planning a second field season to recover the memory of the victims of Spanish fascism in Oleso and to continue a praxis of archaeology.

References

AAUP

    2000 Statement on Graduate Students. American Association of University Professors, http://www.aaup.org/AAUP/pubsres/policydocs/statementon graduatestudents.htm, accessed October 29, 2006.

ACRA

    1996 CRM Salaries and Other Statistics. American Cultural Resources Association, http://www.acra-crm.org/crmstats1996.html, accessed October 1, 2005.

    1997 ACRA Member Questionnaire Results. American Cultural Resources Association, http://www.mindspring.com/~wheaton/questionnaire.html, accessed April 20, 1997.

    2005 ACRA Members. American Cultural Resources Association, http://www.acra-crm.org/ACRAMembership.html, accessed October 1, 2005.

Acuto, Flix

    2003 Archaeology and Political Commitment: The Archaeology of the Disappeared. Paper presented at the Radical Archaeology Theory Symposium Conference, October 17–18, Binghamton, N.Y.

Agger, Ben

    1989 *Fast Capitalism: A Critical Theory of Significance.* University of Illinois Press, Urbana-Champagne.

    1997 *Critical Social Theory: An Introduction.* Westview Press, Boulder, Colo.

    2004 *Speeding Up Fast Capitalism: Cultures, Jobs, Families, Schools, Bodies.* Rowman and Littlefield, Lanham, Md.

Alonso, Ana María

 1988 The Effects of Truth: Re-presentations of the Past and the Imagining of Community. *Journal of Historical Sociology* 1(1):33–58.

 1995 *Thread of Blood: Colonialism, Revolution, and Gender on Mexico's Northern Frontier.* University of Arizona Press, Tucson.

Althusser, Louis

 1969 *For Marx.* Vintage, New York.

Altschul, Jeffrey H.

 2006 The Register: Forward. *SAA Archaeological Record* 6(3):5–6.

Anderson, Benedict

 1983 *Imagined Communities: Reflections on the Origin and Spread of Nationalism.* Verso, London.

Archaeology

 1996 Archaeology Magazine: A Subscriber Profile (information packet to potential advertisers). *Archaeology Magazine,* New York.

Ardren, Tracy

 2004 Where Are the Maya in Ancient Maya Tourism? Advertising and the Appropriation of Culture. In *Marketing Heritage: Archaeology and the Consumption of the Past,* edited by Yorke Rowan and Uzi Baram, pp. 103–116. AltaMira Press, Walnut Creek, Calif.

Arnold, Bettina

 1990 The Past as Propaganda: Totalitarian Archaeology in Nazi Germany. *Antiquity* 64:464–478.

 2004 Dealing with the Devil: The Faustian Bargain of Archaeology under Dictatorship. In *Archaeology under Dictatorship,* edited by M. L. Galaty and Charles Watkinson, pp. 191–212. Kluwer Academic/Plenum Publishers, New York.

Aronowitz, Stanley

 1997 Academic Unionism and the Future of Higher Education. In *Will Teach for Food: Academic Labor in Crisis,* edited by C. Nelson, pp. 181–217. University of Minnesota Press, Minneapolis.

Ashmore, Wendy, and Robert J. Sharer

 1993 *Archaeology: Discovering Our Past.* 2nd ed. Mayfield Publishing, Mountain View, Calif.

Association Research, Inc.

 2005 Salary Survey Conducted for the Society for American Archaeology and the Society for Historical Archaeology. http://www.saa.org/membership/survey/full.pdf, accessed September 5, 2005.

Atalay, Sonya

2006 Indigenous Archaeology as Decolonializing Practice. *American Indian Quarterly* 30(3–4):280–310.

Badillo, J. S.

1995 The Theme of the Indigenous in the National Projects of the Hispanic Caribbean. In *Making Alternative Histories: The Practice of Archaeology and History in Non-Western Society,* edited by P. T. Schmidt and T. Patterson, pp. 25–46. School of American Research, Santa Fe.

Ball, Stephen J.

2003 *Class Strategies and the Education Market: The Middle Classes and Social Advantage.* RoutledgeFalmer, London.

Baram, Uzi, and Yorke Rowan

2004 Archaeology after Nationalism: Globalization and the Consumption of the Past. In *Marketing Heritage: Archaeology and the Consumption of the Past,* edited by Yorke Rowan and Uzi Baram, pp. 3–26. AltaMira Press, Walnut Creek, Calif.

Barbosa, Rodolfo Martínez

2002 One Hundred and Sixty Years of Exile: Vaimaca Pirú and the Campaign to Repatriate His Remains to Uruguay. In *The Dead and Their Possessions: Repatriation in Principle, Policy and Practice,* edited by C. Fforde, J. Hubert and P. Turnbull, pp. 218–221. Routledge, London.

Barbour, Warren T. D.

1994 Musings on a Dream Deferred. *Federal Archaeology Report* 7(1):12–13.

Bardon, Jonathan

1992 *A History of Ulster.* Blackstaff Press, Belfast.

Barker, Frederick

1988 Archaeology and the Heritage Industry. *Archaeological Review from Cambridge* 7(2):141–145.

Barrett, John

1994 *Fragments from Antiquity: An Archaeology of Social Life in Britain, 2900–1200 B.C.* Blackwell Publishers, Oxford, U.K.

2000 A Thesis on Agency. In *Agency in Archaeology,* edited by M. Dobres and J. Robb, pp. 61–68. Cambridge University Press, Cambridge.

Bassett, Everett

1994 "We Took Care of Each Other Like Families Were Meant To": Gender, Social Organization, and Wage Labor Among the Apache at Roosevelt. In *Those of Little Note: Gender, Race, and Class in Historical Archaeology,* edited by Elizabeth Scott, pp. 55–79. University of Arizona Press, Tucson.

Bate, Felipe

1998 *El proceso de investigación en arqueología.* Crítica, Barcelona.

Baxter, Jane Eva

2005 Gendered Perceptions of Archaeology: A Perspective from the SAA Member Needs Assessment Survey. *SAA Archaeological Record* 5(4):7–9.

Beaudry, Mary C.

1994 Women Historical Archaeologists: Who's Counting. In *Equity Issues for Women in Archaeology*, edited by M. C. Nelson, , S. M. Nelson, and A. Wylie, pp. 225–228. Archaeological Papers of the American Anthropological Association 5. American Anthropological Association, Washington, D.C.

Beaudry, Mary (editor)

1988 *Documentary Archaeology in the New World.* Cambridge University Press, Cambridge.

Beaudry, Mary C., and Stephen Mrozowski

1988 The Archaeology of Work and Home Life in Lowell, Massachusetts: An Interdisciplinary Study of the Boott Cotton Mills Corporation. *Industrial Archaeology* 19:1–22.

Benavidas, O. Hugo

2001 Returning to the Source: Social Archaeology as Latin American Philosophy. *Latin American Antiquity* 12(4):355–370.

Bender, Barbara

1998 *Stonehenge: Making Space.* Berg, Oxford, U.K.

Bender, Susan J., and George S. Smith (editors)

2000 *Teaching Archaeology in the Twenty-first Century.* Society for American Archaeology, Washington, D.C.

Benedek, Emily

1999 *The Wind Won't Know Me: A History of the Navajo-Hopi Land Dispute.* University of Oklahoma Press, Norman.

Ben-Yehuda, Nachman

2002 *Sacrificing Truth: Archaeology and the Myth of Masada.* Prometheus/ Humanity Books, New York.

Berggren, Asa, and Ian Hodder

2003 Social Practice, Method, and Some Problems of Field Archaeology. *American Antiquity* 68(3):421–434.

Bernal, Ignacio

1980 *A History of Mexican Archaeology: The Vanished Civilizations of Middle America.* Thames and Hudson, London.

Bernbeck, Reinhard

2003a The Ideologies of Intentionality. *Rundbrief der Arbeltsgemeinschaft Theorie en der Archäologie* 2(2):44–50.

2003b War-Time Academic Professionalism. *Public Archaeology.* 3:112–116.

Bernbeck, Reinhard, and Susan Pollock

1996 Ayodha, Archaeology, and Identity. *Current Anthropology* 37 (supplement):138–142.

Beshoar, Barron B.

1957 *Out of the Depths: The Story of John R. Lawson, A Labor Leader.* Colorado Historical Commission and Denver Trades and Labor Assembly, Denver.

Blakey, Michael L.

2003 Return to the African Burial Ground. *Archaeology Magazine,* http://www.archaeology.org/online/interviews/blakey/, accessed September 15, 2005.

Blakey, Michael, and Cheryl LaRoche

1997 Seizing Intellectual Power: The Dialogue at the New York African Burial Ground. *Historical Archaeology* 31(3):84–106.

Blanton, Dennis B.

1995 The Case for CRM Training in Academic Institutions. *SAA Bulletin* 13(4):40–41

Bloch, Maurice

1985 *Marxism and Anthropology.* Oxford University Press, Oxford, U.K.

Bloom, Allen

1987 *The Closing of the American Mind.* Simon and Schuster, New York.

Bodley, John H.

1983 *Anthropology and Contemporary Human Problems.* Mayfield Publishing, Mountain View, Calif.

Bragg, Billy

1995 *Billy Bragg and the Red Stars Live Bootleg.* Compact disc recording of Phoenix Festival, Stratford upon Avon, U.K., 1993. © Billy Bragg, produced by Union Productions Limited, London.

Brandon, R. Joe

2003 Shovelbums.org. *SAA Archaeological Record* 3(2):38–40.

Braniff, Beatrice, and Richard S. Felger

1976 Sonora: Antropología del desierto. *Noroeste de México 1.* Centro INAH Sonora, Hermosillo.

BRASS El Pilar Project

2006 The BRASS/El Pilar Program: Archaeology under the Canopy. http://www.marc.ucsb.edu/elpilar/brass/phome.shtml, accessed September 1, 2007.

Braverman, Harry

1974 *Labor and Monopoly Capitalism: The Degradation of Work in the Twentieth Century.* Monthly Review Press, New York.

1989 The Degradation of Work in the Twentieth Century. *Monthly Review* 41(5):35–47.

Brumfiel, Elizabeth, M.

1991 Weaving and Cooking: Women's Production in Aztec Mexico. In *Engendering Archaeology*, edited by J. Gero and M. Conkey, pp. 224–254. Blackwell Publishers, Oxford, U.K.

Buchli, Victor

1999 *An Archaeology of Socialism*. Berg, Oxford, U.K.

Cameron, Ardis

1993 *Radicals of the Worst Sort: Laboring Women in Lawrence Massachusetts 1860–1912*. University of Illinois Press, Urbana.

Caso, Alfonso

1958 *Aztecs: People of the Sun*. University of Oklahoma Press, Norman.

Casteñeda, Quetzil E.

1996 *In the Museum of Maya Culture: Touring Chichén Itzá*. University of Minnesota Press, Minneapolis.

2005 Tourism "Wars" in the Yucatán. *Anthropology News* 46(5):8–9.

Castro, P. V., S. Gili, V. Lull, R. Micó, C. Rihuete, R. Risch, and E. S. Yll

1998 Towards a Theory of Social Production and Social Practice. In *Craft Specialization: Operational Sequences and Beyond*, Vol. 4, edited by S. Milliken and M. Vidale, pp. 24–29. BAR International Series 720. Archaeopress, Oxford, U.K.

Castro, P. V., Vicente Lull, and Rafel Micó Pérez

1992 La fragilidad del método hipotético-deductivo en la arqueología procesual. *Boletín de Antropología Americana* 26:33–48.

CGEU

2006 The Coalition of Graduate Employee Unions. http://cgeu.org/index.php, accessed July 18, 2006.

Chernykh, E. N.

1995 Postscript: Russian Archaeology after the Collapse of the USSR—Infrastructural Crisis and the Resurgence of Old and New Nationalisms. In *Nationalism, Politics and the Practice of Archaeology*, edited by P. L. Kohl and C. Fawcett, pp. 139–148. Cambridge University Press, Cambridge.

Chester, Hilary, Nan A. Rothchild, and Diana diZerega Wall

1994 Women in Historical Archaeology: The SHA Survey. In *Equity Issues for Women in Archaeology*, edited by M. C. Nelson, S. M. Nelson, and A. Wylie, pp. 213–218. Archaeological Papers of the American Anthropological Association 5. American Anthropological Association, Washington, D.C.

Chicone, Sarah

2006 Feeding, Clothing and Sheltering Southern Colorado's Working Poor:

Towards an Archaeological Analysis of Poverty. Ph.D. dissertation, Department of Anthropology, Binghamton University, Binghamton, N.Y.

Childe, V. G.

1947 *History.* Cobbett Press, London.

1949 The Sociology of Knowledge. *Modern Quarterly,* n.s.(4):302–309.

1956 *Society and Knowledge.* Harper and Brothers, New York.

1979 Prehistory and Marxism. *Antiquity* 53:93–95.

1989 Retrospective. In *The Pastmasters: Eleven Modern Pioneers of Archaeology,* edited by G. Daniels and C. Chippendale, pp. 10–19. Thames and Hudson, London.

Chippendale, Christopher

1983 *Stonehenge Complete.* Thames and Hudson, London.

1986 Stoned Henge: Events and Issues at the Summer Solstice. *World Archaeology* 18(1):38–58.

Clark, G. A.

1996 NAGPRA and the Demon Haunted World. *Archaeological Record* 14(5):3.

Clifford, James

2004 Looking Several Ways: Anthropology and Native Heritage in Alaska. *Current Anthropology* 45(1):5–30.

Collier, George A.

1994 *Basta! Land and the Zapatista Rebellion in Chiapas.* Institute for Food and Development Policy, Oakland.

Colwell-Chanthaphonh, Chip

2006 Dreams at the Edge of the World and Other Evocations of O'odham History. *Archaeologies: Journal of the World Archaeological Congress* 2(1):20–44.

Colwell-Chanthaphonh, Chip, and T. J. Ferguson

2004 Virtue Ethics and the Practice of History: Native Americans and Archaeologists along the San Pedro Valley of Arizona. *Journal of Social Archaeology* 4(1):5–27.

2006 Memory Pieces and Footprints: Multivocality and the Meanings of Ancient Times and Ancestral Places among the Zuni and Hopi. *Current Anthropology* 108(1):148–162.

Conkey, Margaret W.

2005a Doing Theory: A Feminist Perspective. Paper presented at the annual meeting of the Society for American Archaeology, April, Salt Lake City.

2005b Dwelling at the Margins, Action at the Intersection? Feminist and Indigenous Archaeologies, 2005. *Archaeologies* 1(1):9–59.

Conkey, Margaret, and Joan Gero

1991 Tensions, Pluralities, and Engendering Archaeology: An Introduction to Women and Prehistory. In *Engendering Archaeology*, edited by J. Gero and M. Conkey, pp. 3–30. Blackwell Publishers, Oxford, U.K.

Conkey, Margaret W., and Janet Spector

1984 Archaeology and the Study of Gender. *Advances in Archaeological Method and Theory* 7:1–29.

Conkey, Margaret, and Sarah Williams

1991 Original Narratives: The Political Economy of Gender in Archaeology. In *Gender at the Crossroads of Knowledge: Feminist Anthropology in the Postmodern Era*, edited by M. di Leonardo, pp. 102–139. University of California Press, Berkeley.

Conklin, Beth A.

2003 Speaking Truth to Power. *Anthropology News* 44(7):5.

Cox, Susan Jane Buck

1985 No Tragedy on the Commons. *Environmental Ethics* 7:49–62.

Crehan, Kate

2002 *Gramsci, Culture and Anthropology*. University of California Press, Berkeley.

Daniel, Glyn

1981 *A Short History of Archaeology*. Thames and Hudson, London.

de Boer, Trent

2004 *Shovel Bum: Comix of Archaeological Field Life*. AltaMira Press, Walnut Creek, Calif.

DeCicco, Gabriel

1988 A Public Relations Primer. *American Antiquity* 53(4):840–856.

De Cunzo, Lu Ann, and Bernard L. Herman (editors)

1996 *Historical Archaeology and the Study of American Culture*. Henry Francis du Pont Winterthur Museum, Winterthur, Del.

Deetz, James

1993 *Flowerdew Hundred: The Archaeology of a Virginia Plantation, 1619–1864*. University of Virginia Press, Charlottesville.

Delle, James A.

1994 The Dane's Cast and Black Pig's Dyke: Politics, Nation Building and Archaeology in Ireland, 1894–1994. Paper presented at the Theoretical Archaeology Group Conference, December, University of Bradford, U.K.

Delle, J. A., S. A. Mrozowski, and R. Paynter (editors)

2000 *Lines That Divide: Historical Archaeologies of Race, Class, and Gender*. University of Tennessee Press, Knoxville.

Deloria, Vine, Jr.

1993 *God Is Red: A Native View of Religion.* 2nd ed. North American Press, Golden, Colo.

1997 Conclusion: Anthros, Indians, and Planetary Reality. In *Indians and Anthropologists: Vine Deloria Jr. and the Critique of Anthropology,* edited by T. Biolsi and L. J. Zimmerman, pp. 209–221. University of Arizona Press, Tucson.

2002 *Evolution, Creationism, and Other Modern Myths.* Fulcrum Publishing, Golden, Colo.

Deloria, Vine, Jr., and Clifford M. Lytle

1984 *The Nations Within: The Past and Future of American Indian Sovereignty.* Pantheon Books, New York.

Díaz-Andreu, Margarita, and Timothy Champion

1996 *Nationalism and Archaeology in Europe.* Westview Press, Boulder, Colo.

DiGiacomo, Susan

1996 The "Other" Within. *NEAA Newsletter* 20(3):2–5.

Dobres, Marcia-Anne, and John Robb

2000 *Agency in Archaeology.* Routledge, London.

DOL (U.S. Department of Labor)

2005 Service Contract Act Directory of Occupations 29000 TECHNICAL OCCUPATIONS, U.S. Department of Labor. http://www.dol.gov/esa/regs/compliance/whd/wage/p29000.htm, accessed October 1, 2005.

Domhoff, G. William

1983 *Who Rules America Now?* Simon and Schuster, New York.

1996 *State Autonomy or Class Dominance?* Aldine De Gruyter, New York.

Dowson, T. A. (editor)

2000 Queer Archaeologies. *World Archaeology* 32(2):161–274.

Duke, Philip

1991 Cultural Resource Management and the Professional Archaeologist. *SAA Bulletin* 9(4):10–11.

2007 *The Tourist's Gaze, the Cretan's Glance: Archaeology and Tourism on a Greek Island.* Left Coast Press, Walnut Creek, Calif.

Duke, Philip, and Gary Matlock

N.d. The Town Built on a Pithouse: The Archaeology of Durango, Colorado. Manuscript. Fort Lewis College, Durango.

Duke, Philip, and Dean Saitta

1998 An Emancipatory Archaeology for the Working Class. *Assemblage* 4, http://www.shef.ac.uk/~assem/4/4duk_sai.html, accessed March 27, 2000.

Dunn, John

　1994 Crisis of the Nation State? *Political Studies* 42(1):3–15.

Durrenberger, Paul

　2006 On the Invisibility of Class in America. *Anthropology News* 47(8):9–10.

EAAF (Equipo Argentina de Antropolgía Forense)

　2005 *Argentine Forensic Anthropology Team Annual Report.* Buenos Aires.

Eagleton, Terry

　1996 *The Illusions of Postmodernism.* Blackwell Publishers, Oxford, U.K.

　2002 *After Theory.* Basic Books, New York.

Ehrenreich, Barbara

　1989 *Fear of Falling: The Inner Life of the Middle Class.* Pantheon Books, New York.

Ehrenreich, Barbara, and John Ehrenreich

　1979 The Professional Managerial Class. In *Between Labor and Capital,* edited by P. Walker, pp. 5–45. South End Press, Boston.

Elkin, Mike

　2006 Opening Franco's Graves. *Archaeology* 59(5):85–86.

Endere, María Luz

　2002 The Reburial Issue in Argentina: A Growing Conflict. In *The Dead and Their Possessions: Repatriation in Principle, Policy and Practice,* edited by C. Fforde, J. Hubert, and P. Turnbull, pp. 266–283. Routledge, London.

Engels, Friedrich

　1927 *The Dialectics of Nature.* Foreign Language Publishers, Moscow.

Enloe, Cynthia

　2004 *The Curious Feminist.* University of California Press, Berkeley.

Ensor, B. E.

　2000 Social Formations, Modo de Vida, and Conflict in Archaeology. *American Antiquity* 65(1):15–42.

Erickson, Winston P.

　1994 *Sharing the Desert: The Tohono O'odham in History.* University of Arizona Press, Tucson.

Estévež, Jordi, and Assumpció Vila

　1999 *Piedra a piedra: Historia de la construcción del paleolítico en la Península Ibérica.* BAR International Series 805. Oxford, U.K.

　2006 *Una historia de la investigación sobre el paleolítica en la Península Ibérica.* Editorial Sintesis, Madrid.

Evens, Patsy, Dave Givens, and Timothy Jablonski

　1997 Anthropology PhDs: Findings from the AAA Biennial Survey. *Anthropology Newsletter* 38(6):17–18.

Fagan, Brian

2006 So You Want to Be an Archaeologist? *Archaeology Magazine* 59(3): 59–64.

Falk, John H., and Lynn D. Dierking

1992 *The Museum Experience.* Whalesback Books, Washington, D.C.

Fantasia, Rick, and Kim Voss

2004 *Hard Work: Remaking the American Labor Movement.* University of California Press, Berkeley.

Faulkner, Neil

2000 Archaeology from Below. *Public Archaeology* 1(1):21–33.

Fernández, Victor M.

2006 *Una arqueología crítica: Ciencia, ética y política en la construcción pasado.* Crítica, Barcelona.

Fforde, Cressida

2004 *Collecting the Dead: Archaeology and the Reburial Issue.* Duckworth, London.

Fforde, Cressida, Jane Hubert, and Paul Turnbull

2002 *The Dead and Their Possessions: Repatriation in Principle, Policy and Practice.* Routledge, London.

Fine-Dare, Kathleen S.

2002 *Grave Injustice: The American Indian Repatriation Movement and NAGPRA.* University of Nebraska Press, Lincoln.

Finn, Christine

1997 Leaving More Than Footprints: Modern Votive Offerings at Chaco Canyon Prehistoric Site. *Antiquity* 71:169–178.

Fitting, James C., and Albert C. Goodyear

1979 Client-Oriented Archaeology: An Exchange of Views. *Journal of Field Archaeology* 6:352–360.

Fontana, Bernard, L.

1981 *Of Earth and Little Rain: The Papago Indians.* Northland Press, Flagstaff.

Ford, Richard I.

1973 Archaeology Serving Humanity. In *Research and Theory in Current Archaeology*, edited by C. Redman, pp. 83–93. John Wiley, New York.

Foster, John Bellamy

2006 Aspects of Class in the United States: An Introduction. *Monthly Review* 58(3):1–5.

Foster, John Bellamy, Harry Magdoff, and Michael D. Yates

2001 The New Economy: Myth and Reality. *Monthly Review* 52(11):1–15.

2002 The New Face of Capitalism: Slow Growth, Excess Capital, and a Mountain of Debt. *Monthly Review* 53(11):1–14.

Foundation Topography of Terror

2002 Foundation Topography of Terror in Berlin: New Exhibition and Documentation Center. http://www.topographie.de/en/index.htm#, accessed July 11, 2005.

Fowler, Donald

1987 Uses of the Past: Archaeology in the Service of the State. *American Antiquity* 52(2):229–248.

Franklin, Maria

1997 Why Are There So Few Black American Archaeologists? *Antiquity* 71:799–801.

2001 A Black Feminist Inspired Archaeology? *Journal of Social Archaeology* 1(1):108–125.

Fried, Morton H.

1967 *The Evolution of Political Society.* Random House, New York.

Fritz, John M.

1973 Relevance, Archeology and Subsistence Theory. In *Research and Theory in Current Archeology,* edited by C. L. Redman, 59–82. John Wiley and Sons, New York.

Frohlich, Bruno, and David Hunt

2006 A History Not to Be Forgotten: Mass Burials in Mongolia. *AnthroNotes* 27(1):1–5.

Frykman, Jonas

1987 *Culture Builders: A Historical Anthropology of Middle Class Life.* Rutgers University Press, New Brunswick, N.J.

1990 What People Do but Seldom Say. *Ethnologia Scandinavica* 20:50–62.

Galaty, Michael L., and Charles Watkinson (editors)

2004 *Archaeology under Dictatorship.* Kluwer Academic/Plenum Publishers, New York.

Gamble, Clive

2001 *Archaeology: The Basics.* Routledge, London.

Gandara, Manuel

1980 La vieja "nueva arqueología." *Boletín de Antropología Americana* 2:7–45

1992 *La arqueología oficial mexicana: Causas y efectos.* Colección Divulgación del INAH, Mexico.

Gassiot, Ermengol

2005 Arqueología forense de la Guerra Civil: Justícia y memoria de la represión fascista. *Mientras Tanto* 97:95–112.

Gassiot, Ermengol, Joaquim Oltra, and Elena Sintes

2005 Recuperació de la memòria dels afusellaments de febrero de 1939 a Olesa de Montserrat: Informe preliminar de la intervenció al Cementiri Vell (novembre de 2004). Manuscript on file, Departament de Prehistòria de la Universitat Autònoma de Barcelona, Bella Terra, Catalunya.

Gassiot, Ermengol, and Beatrice Palomar

2000 Arqueología de la praxis: Información histórica de la acción social. *Complutum* 11:87–99.

Gassiot, Ermengol, Beatrice Palomar, and Gustavo Ruiz

1999 Brief Outline of the Marxist Archeology in the Spanish State. *European Journal of Archaeology* 2(3):234–236.

Gellately, Robert

2002 *Backing Hitler: Consent and Coercion in Nazi Germany*. Oxford University Press, Oxford, U.K.

Gero, Joan M.

1983 Gender Bias in Archaeology: A Cross-Cultural Perspective. In *The Socio-politics of Archaeology*, edited by J. M. Gero, D. Lacey, and M. Blakey, pp. 51–57. University of Massachusetts, Department of Anthropology Research Report 23. Amherst.

1985 Socio-politics and the Women-at-Home Ideology. *American Antiquity* 50:342–350.

1989 Producing Prehistory, Controlling the Past: The Case of New England Beehives. In *Critical Traditions in Contemporary Archaeology: Essays in the Philosophy, History and Socio-politics of Archaeology*, edited by V. Pinsky and A. Wylie, pp. 96–103. Cambridge University Press, Cambridge.

Gilchrist, Roberta

1994 *Gender and Material Culture: The Archaeology of Religious Women*. Routledge, London.

1999 *Gender and Archaeology: Contesting the Past*. Routledge, London.

Gilman, Antonio

1989 Marxism in American Archaeology. In *Archaeological Thought in America*, edited by C. C. Lamberg-Karlovsky, pp. 63–73. Cambridge University Press, Cambridge.

1993 Historia y Marxismo en la arqueología anglo-sajona. *Arqrítica* 6:6–7.

Gitelman, Howard

1988 *Legacy of the Ludlow Massacre: A Chapter in American Industrial Relations*. University of Pennsylvania Press, Philadelphia.

Given, Michael

2004 *The Archaeology of the Colonized*. Routledge, London.

Givens, David B., and Timothy Jablonski

  1996 Applied/Practicing Anthropology: 1996–2000. *Anthropology Newsletter* 37(8):5.

Godelier, Maurice

  1986 *The Mental and the Material: Thought, Economy, and Society.* Verso, London.

Golden, Jonathan

  2004 Targeting Heritage: The Abuse of Symbolic Sites in Modern Conflicts. In *Marketing Heritage: Archaeology and the Consumption of the Past,* edited by Yorke Rowan and Uzi Baram, pp. 183–202. AltaMira Press, Walnut Creek, Calif.

Gonzales, Michael J.

  2002 *The Mexican Revolution, 1910–1940.* University of New Mexico Press, Albuquerque.

Gottlieb, Roger (editor)

  1989 *An Anthology of Western Marxism: From Lukacs and Gramsci to Socialist-Feminism.* Oxford University Press, Oxford, U.K.

Gramsci, Antonio

  1971 *Selections from the Prison Notebooks.* International Publishers, New York.

  1994 *Letters from Prison,* Vol. 2. Edited by F. Rosengarten. Columbia University Press, New York.

Griswold del Castillo, Richard

  1990 *The Treaty of Guadalupe Hidalgo: A Legacy of Conflict.* University of Oklahoma Press, Norman.

Grosby, Steven

  2005 *Nationalism: A Very Short Introduction.* Oxford University Press, Oxford, U.K.

Habermas, Jürgen

  1984 *The Theory of Communicative Action.* Beacon Press, Boston.

Hall, Martin, and Pia Bombardella

  2005 Las Vegas in Africa. *Journal of Social Archaeology* 5(1):5–24.

Hamilakis, Yannis

  1996 Through the Looking Glass: Nationalism, Archaeology and the Politics of Identity. *Antiquity* 70:975–978.

  2003 Antiquities and National Imagination in Greece. In *The Politics of Archaeology and Identity in a Global Context,* edited by Susan Kane, pp. 51–78. Archaeological Institute of America, Boston.

  2005 Whose World and Whose Archaeology? The Colonial Present and the

Return of the Political. *Archaeologies: Journal of the World Archaeology Congress* 1(2):94–101.

Hamilakis, Yannis, and Phil Duke (editors)

2007 *Archaeology and Capitalism.* Left Coast Press, Walnut Creek, Calif.

Hammond, Guyton B.

1993 *Conscience and Its Recovery: From the Frankfurt School to Feminism.* University Press of Virginia, Charlottesville.

Hardesty, Donald L.

1988 *The Archaeology of Mines and Mining: The View from the Silver State.* Society for Historical Archaeology, Pleasant Hill, Calif.

Hardin, Garrett

1968 The Tragedy of the Commons. *Science* 162:1243–1248.

Harding, Sandra

1986 *The Science Question in Feminism.* Cornell University Press, Ithaca, N.Y.

Hardt, Michael, and Antonio Negri

2000 *Empire.* Harvard University Press, Cambridge, Mass.

Harris, Nigel

1990 *National Liberation.* University of Nevada Press, Reno.

Hartman, Heidi

1981 The Unhappy Marriage of Marxism and Feminism: Towards a More Progressive Union. In *Women and Revolution,* edited by L. Sargent, pp. 1–4. South End Press, Boston.

Harvey, David

2000 *Spaces of Hope.* University of California Press, Berkeley.

Hawkes, David

2003 *Ideology.* 2nd ed. Routledge, London.

Hays-Gilpin, Kelley, and David S. Whitley

1998 *Reader in Gender Archaeology.* Routledge, London.

Hegmon, Michelle

2003 Setting Theoretical Egos Aside: Issues and Theories in North American Archaeology. *American Antiquity* 68(2):213–244.

Hesse, Herman

1969 *The Glass Bead Game.* Holt, Rinehart and Winston, New York.

Hetherington, Kevin

2000 *New Age Travellers: Vanloads of Uproarious Humanity.* Continuum International Publishing Group, London.

Hewison, Robert

1987 *The Heritage Industry: Britain in a Climate of Decline.* Methuen, London.

Hill, James N.

1970 Prehistoric Social Organization in the American Southwest: Theory and Method. In *Reconstructing Prehistoric Pueblo Societies,* edited by W. A. Longacre, pp. 11–58. University of New Mexico Press, Albuquerque.

Hill, Rick

1994 Repatriation Must Heal Old Wounds. In *Reckoning with the Dead,* edited by T. L. Bray and T. W. Killion, pp. 184–186. Smithsonian Institution Press, Washington, D.C.

Hirst, K. Kris

2005 Have Trowel Will Travel. *About Archaeology,* http://archaeology.about .com/cs/fieldlabgear/a/havetrowel1.htm, accessed October 1, 2005.

Hobart, Mark

1993 *An Anthropological Critique of Development.* Taylor and Francis, London.

Hobsbawm, Eric J.

1983 Mass-Producing Traditions: Europe, 1870–1914. In *The Invention of Tradition,* edited by E. Hobsbawm and T. Ranger, pp. 263–308. Cambridge University Press, Cambridge.

Hodder, Ian

1984 Archaeology in 1984. *Antiquity* 58:25–32.

1991 *Archaeological Theory in Europe: The Last Three Decades.* Routledge, London.

1998 The Past as Passion and Play: Çatalhöyük as a Site of Conflict in the Construction of Multiple Pasts. *Archaeology under Fire: Nationalism, Politics and Heritage in the Eastern Mediterranean and Middle East,* edited by Lynn Meskell, pp. 111–123. Routledge, London.

1999 *The Archaeological Process: An Introduction.* Blackwell Publishers, Oxford, U.K.

2006 *The Leopard's Tale: Revealing the Mysteries of Çatalhöyük.* Thames and Hudson, London.

Hodder, Ian (editor)

1982 *Symbolic and Structural Archaeology.* Cambridge University Press, Cambridge.

2000 *Towards Reflexive Method in Archaeology: The Example at Çatalhöyük.* McDonald Institute for Archaeological Research/British Institute of Archaeology at Ankara, Monograph no. 28, Ankara.

Holmes, Douglas R.

2000 *Integral Europe: Fast-Capitalism, Multiculturalism, Neofascism.* Princeton University Press, Princeton, N.J.

hooks, bell

2000 *Feminism is for Everybody.* South End Press, Cambridge, Mass.

Hooper-Greenhill, Eilean

1994 *Museums and Their Visitors*. Routledge, London.

Horkheimer, Max

1982 *Dialectics of Enlightenment*. Continuum, London.

INAH (Instituto Nacional de Antropología y Historia)

1994 *Reglamento del Consejo de Arqueología*. INAH, México.

Indian Claims Commission

1978 *United States Indian Claims Commission Final Report*. U.S. Government Printing Office, Washington, D.C.

Isaacson, Ken, and Stephanie Ford

2005 Looking Forward—Looking Back: Shaping a Shared Future. In *Indigenous Archaeologies: Decolonizing Theory and Practice,* edited by C. Smith and H. M. Wobst, pp. 354–367. Routledge, London.

Jacobe, Monica

2006 Contingent Faculty across the Disciplines. *Academe* 92(6):43–49.

Jacobson, Michael

2006 The Rise and Fall of Place: The Development of a Sense of Place and Community in Colorado's Southern Coalfields, 1890–1930. Ph.D. dissertation. Department of Anthropology, Binghamton University, Binghamton, N.Y.

Jacoby, Russell

2002 *Dialectic of Defeat: Contours of Western Marxism*. Cambridge University Press, Cambridge.

Jameson, Frederic

1992 *Postmodernism, or, the Cultural Logic of Late Capitalism*. Duke University Press, Durham, N.C.

1997 Five Theses on Actually Existing Marxism. In *In Defense of History: Marxism and the Postmodern Agenda,* edited by E. M. Wood and J. B. Foster, pp. 175–183. Monthly Review Press, New York.

Jameson, John H., Jr. (editor)

1997 *Presenting Archaeology to the Public: Digging for Truths*. AltaMira, Walnut Creek, Calif.

Jancius, Angela

2006 Class in the Academy: Our Achilles' Heel. *Anthropology News* 47(8): 11–12.

Johnson, Matthew H.

1989 Conceptions of Agency in Archaeological Interpretation. *Journal of Anthropological Archaeology* 8:189–211.

1999 *Archaeological Theory: An Introduction*. Blackwell Publishers, Oxford, U.K.

Jones, Mary Harris

   2004 Autobiography *of Mother Jones.* Dover Publications, Mineola, N.Y. Originally published 1925.

Jones, Sian

   1997 *The Archaeology of Ethnicity: Constructing Identities in the Past and Present.* Routledge, London.

Joseph, Tamara, and Jon Curtiss

   1997 Why Graduate Student Unions Need Your Support. *On Campus* 16(8):14.

Joyce, Rosemary A.

   2002 *The Languages of Archaeology.* Blackwell Publishing, Oxford, U.K.

   2003 Archaeology and Nation Building: A View from Central America. In *The Politics of Archaeology and Identity in a Global Context,* edited by S. Kane, pp. 79–100. Archaeological Institute of America, Boston.

   2004 Embodied Subjectivity: Gender, Femininity, Masculinity, Sexuality. In *A Companion to Social Archaeology,* edited by L. Meskell and R. W. Preucel, pp. 82–95. Blackwell Publishers, Oxford, U.K.

   2005 Solid Histories for Fragile Nation: Archaeology as Cultural Patrimony. In *Embedded Ethics,* edited by L. Meskell and P. Pels, pp. 253–274. Berg, Oxford, U.K.

Judge, W. J.

   1989 The View from Taos. *Bulletin of the Society for American Archaeology* 7(5):4.

Juliá, Santos (coordinator)

   1999 *Victimas de la Guerra Civil.* Temas de Hoy, Madrid.

Kadir, Nazima

   2006 Class War at Yale. *Anthropology News* 47(8):12–13.

Kampschror, Beth

   2007 Ghosts of Kosovo. *Archaeology* 60(4):44–49.

Kane, Susan (editor)

   2003 *The Politics of Archaeology and Identity in a Global Context.* Archaeological Institute of America, Boston.

Keat, Russell, and John Urry

   1983 *Social Theory as Science.* Routledge and Kegan Paul, London.

Kehoe, Alice Beck

   1998 *The Land of Prehistory: A Critical History of American Archaeology.* Routledge, London.

Keller, Bill

   2005 *Class Matters.* Times Books, New York.

Kelley, Robin D. G.

1997 The Proletariat Goes to College. In *Will Teach for Food: Academic Labor in Crisis,* edited by C. Nelson, pp. 145–152. University of Minnesota Press, Minneapolis.

Kennedy, Duncan

1997 Boola. In *Will Teach for Food: Academic Labor in Crisis,* edited by C. Nelson, pp. 129–136. University of Minnesota Press, Minneapolis.

Kennedy, Roger G.

1996 *Hidden Cities: The Discovery and Loss of Ancient North American Civilization.* Penguin Books, New York.

Kershaw, Ian

1987 *The "Hitler Myth": Image and Reality in the Third Reich.* Oxford University Press, Oxford, U.K.

Kintz, Theresa

1995 The '95 Underground Survey Results Issue. *Underground* 19 (July):1–4.

1996 Underground at the Society for American Archaeology Meeting. *Underground* 23 (May):1.

Klejn, Leo S.

1993 *La arqueología soviética: Historia y teoría de una escuela desconocida.* Crítica, Barcelona.

Kohl, Phil

1975 The Archaeology of Trade. *Dialectical Anthropology* 1(1):43–50.

1985 Symbolic and Cognitive Archaeology: A New Loss of Innocence. *Dialectical Anthropology* 9:105–117.

2004 Making the Past Profitable in an Age of Globalization and National Ownership: Contradictions and Considerations. In *Marketing Heritage: Archaeology and the Consumption of the Past,* edited by Yorke Rowan and Uzi Baram, pp. 295–302. AltaMira Press, Walnut Creek, Calif.

Kohl, Phil, and C. Fawcett (editors)

1995 *Nationalism, Politics, and the Practice of Archaeology.* Cambridge University Press, Cambridge.

Kohl, Phil, and Gocha R. Tsetskhladze

1995 Nationalism, Politics, and the Practice of Archaeology in the Caucasus. In *Nationalism, Politics and the Practice of Archaeology,* edited by P. L. Kohl and C. Fawcett, pp. 149–176. Cambridge University Press, Cambridge.

Kramer, Carol, and Miriam Stark

1994 The Status of Women in Archaeology. In *Equity Issues for Women in Archaeology,* edited by M. C. Nelson, S. M. Nelson, and A. Wylie, pp. 17–22. Archaeological Papers of the American Anthropological Association 5. American Anthropological Association, Washington, D.C.

Lacey, David, M., and Robert L. Hasenstab

1983 The Development of Least Effort Strategies in CRM: Competition for Scarce Resources in Massachusetts. In *The Socio-politics of Archaeology,* edited by J. Gero, D. Lacey, and M. Blakey, pp. 31–50. University of Massachusetts, Department of Anthropology. Amherst.

Langford, Ros F.

1983 Our Heritage—Your Playground. *Australian Archaeology* 16:1–6.

Lareau, Annette

2003 *Unequal Childhoods: Class, Race, and Family Life.* University of California Press, Berkeley.

LaRoche, Cheryl J., and Michael L. Blakey

1997 Seizing Intellectual Power: The Dialogue at the New York African Burial Ground. *Historical Archaeology* 31(3):84–106.

Larrain, Jorge

1995 Identity, the Other, and Postmodernism. In *Post-ality: Marxism and Postmodernism,* edited by M. U. Zavarzadeh, T. L. Ebert, and D. Morton, pp. 271–289. Transformations, Vol. 1. Maisonneuve Press, Washington, D.C.

LeBlanc, Steven A.

1999 *Prehistoric Warfare in the American Southwest.* University of Utah Press, Salt Lake City.

Lee, Richard

forthcoming The Modern World-System: Its Structures, Its Geoculture, Its Crisis and Transformation. In *World-Scale Ambitions,* edited by Nirvana Tanoukhi and David Palumbo-Liu. Duke University Press, Durham, N.C.

Leone, Mark

1981 The Relationship between Artifacts and the Public in Outdoor History Museums. *Annuals of the New York Academy of Sciences* 376:301–314.

1986 Symbolic, Structural, and Critical Archaeology. In *American Archaeology Past and Future,* edited by D. Meltzer, D. Fowler, and J. Sabloff, pp. 415–438. Smithsonian Institution Press, Washington, D.C.

1995 A Historical Archaeology of Capitalism. *American Anthropologist* 97(2):251–268.

2005 *The Archaeology of Liberty in an American Capital: Excavations in Annapolis.* University of California Press, Berkeley.

Leone, Mark, and Barbara Little

1993 Artifacts as Expressions of Society and Culture: Subversive Genealogy and the Value of History. In *History from Things: Essays on Material Culture,* edited by S. Lubar and W. D. Kingery, pp. 160–181. Smithsonian Institution Press, Washington, D.C.

Leone, Mark P., and Parker B. Potter Jr.

1984 *Archaeological Annapolis: A Guide to Seeing and Understanding Three Centuries of Change.* Mark P. Leone and Parker Potter Jr., Annapolis.

1988 Introduction: Issues in Historical Archaeology. In *The Recovery of Meaning: Historical Archaeology in the Eastern United States,* edited by Mark P. Leone and Parker B. Potter Jr., pp. 1–26. Smithsonian Institution Press, Washington, D.C.

——— (editors)

1999 *Historical Archaeologies of Capitalism.* Kluwer Academic, New York.

Leone, Mark P., Parker B. Potter Jr., and Paul A. Shackel

1987 Toward a Critical Archaeology. *Current Anthropology* 28(3):283–302.

Leonhardt, David

2005 The College Drop Out Boom. In *Class Matters,* edited by B. Keller, pp. 87–104. Times Books, New York.

León-Portilla, Miguel

1972 The Norteño Variety of Mexican Culture: An Ethnohistorical Approach. In *Plural Society in the Southwest,* Ed. by E. H. Spicer, Weatherhead Foundation, New York.

Levy, Janet E.

2006 Prehistory, Identity, and Archaeological Representation in Nordic Museums. *Current Anthropology* 108(1):135–147.

Lilley, Ian

2006 Archaeology, Diaspora and Decolonization. *Journal of Social Archaeology* 6(1):28–47.

Lippert, Dorothy

1997 In Front of the Mirror: Native Americans and Academic Archaeology. In *Native Americans and Archaeologists: Stepping Stones to Common Ground,* edited by N. K. Swindler, K. E. Dongoske, R. Anyon, and A. S. Downer, pp. 120–132. AltaMira Press, Walnut Creek, Calif.

2005 Comments on "Dwelling at the Margins, Action at the Intersection? Feminist and Indigenous Archaeologies, 2005." *Archaeologies: Journal of the World Archaeological Congress* 1(1):63–66.

Little, Barbara (editor)

1992 *Text-Aided Archaeology.* CRC Press, Boca Raton, Fla.

Lloyd, William F.

1833 *Two Lectures on the Checks to Population.* Oxford University Press, Oxford.

Long, Priscilla

1985 The Women of the CF&I Strike, 1913–1914. In *Women, Work, and*

Protest: A Century of U.S. Women's Labor History, edited by R. Milkman, pp. 62–85. Routledge and Kegan Paul, London.

1991 *Where the Sun Never Shines: A History of America's Bloody Coal Industry.* Paragon Books, New York.

Lorenzo, José L.

1976 *La arqueología mexicana y los arqueólogos morteamericanos.* Departmento de Prehistoria INAH, Cuadernos de Trabajo 14. México City.

1982 Archaeology South of the Rio Grande. *World Archaeology* 13(2):190–208.

1998 *La arqueología y México.* Instituto Nacional de Antropología y Historia, México City.

Lorenzo, J. L., A. P. Lias, and J. García-Bárcena

1976 *Hacia una arqueología social: Reunión de Teotihuacan.* INAH, México City.

Lowenthal, David

1985 *The Past Is a Foreign Country.* Cambridge University Press, Cambridge.

Lucas, Gavin

2001 *Critical Approaches to Archaeology: Contemporary and Historical Archaeological Practice.* Routledge, London.

Ludlow Collective

2001 Archaeology of the Colorado Coal Field War, 1913–1914. In *Archaeologies of the Contemporary Past,* edited by V. Buchli and G. Lucas, pp. 94–107. Routledge, London.

Lukács, Georg

1971 *History and Class Consciousness.* MIT Press, Cambridge, Mass.

Lull, Vicente

2000 Death and Society: A Marxist Approach. *Antiquity* 74:576–580.

Lumbreras, Luis Guillermo

2005 *Arqueología y sociedad.* Instituto de Estudios Peruanos, Lima.

Lutz, Catherine A., and Jane L. Collins

1993 *Reading National Geographic.* University of Chicago Press, Chicago.

Lynott, Mark J.

1990 Archaeology and Public Relations. *Bulletin of the Society for American Archaeology* 8(3):2.

Lyons, C. L., and J. K. Papadopoulos (editors)

2002 *The Archaeology of Colonialism.* Getty Research Institute, Los Angeles.

Magdoff, Fred, and Harry Magdoff

2004 Disposable Workers: Today's Reserve Army of Labor. *Monthly Review* 55(11):18–35.

Mandal, D.

   1993 *Ayodhya: Archaeology after Demolition.* Orient Longman, New Delhi.

Marcuse, Herbert

   1955 *Eros and Civilization.* Vintage, New York.

Marshall, Yvonne

   2002 What Is Community Archaeology? *World Archaeology* 34(2):211–219.

   2004 Archaeologies of Resistance. Paper presented at the thirty-seventh
   Annual Chacmool Conference, Calgary.

Martin, Paul S., and David A. Gregory

   1973 Prehistoric and Contemporary Problems. In *The Archaeology of Arizona: A Study of the Southwest Region,* edited by P. S. Martin and F. Plog,
   pp. 361–368. Doubleday, Garden City, N.Y.

Martin, Paul S., and F. Plog

   1973 *The Archaeology of Arizona: A Study of the Southwest Region.* Doubleday, Garden City, N.Y.

Martinez, Desireé Reneé

   2006 Overcoming Hindrances to Our Enduring Responsibility to the Ancestors: Protecting Traditional Cultural Places. *American Indian Quarterly*
   30(3–4):486–506.

Marx, Karl

   1906 *Capital: A Critique of Political Economy.* Modern Library, New York.
   Originally published 1867.

   1938 *Critique of the Gotha Programme.* International Publishers, New York.
   Originally published 1891.

   1959 *Economic and Philosophic Manuscripts of 1844.* Progress Publishers,
   Moscow. Originally published 1844.

   1978 *The Eighteenth Brumaire of Louis Bonaparte.* Foreign Language Press,
   Peking. Originally published 1852.

Marx, Karl, and Friedrich Engels

   1947 *The German Ideology.* International Publishers, New York. Originally
   published 1846.

Matos, Eduardo

   1988 *The Great Temple of the Aztecs.* Translated by Doris Heyden. Thames
   and Hudson, New York.

McClung, Emily de Tapia

   1999 Cultural Patrimony in Mexico: Proposal for a New Law to Replace the
   1972 Legislation. *SAA Bulletin* 17(5):28–29.

McDavid, Carol

   2002 Archaeologies That Hurt, Descendents That Matter: A Pragmatic

Approach to Collaboration in the Public Interpretation of African-American Archaeology. *World Archaeology* 34(2):303–314.

McGaw, J. A.

1989 No Passive Victims, No Separate Spheres: A Feminist Perspective on Technology's History. In *In Context: History and the History of Technology*, edited by S. H. Cutcliffe and R. Post, pp. 172–191. Lehigh University Press, Bethlehem, Pa.

McGovern, George S., and Leonard F. Guttridge

1972 *The Great Coalfield War.* Houghton Mifflin, Boston.

McGuire, Randall H.

1984 Demystifying Contract Archaeology. Paper presented at the annual meeting of the American Anthropological Association, Denver, Colo.

1988 Dialogues with the Dead, Ideology and the Cemetery. In *The Recovery of Meaning, Historical Archaeology in the Eastern United States*, edited by M. P. Leone and P. B. Potter Jr., 435–480. Smithsonian Institution Press, Washington, D.C.

1992a Archaeology and the First Americans. *American Anthropologist* 94(4):816–836.

1992b *A Marxist Archaeology.* Academic Press, Orlando, Fla.

1997 Crossing the Border. In *Prehistory of the Borderlands,* edited by J. Carpenter and G. Sanchez, pp. 130–137. Arizona State Museum Archaeological Series 186, Tucson.

2002a The Meaning and Limits of the Southwest/Northwest. In *Boundaries and Territories: Prehistory of the U.S. Southwest and Northern Mexico,* edited by M. E. Villalpando, pp. 173–183. Arizona State University Anthropological Research Papers 54. Arizona State University, Tempe.

2002b Prologue to the Percheron Press edition. In *A Marxist Archaeology.* Percheron Press, Clinton Corners, N.Y.

2002c Stories of Power, Powerful Tales: A Commentary on Ancient Pueblo Violence. In *The Dynamics of Power,* edited by Maria O'Donovan, pp. 126–150. Center for Archaeological Investigations, Occasional Paper 30. Southern Illinois University, Carbondale.

McGuire, Randall H., and Rodrigo Navarrete

1999 Entre motocicletas y fusiles: Las arqueologías radicales anglo-sajona y latinoamericana. *Boletín de Antropología Americana* 34:89–110.

2004 Between Motorcycles and Rifles: Anglo-American and Latin American Radical Archaeologies. In *Global Archaeological Theory,* edited by P. Funari, A. Zarankin, and E. Stoval, pp. 309–336. Routledge, London.

McGuire, Randall H., Maria O'Donovan, and LouAnn Wurst

2005 Praxis in Archaeology: The Last Eighty Years. *Rethinking Marxism* 17(3):355–372.

McGuire, Randall H., and Paul Reckner

2002 The Unromantic West: Labor Capital, and Struggle. *Historical Archaeology* 36(3):44–58.

2003 Building a Working Class Archaeology: The Colorado Coal Field War Project. *Industrial Archaeology Review* 25(2):83–95.

McGuire, Randall H., and Ruth M. Van Dyke

Forthcoming. Dismembering the Trope: Imagining Cannibalism in the Ancient Pueblo World. In *Multidisciplinary Approaches to Social Violence in the Prehispanic Southwest,* edited by Deborah Nichols and Patricia Crown. University of Arizona Press, Tucson.

McGuire, Randall H., and María Elisa Villalpando

1993 *An Archaeological Survey of the Altar Valley, Sonora, Mexico.* Arizona State Museum Archaeological Series 184. Arizona State Museum, Tucson.

Forthcoming. Excavations at Cerro de Trincheras. In *Enduring Borderlands Traditions: Trincheras Sites in Time, Space, and Society,* edited by Suzanne K. Fish, Paul R. Fish, and Elisa Villalpando. University of Arizona Press, Tucson.

McGuire, Randall H., and Mark Walker

1999 Class Confrontations in Archaeology. *Historical Archaeology* 33(1):159–183.

McGuire, Randall H., and LouAnn Wurst

2002 Struggling with the Past. *International Journal of Historical Archaeology* 6:85–94.

McKenna, Barbara

1997 Off the Tenure Track. *On Campus* 16(8):6–7, 15.

McManamon, Francis P.

2000 Archaeological Messages and Messengers. *Public Archaeology* 1(1):5–20.

2003 Archaeology, Nationalism, and Ancient America. In *The Politics of Archaeology and Identity in a Global Context,* edited by Susan Kane, pp. 115–137. Archaeological Institute of America, Boston.

McNiven, Ian, and Lynette Russell

2005 *Appropriated Pasts: Indigenous Peoples and the Colonial Culture of Archaeology.* AltaMira Press, Lanham, Md.

Menand, Louis

1997 Everybody Else's College Education. *New York Times Magazine,* April 20:48–49.

Merriman, Nick

1987 Museums and Archaeology: The Public Point of View. Paper presented at the annual conference of the Society of Museum Archaeologists, March, Lincoln, Neb.

1988 The Heritage Industry Reconsidered. *Archaeological Review from Cambridge* 7(2):146–156.

1991 *Beyond the Glass Case: The Past, the Heritage and Public in Britain.* Leicester University Press, Leicester, U.K.

Meskell, Lynn

1995 Goddesses, Gimbutas, and New Age Archaeology. *Antiquity* 69:74–86.

1998 Twin Peaks: The Archaeologies of Çatalhöyük. In *Ancient Goddesses: The Myths and Evidence,* edited by C. Morris and L. Goodison, pp. 46–62. British Museum Press, London.

1999 *Archaeologies of Social Life: Age, Sex, Class in Ancient Egypt.* Blackwell Publishers, Oxford, U.K.

2002a The Intersections of Identity and Politics in Archaeology. *Annual Review of Anthropology* 31:279–301.

2002b *Private Life in New Kingdom Egypt.* Princeton University Press, Princeton, N.J.

2003 Pharaonic Legacies: Postcolonialism, Heritage, and Hyperreality. In *The Politics of Archaeology and Identity in a Global Context,* edited by S. Kane, pp. 149–171. Archaeological Institute of America, Boston.

2005 Sites of Violence: Terrorism, Tourism, and Heritage in the Archaeological Present. In *Embedded Ethics,* edited by L. Meskell and P. Pels, pp. 123–146. Berg, Oxford, U.K.

Meskell, Lynn (editor)

1998 *Archaeology under Fire: Nationalism, Politics and Heritage in the Eastern Mediterranean and Middle East.* Routledge, London

Meskell, Lynn, and Peter Pels

2005 *Embedded Ethics.* Berg, Oxford, U.K.

Meskell, Lynn, and Robert W. Preucel

2004 Politics. In *A Companion to Social Archaeology,* edited by L. Meskell and R. W. Preucel, pp. 315–334. Blackwell Publishing, Oxford, U.K.

Meyer, Karl E.

1992 Digging Berlin's Chamber of Horrors. *Archaeology* 45(4):25–29.

Middlebrook, Kevin J., and Eduardo Zepeda

2003 *Confronting Development: Assessing Mexico's Economic and Social Policy Challenges.* Stanford University Press, Palo Alto, Calif.

Mills, C. Wright

1956 *The Power Elite.* Oxford University Press, New York.

Minnis, Paul

1985 *Social Adaptation to Food Stress: A Prehistoric Southwestern Example.* University of Chicago Press, Chicago.

Mintz, Sidney W.

1986 *Sweetness and Power.* Penguin, New York.

Mohanty, Chandra Talpade

2003 *Feminism without Borders: Decolonizing Theory, Practicing Solidarity.* Duke University Press, Durham, N.C.

Montané, Julio

1980 *Marxismo y arqueología.* Ediciones de Cultura Popular, México City.

Moore, Lawrence E.

2006 Insights: CRM beyond Its Peak. *SAA Archaeological Record* 6(1):30–33.

Moser, Stephanie, Darren Glaizer, James E. Phillips, Lamya Nasser el Nemr, Mohammed Saleh Mousa, Rascha Nasr Aiesh, Susan Richardson, Andrew Conner, and Michael Seymour

2002 Transforming Archaeology through Practice: Strategies for Collaborative Archaeology and the Community Archaeology Project at Quseir, Egypt. *World Archaeology* 34(2):220–248.

Mrozowski, Stephen, Grace H. Ziesing, and Mary C. Beaudry

1996 *Living on the Boott: Historical Archaeology at the Boott Mills Boardinghouses, Lowell, Massachusetts.* University of Massachusetts Press, Amherst.

Muller, John

1997 *Mississippian Political Economy.* Plenum Press, New York.

Mullins, Paul

1999 *Race and Affluence: An Archaeology of African America and Consumer Culture.* Plenum Press, New York.

Murolo, Priscilla

1996 What Kind of Alliance? *Radical Historian's Newsletter* 75:1, 4, 15.

Nabhan, Gary

1998 Sonora Querida: The Visual Celebrations and Laments of David Burckhalter. In *La Vida Nortaña: Photographs of Sonora Mexico,* by David Burckhalter, pp. 3–12. University of Arizona Press, Tucson.

NATHPO

2006 Map of Currently Recognized THPOs. National Association of Tribal Historic Preservation Officers. http://www.nathpo.org/map.html, accessed June 27, 2006.

Neeson, J. M.

2004 *Commoners: Common Right, Enclosure and Social Change in England, 1700–1820.* Cambridge University Press, Cambridge.

Nelson, Cary (editor)

1997a *Manifesto of a Tenured Radical.* New York University Press, New York.

1997b *Will Teach for Food: Academic Labor in Crisis*. University of Minnesota Press, Minneapolis.

Nelson, Cary, and Stephen Watt

2004 *Office Hours: Activism and Change in the Academy*. Routledge, New York.

Nelson, Margaret C., Sarah M. Nelson, and Alison Wylie (editors)

1994 *Equity Issues for Women in Archaeology*. Archaeological Papers of the American Anthropological Association 5. American Anthropological Association, Washington, D.C.

Nelson, Sarah M.

2004 *Gender in Archaeology: Analysing Power and Prestige*. 2nd ed. AltaMira Press, Walnut Hills, Calif.

Nelson, Sarah M., and Margaret C. Nelson

1994 Conclusions. In *Equity Issues for Women in Archaeology*, edited by M. C. Nelson, S. M. Nelson, and A. Wylie, pp. 229–235. Archaeological Papers of the American Anthropological Association 5. American Anthropological Association, Washington D.C.

Nemaheni, Tshimangadzo Israel

2002 The Reburial of Human Remains at Thulamela, Kruger National Park, South Africa. In *The Dead and Their Possessions: Repatriation in Principle, Policy and Practice*, edited by C. Fforde, J. Hubert, and P. Turnbull, pp. 256–260. Routledge, London.

Newell, Gillian E.

1999 American and Mexican Archaeology: Differences in Meaning and Teaching. *SAA Bulletin* 17(5):29–31.

Nichols, George P., and Thomas D. Andrews (editors)

1997 *At a Crossroads: Archaeology and First Peoples in Canada*. Archaeology Press, Department of Archaeology, University of Simon Fraser, Burnaby, B.C.

Nobel, David F.

2003 *Digital Diploma Mills: The Automation of Higher Education*. Monthly Review Press, New York.

Noel-Hume, Ivor

1969 *Historical Archaeology*. Alfred A. Knopf, New York.

Northeastern University

2001 The Campus Charter, Northeastern University in Boston. http://www.cewaction.org/2001SiteFiles/resources/charter.html, accessed October 29, 2006.

O'Donovan, Maria

2002 *The Survey of Cerro de Trincheras: New Perspectives on Site Function and Scale.* Arizona State Museum Technical Series 190, University of Arizona, Tucson.

Ollman, Bertell

1976 *Alienation.* 2nd ed. Cambridge University Press, Cambridge.

1992 *Dialectical Investigations.* Routledge, New York.

2003 *Dance of the Dialectic: Steps in Marx's Method.* University of Illinois Press, Urbana-Champagne.

Orser, Charles

1996 *A Historical Archaeology of the Modern World.* Plenum Press, New York.

Ouzman, Sven

2005 Silencing and Sharing Southern African Indigenous and Embedded Knowledge. In *Indigenous Archaeologies: Decolonizing Theory and Practice,* edited by C. Smith and H. M. Wobst, pp. 208–225. Routledge, London.

Palerm, Ángel

1980 *Antropología y Marxismo.* Editorial Nueva Imagen, México City.

Palus, Matthew M., Mark P. Leone, and Matthew D. Cochran

2006 Critical Archaeology: Politics Past and Present. In *Historical Archaeology,* edited by M. Hall and S. W. Silliman, pp. 84–106. Blackwell Publishing, Oxford, U.K.

Panameno, Rebeca, and Enrique Nalda

1978 Arqueología, para quien? *Nueva Antropología* 12:111–124.

Papanikolas, Zeese

1982 *Buried Unsung: Louis Tikas and the Ludlow Massacre.* University of Utah Press, Salt Lake City.

Pape, Kevin

1996a ACRA Committee Reports: Labor Relations Committee. *ACRA Edition* 2(2):6–7.

1996b ACRA Committee Reports: Labor Relations Committee. *ACRA Edition* 2(3):9.

1996c ACRA Committee Reports: Labor Relations Committee—Summary. *ACRA Edition* 2(9):6–7.

1997a A Summary of ACRA's Involvement in the Archaeological Technician Position Descriptions and Wage Determination Issue. *ACRA Edition* 3(6):5–7.

1997b A Summary of ACRA's Involvement in the Archaeological Technician Position Descriptions and Wage Determination Issue. http://mindspring .com/~wheaton/wagedetermination.html, accessed September 16, 2005.

Parsons, Neil, and Alinah Kelo Segobye

2002 Missing Persons and Stolen Bodies: The Repatriation of "El Negro" to

Botswana. In *The Dead and Their Possessions: Repatriation in Principle, Policy and Practice,* edited by C. Fforde, J. Hubert, and P. Turnbull, pp. 245–255. Routledge, London.

Patterson, Thomas C.

1973 *America's Past: A New World Archaeology.* Scott Foresman, London.

1986 The Last Sixty Years: Towards a Social History of Archaeology in the United States. *American Anthropologist* 88(1):7–26.

1989 Political Economy and a Discourse Called "Peruvian Archaeology." *Culture and History* 4:35–64.

1994 Social Archaeology in Latin America: An Appreciation. *American Antiquity* 59(3):531–537.

1995a Archaeology, History, *Indigenismo* and the State in Peru and Mexico. In *Making Alternative Histories: The Practice of Archaeology and History in Non-Western Societies,* edited by P. R. Schmidt and T. Patterson, pp. 69–85. School of American Research Press, Santa Fe.

1995b *Toward a Social History of Archaeology in the United States.* Harcourt Brace, Orlando, Fla.

1997 *Inventing Western Civilization.* Monthly Review Press, New York.

2003 *Marx's Ghost: Conversations with Archaeologists.* Berg, Oxford, U.K.

Pauketat, Timothy

2000 The Tragedy of the Commoners. In *Agency in Archaeology,* edited by M-A. Dobres and J. Robb, pp. 113–129. Routledge, London.

Paynter, Robert

1983 Field or Factory? Concerning the Degradation of Archaeological Labor. In *The Socio-politics of Archaeology,* edited by J. M. Gero, D. M. Lacy, and M. L. Blakey, pp. 17–30. University of Massachusetts, Department of Anthropology, Amherst.

Perkins, John H.

1998 *Geopolitics and the Green Revolution.* University of Oxford Press, Oxford.

Pinkoski, Marc, and Michael Asch

2004 Anthropology as Science or Politics? Julian Steward and the Doctrine of Terra Mullius. In *Hunter-Gatherers in History, Archaeology and Anthropology,* edited by A. Barnard, pp. 187–200. Berg Publishers, New York.

Plog, Fred

1974 *A Study of Prehistoric Change.* Academic Press, New York.

Poggie, John J., and Robert N. Lynch (editors)

1974 *Rethinking Modernization: Anthropological Perspectives.* Greenwood Press, Westport, Conn.

Politis, Gustavo

2003 The Theoretical Landscape and the Methodological Development of Archaeology in Latin America. *American Antiquity* 68(2):245–272.

Politis, Gustavo, and Benjamin Alberti (editors)

1999 *Archaeology in Latin America.* Routledge, London.

Pollock, Susan

2003 The Looting of the Iraq Museum: Thoughts on Archaeology in a Time of Crisis. *Public Archaeology* 3:117–124.

Poole, Ross

1999 *Nation and Identity.* Routledge, London.

Potter, Parker B., Jr.

1994 *Public Archaeology in Annapolis.* Smithsonian Institution Press, Washington, D.C.

Pratt, Linda Ray

1997 Disposable Faculty: Part-Time Exploitation as Management Strategy. In *Will Teach for Food: Academic Labor in Crisis,* edited by C. Nelson, pp. 264–277. University of Minnesota Press, Minneapolis.

Price, Brian R.

2002 *The Book of the Tournament.* Chivalry Bookshelf, Highland Village, Tex.

Price, David

2003 Cloak and Trowel. *Archaeology* 56(5):27–31.

Prince, Gene

1988 Photography for Discovery and Scale by Superimposing Old Photographs on the Present-Day Scene. *Antiquity* 62:12–116.

Pullar, Gordon L.

1994 The Qikertarmiut and the Scientist: Fifty Years of Clashing World Views. In *Reckoning with the Dead,* edited by T. L. Bray and T. W. Killion, pp. 15–25. Smithsonian Institution Press, Washington, D.C.

Pyburn, Anne K.

2005 Past Pedagogy. *Archaeologies: Journal of the World Archaeological Congress* 1(2):1–6.

Rathje, William, and Cullen Murphy

1992 *Rubbish: The Archaeology of Garbage.* Harper Collins Publishers, New York.

Ratnagar, Shereen

2004 Archaeology at the Heart of a Political Confrontation: The Case of Ayodhya. *Current Anthropology* 45(2):239–260.

Ravesloot, John C.

1990 On the Treatment and Reburial of Human Remains: The San Xavier Project, Tucson, Arizona. *American Indian Quarterly* 14(1):35–50.

Redman, Charles L.

1973 *Research and Theory in Current Archaeology.* John Wiley and Sons, New York.

1991 In Defense of the 70s—the Adolescence of New Archaeology. *American Anthropologist* 93:295–307.

Ren, Avexnim Coijti

2006 Maya Archaeology and the Political and Cultural Identity of Contemporary Maya in Guatemala. *Archaeologies: Journal of the World Archaeological Congress* 2(1):8–19.

Renfrew, Colin

1982 Explanation Revisited. In *Theory and Explanation in Archaeology,* edited by Colin Renfrew, M. J. Rowlands, and B. A. Segraves, pp. 5–24. Academic Press, New York.

1989 Comments on Archaeology into the 1990's. *Norwegian Archaeological Review* 22:33–41.

Ridge, John Rollin

1955 *Joaquín Murieta.* University of Oklahoma Press, Norman. Originally published 1855.

Romey, Kristin

2004 Flashpoint Ayodhya. *Archaeology* (July/August):49–55.

Roseberry, William

1996 The Unbearable Lightness of Anthropology. *Radical History Review* 65:5–25.

1997 Marx and Anthropology. *Annual Review of Anthropology* 26:25–46.

Rowan, Yorke, and Uzi Baram (editors)

2004 *Marketing Heritage: Archaeology and the Consumption of the Past.* AltaMira Press, Walnut Creek, Calif.

Rürup, Reinhard

2002 *Topographie des Terrors: Gestapo, SS und Reichssicherheitshauptamt auf dem "Prinz-Albrecht-Gelände," eine Dokumentation.* Verlag Willmuth Arenhövel, Berlin.

Russell, Lynette

2001 *Savage Imaginings: Historical and Contemporary Constructions of Australian Aboriginalities.* Australian Scholarly Publications, Melbourne.

Ryan, Jake, and Charles Sackrey

1996 *Strangers in Paradise: Academics from the Working Class.* University Press of America, Lanham, Md.

Saitta, Dean J.

2004 Desecration at Ludlow. *New Labor Forum* 13:86–89.

2005 Labor and Class in the American West. In *North American Archaeology*, edited by T. R. Pauketat and D. D. Loren, pp. 359–385. Blackwell Publishing, Oxford, U.K.

2007 *The Archaeology of Collective Action*. University Press of Florida, Tallahassee.

Salmon, Merrilee H.

1982 *Philosophy and Archaeology*. Academic Press, New York.

Sanahuja, M. E.

2002 *Cuerpos sexuados, objetos, y prehistoria*. Ediciones Cátedra, Universitat de Valéncia, España.

Sargent, Lydia (editor)

1981 *Women and Revolution: A Discussion of the Unhappy Marriage of Marxism and Feminism*. South End Press, Boston.

Sayer, Derek

1979 *Marx's Method: Ideology, Science and Critique in Capital*. Harvester Press, Brighton, U.K.

1987 *Violence of Abstraction*. Blackwell Publishers, Oxford, U.K.

Scham, Sandra Arnold

2001 The Archaeology of the Disenfranchised. *Journal of Archaeological Method and Theory* 8(2):183–213.

Scham, Sandra Arnold, and Adel Yahya

2003 Heritage and Reconciliation. *Journal of Social Archaeology* 3(2):399–416.

Schiffer, Michael B.

1988 The Structure of Archaeological Theory. *American Antiquity* 53(3):461–486.

Schmidt, Peter R.

2005 Teaching Revolutionary Archaeology: African Experiments in History Making and Heritage Management. *Archaeologies: Journal of the World Archaeological Congress* 1(2):46–59.

Schmidt, Peter R., and Thomas C. Patterson (editors)

1995 *Making Alternative Histories: The Practice of Archaeology and History in Non-Western Settings*. School of American Research, Santa Fe.

Schmidt, R. A., and Barbara L. Voss (editors)

2000 *Archaeologies of Sexuality*. Routledge, London.

Schmitt, Richard

2002 *Alienation and Freedom*. Westview Press, Boulder, Colo.

Schmitt, Richard, and Thomas E. Moody (editors)

1994 *Alienation and Social Criticism*. Humanity Books, Amherst, N.Y.

Schuldenrein, Joseph

1992 Cultural Resource Management and Academic Responsibility in Archaeology: A Rejoinder to Duke. *SAA Bulletin* 10(5):3.

1995 The Care and Feeding of Archaeologists: A Plea for Pragmatic Training in the 21st Century. *SAA Bulletin* 13(3):22–24.

Seligman, Edwin R.

1914 The Crisis in Colorado. *Annalist* (May 4):552–553.

Sen, Swadhin

2002 Community Boundary, Secularized Religion and Imagined Past in Bangladesh: Archaeology and Historiography of Unequal Encounter. *World Archaeology* 34(2):346–362.

Sennett, Richard, and Jonathan Cobb

1972 *The Hidden Injuries of Class*. Vintage Books, New York.

Shackel, Paul

1994 A Material Culture of Armory Workers. In *Domestic Responses to Nineteenth-Century Industrialization: An Archaeology of Park Building 48, Harper's Ferry National Historical Park*, edited by Paul Shackel, pp. 10.1–10.7. U.S. Department of the Interior, National Park Service, National Capital Region, Regional Archaeology Program, Washington, D.C.

1996 *Culture Change and the New Technology: An Archaeology of the Early American Industrial Era*. Plenum Press, New York.

Shackel, Paul, and Matthew Palus

2006 Remembering an Industrial Landscape. *International Journal of Historical Archaeology* 10(1):49–72.

Shanks, Michael

1992 *Experiencing the Past: On the Character of Archaeology*. Routledge, London.

2001 The Future of the Past in Post Industrial Society. Paper presented at the conference Industrial Heritage as a Force in Democratic Society, Council of Europe, National Heritage Board, Orebro, Sweden. http://traumwerk.stanford.edu/~mshanks/writing/Future_past.pdf, accessed September 23, 2003.

2004 Archaeology and Politics. In *A Companion to Archaeology*, edited by J. Bintliff, pp. 490–508. Blackwell Publishing, Oxford, U.K.

Shanks, Michael, and Randall H. McGuire

1996 The Craft of Archaeology. *American Antiquity* 61(1):75–88.

Shanks, Michael, and Christopher Tilley

1987 *Social Theory and Archaeology*. Polity Press, Cambridge.

1992 *Reconstructing Archaeology: Theory and Practice.* 2nd ed. Routledge, London.

Sheridan, Thomas E.

1998 Another Country. In *La Vida Nortaña: Photographs of Sonora Mexico,* by David Burckhalter, pp. 13–37. University of Arizona Press, Tucson.

Sheridan, Thomas E., and Nancy J. Parezo

1996 *Paths of Life: American Indians of the Southwest and Northern Mexico.* University of Arizona Press, Tucson.

Sherman, Howard J.

1995 *Reinventing Marxism.* Johns Hopkins University Press, Baltimore, Md.

Shnirelman, Victor A.

1995 From Internationalism to Nationalism: Forgotten Pages of Soviet Archaeology in the 1930s and 1940s. In *Nationalism, Politics and the Practice of Archaeology,* edited by P. L. Kohl and C. Fawcett, pp. 120–138. Cambridge University Press, Cambridge.

Shott, Michael J.

1992 Commerce or Service: Models of Practice in Archaeology. In *Quandaries and Quests: Visions of Archaeology's Future,* edited by L. Wandsnider, pp. 9–24. Center for Archaeological Investigations, Southern Illinois University, Carbondale.

2004 Guilt by Affiliation: Merit and Standing in Academic Archaeology. *SAA Archaeological Record* 4(2):30–37.

Sider, Gerald M.

1996 Cleansing History: Lawrence, Massachusetts, the Strike for Four Loaves of Bread and No Roses, and the Anthropology of Working-Class Consciousness. *Radical History* 65:48–83.

Sieder, Rachel (editor)

2002 *Multiculturalism in Latin America: Indigenous Rights, Diversity and Democracy.* Palgrave Macmillan, New York.

Siegel, David J.

2006 Minding the Academy's Business. *Academe* 92(6):54–57.

Silberman, Neal Asher

1993 *A Prophet from amongst You: The Life of Yigael Yadin: Soldier, Scholar, and Mythmaker of Modern Israel.* Addison Wesley, Boston.

1995 Promised Lands and Chosen Peoples: The Politics and Poetics of Archaeological Narrative. In *Nationalism, Politics and the Practice of Archaeology,* edited by P. L. Kohl and C. Fawcett, pp. 249–262. Cambridge University Press, Cambridge.

Silliman, Stephen

2001 Agency, Practical Politics, and the Archaeology of Cultural Contact. *Journal of Social Archaeology* 1(2):184–204.

Silverberg, Robert

1968 *The Mound Builders: The Archaeology of a Myth*. New York Graphic Society, New York.

Singleton, Theresa, and Charles E. Orser Jr.

2003 Descendant Communities: Linking People in the Present to the Past. In *Ethical Issues in Archaeology*, edited by L. J. Zimmerman, K. D. Vitelli, and J. Hollowell-Zimmer, pp. 143–152. AltaMira Press, Walnut Creek, Calif.

Smardz, Karolyn, and Shelley J. Smith

2000 *The Archaeology Education Handbook*. AltaMira Press, Walnut Creek, Calif.

Smith, Anthony D.

1991 *National Identity*. University of Nevada Press, Reno.

Smith, Claire, and H. Martin Wobst (editors)

2005 *Indigenous Archaeologies: Decolonizing Theory and Practice*. Routledge, London.

Sorensen, N. N.

1997 There Are No Indians in the Dominican Republic: The cultural Construction of Dominican Identities. *Siting Culture*, edited by K. F. Olwig and K. Harstrup, pp. 292–310. Routledge, London.

Spector, Janet D.

1993 *What This Awl Means: Feminist Archaeology at a Wahpeton Dakota Village*. Minnesota Historical Society Press, Minneapolis.

Spencer-Wood, Suzanne

1994 The Historical Archaeology Women's Caucus and the SHA Committee on Gender Issues. In *Equity Issues for Women in Archaeology*, edited by M. C. Nelson, S. M. Nelson, and A. Wylie, pp. 219–224. Archaeological Papers of the American Anthropological Association 5. American Anthropological Association, Washington D.C.

Sprague, Roderick

1974 American Indians and American Archaeology. *American Archaeology* 39(1):1–2.

Stapp, Darby C., and Michael S. Burney

2002 *Tribal Cultural Resource Management*. AltaMira Press, Walnut Creek, Calif.

Stover, Eric

1998 *The Graves: Srebrenica and Vukovar*. Scalo Publishers, Zürich.

Sugrue, Thomas J.

1996 The Long Road Ahead. *Radical Historian's Newsletter* 75:1, 14–15.

Sullivan, James D.

1997 Gender and Status in Academe. In *Will Teach for Food: Academic Labor in Crisis,* edited by C. Nelson, pp. 254–263. University of Minnesota Press, Minneapolis.

Sullivan, Teresa A., Elisabeth Warren, and Jay Westbrook

2001 *The Fragile Middle Class: Americans in Debt.* Yale University Press, New Haven, Conn.

Swartley, Lynn

2002 *Inventing Indigenous Knowledge: Archaeology, Rural Development and the Raised Field Rehabilitation Project in Bolivia.* Routledge, London.

Sykes, C. J.

1988 *ProfScam: Professors and the Demise of Higher Education.* Regenery Gateway, Washington, D.C.

Tapsell, Paul

2002 Partnership in Museums: A Tribal Maori Response to Repatriation. In *The Dead and Their Possessions: Repatriation in Principle, Policy and Practice,* edited by C. Fforde, J. Hubert, and P. Turnbull, pp. 284–292. Routledge, London.

Taylor, Sarah

1990 "Brothers" in Arms? Feminism, Post-structuralism, and the Rise of "Civilization." In *Writing the Past in the Present,* edited by F. Baker and J. Thomas, pp. 32–41. St. David's University College, Lampeter, Wales.

Thomas, David Hurst

2000 *Skull Wars.* Basic Books, New York.

Thomas, Julian

1990 Same, Other, Analogue: Writing the Past. In *Writing the Past in the Present,* edited by F. Baker and J. Thomas, pp. 18–23. Saint David's University College, Lampeter, Wales.

2000 Reconfiguring the Social, Reconfiguring the Material. In *Social Theory in Archaeology,* edited by M. Shiffer, pp. 143–155. University of Utah Press, Salt Lake City.

2004 *Archaeology and Modernity.* Routledge, London.

Thomas, Mary

1971 *Those Damn Foreigners.* Self-published, Hollywood, Calif.

Thompson, Karen

1997 Alchemy in the Academy: Moving Part-Time Faculty from Piece Work to Parity. In *Will Teach for Food: Academic Labor in Crisis,* edited by C. Nelson, pp. 278–290. University of Minnesota Press, Minneapolis.

Tilley, Christopher

1989 Archaeology as Socio-political Action in the Present. In *Critical Tradi-*

tions in Contemporary Archaeology: Essays in the Philosophy, History and Socio-politics of Archaeology, edited by V. Pinsky and A. Wylie, pp. 104–116. Cambridge University Press, Cambridge.

Tomasky, Michael

    1997 Waltzing with Sweeny: Is the Academic Left Ready to Join the AFL-CIO? *Lingua Franca* (February):40–47.

Trigger, Bruce

    1978 *Time and Traditions: Essays in Archaeological Interpretation.* Columbia University Press, New York.

    1980a Archaeology and the Image of the American Indian. *American Antiquity* 45:662–676.

    1980b *Gordon Childe: Revolutions in Archaeology.* Columbia University Press, New York.

    1984a Alternative Archaeologies: Nationalist, Colonialist, Imperialist. *Man* 19:355–370.

    1984b Marxism and Archaeology. In *On Marxian Perspectives in Anthropology: Essays in Honor of Harry Hoijer 1981,* by S. Mintz, M. Godelier, and B. Trigger, pp. 59–97. Undena Publications, Malibu, Calif.

    1985 Marxism in Archaeology: Real or Spurious. *Reviews in Anthropology* 12:114–123.

    1989a *A History of Archaeological Thought.* University of Cambridge Press, Cambridge.

    1989b Hyperrelativism, Responsibility, and the Social Sciences. *Canadian Review of Sociology and Anthropology* 26:776–797.

    1993a *Early Civilizations Ancient Egypt in Context.* American University in Cairo Press, Cairo.

    1993b Marxism in Contemporary Western Archaeology. *Archaeological Method and Theory* 5:159–200.

    1995a Archaeology and the Integrated Circus. *Critique of Anthropology* 15(4):319–335.

    1995b A Reply to Tilley and Nencel. *Critique of Anthropology* 15(4):347–350.

    1998 *Sociocultural Evolution.* Blackwell Publishers, Oxford, U.K.

    2003a All People Are [Not] Good. *Anthropologica* 45:39–44.

    2003b *Artifacts and Ideas.* Transaction Publishers, New Brunswick, N.J.

    2003c *Understanding Early Civilizations: A Comparative Study.* Cambridge University Press, Cambridge.

    2006 *A History of Archaeological Thought.* 2nd ed. Cambridge University Press, Cambridge.

Trotter, Robert T.

    1989 Summary: Results of Wupatki National Monument Summer Ethnographic Field School. Ms on file, Wupatki National Monument, Flagstaff, Ariz.

Turner, Christy G., II, and Jacqueline A. Turner

1999 *Man Corn: Cannibalism and Violence in the Prehistoric American Southwest.* University of Utah Press, Salt Lake City.

Two Bears, Davina

2006 Navajo Archaeologist Is Not an Oxymoron: A Tribal Archaeologist's Experience. *American Indian Quarterly* 30(3–4):381–387.

UAFT (United Archaeological Field Technicians)

1996 Answers the Question: What Is an Archaeological Field Technician? United Archaeological Field Technicians, Middletown, Ohio, http://members.aol.com/uaft/handbook.htm, accessed October 1, 2005.

1997 Archaeological Field Technician's Handbook. A Guide to Your Union: Its History *and* Administration, Out Place in the Labor Movement, Your Labor and Safety Rights, Membership Duties and Membership Privileges. United Archaeological Field Technicians Membership Committee, Middletown, Ohio, http://members.aol.com/UAFT/handbook.htm, accessed October 1, 2005.

U.S. Congress, Senate

1916 Industrial Relations: Final Report and Testimony Submitted to Congress by the Commission on Industrial Relations, Created by the Act of August 23, 1912. 64th Cong., 1st session, 1916, Doc. 415, VII–IX.

Van Dyke, Ruth M., and Susan E. Alcock (editors)

2003 *Archaeologies of Memory.* Blackwell Publishers, Oxford, U.K.

Vargas, Irada

1990 *Arqueología, ciencia y sociedad: Ensayo sobre teoría arqueológica y la formación económico social tribal en Venezuela.* Editorial Abrebrecha, Caracas.

Vargas, Irada, and Mario Sanoja

1999 Archaeology as Social Science: Its Expression in Latin America. In *Archaeology in Latin America*, edited by G. G. Politis and B. Alberti, pp. 59–75. Routledge, London.

Vázquez, J. M., and Roberto Risch

1991 Theory in Spanish Archaeology since 1960. In *Archaeological Theory in Europe: The Last Three Decades,* edited by I. Hodder, pp. 25–51. Routledge, London.

Villalobos, César Acosta

2004 La diversidad emergente: Complejidad y metáforas textuales en la investigación arqueológica de Sonora, México. Tesis de maestro en antropología, Universidad Nacional Autónoma de México, Ciudad de México.

Voss, Barbara L.

2006 Engendered Archaeology: Men, Women, and Others. In *Historical Archaeology,* edited by M. Hall and S. W. Silliman, pp. 107–127. Blackwell Publishing, Oxford, U.K.

Walker, Mark

2000 Labor History at the Ground Level. *Labor's Heritage* 11:60–75.

2003 The Ludlow Massacre: Class, Warfare, and Historical Memory in Southern Colorado. *Historical Archaeology* 37:66–80.

Walker, Mark, and Dean Saitta

2002 Teaching the Craft of Archaeology: Theory, Practice, and the Field School. *International Journal of Historical Archaeology* 6:199–207.

Wallace, Anthony J. C.

1999 *Jefferson and the Indians: The Tragic Fate of the First Americans.* Belknap Press of Harvard University, Cambridge, Mass.

Wallace, Mike

1996 *Mickey Mouse History and Other Essays on American Memory.* Temple University Press, Philadelphia.

Wallach, Janet

1999 *Desert Queen: The Extraordinary Life of Gertrude Bell: Adventurer, Adviser to Kings, Ally of Lawrence of Arabia.* Anchor Books, New York.

Wallerstein, Immanuel M.

2000 *The Essential Wallerstein.* New Press, New York.

Watkins, Joe

2000 *Indigenous Archaeology: American Indian Values and Scientific Practice.* AltaMira Press, Walnut Creek, Calif.

Watson, Patty Jo, Steven A. LeBlanc, and Charles L. Redman

1984 *Archaeological Explanation: The Scientific Method in Archaeology.* Columbia University Press, New York.

Wegars, Priscilla

1991 Who's Been Workin' on the Railroad: An Examination of the Construction, Distribution, and Ethnic Origins of Domed Rock Ovens on Railroad-Related Sites. *Historical Archaeology* 25:37–65.

Weissel, Marcelo N.

2003 A Needle in a Haystack: Buenos Aires Historical Archaeology. *SAA Archaeological Record* 3(4):28–30.

West, Bryan

1994 Letter. *Underground* 20 (March):10.

Whiteside, James

1990 *Regulating Danger: The Struggle for Mine Safety in the Rocky Mountain Coal Industry.* University of Nebraska Press, Lincoln.

Whitley, Thomas G.

2004 CRM Training in Academic Archaeology: A Personal Perspective. *SAA Archaeological Record* 4(2):20–25.

Wildesen, Leslie E.

1994 The Status of Women in Archaeology: Results of a Preliminary Survey. In *Equity Issues for Women in Archaeology,* edited by M. C. Nelson, S. M. Nelson, and A. Wylie, pp. 23–37. Archaeological Papers of the American Anthropological Association 5. American Anthropological Association, Washington D.C.

Wilkie, Laurie A., and Kevin M. Bartoy

2000 A Critical Archaeology Revisited. *Current Anthropology* 41(5):747–778.

Wilkinson, John Bernard

1992 *The Annals of Binghamton of 1840.* Broome County Historical Society, Binghamton, N.Y. Originally published 1840.

Willey, Gordon R., and Jeremy A. Sabloff

1993 *A History of American Archaeology.* 3rd edition. W. H. Freeman, New York.

Wilson, Jeremy

1989 *Lawrence of Arabia: The Authorized Bibliography.* N. Helari, London.

Wilson, Michele L.

2001a Tales from the Trenches: The People, Policies, and Procedures of Cultural Resource Management, Part 1. *SAA Archaeological Record* 1(2):30–33.

2001b Tales from the Trenches: The People, Policies, and Procedures of Cultural Resource Management, Part 2. *SAA Archaeological Record* 1(3):37–38.

Wiseman, Frederick Matthew

2005 *Reclaiming the Ancestors: Decolonizing a Taken Prehistory of the Far Northeast.* University Press of New England, Lebanon, N.H.

Wiynjorroc, Phyllis, Peter Manabaru, Nell Brown, and Andrew Warner

2005 We Just Have to Show You: Research Ethics Blekbalawei. In *Indigenous Archaeologies: Decolonizing Theory and Practice,* edited by C. Smith and H. M. Wobst, pp. 316–327. Routledge, London.

Wobst, H. Martin

1989 Commentary: A Socio-politics of Socio-politics in Archaeology. In *Critical Traditions in Contemporary Archaeology: Essays in the Philosophy, History and Socio-politics of Archaeology,* edited by V. Pinsky and A. Wylie, pp. 136–140. Cambridge University Press, Cambridge.

2005 Power to the (Indigenous) Past and Present! Or: The Theory and Method behind Archaeological Theory and Method. In *Indigenous*

Archaeologies: Decolonizing Theory and Practice, edited by C. Smith and H. M. Wobst, pp. 17–32. Routledge, London.

Wolf, Eric R.

1976 Introduction. In *The Valley of Mexico: Studies in Prehispanic Ecology and Society,* edited by E. R. Wolf, pp. 1–10. University of New Mexico Press, Albuquerque.

Wolff, Robert Paul

1969 *The Ideal of the University.* Beacon Press, Boston.

Wood, Margaret

2002a A House Divided: Changes in Women's Power within and outside the Household, 1900–1930. In *The Dynamics of Power,* edited by M. O. Donovan. Center for Archaeological Investigations, Carbondale, Ill.

2002b Moving towards Transformative Action through Archaeology. *International Journal of Historical Archaeology* 6(2):187–198.

Woods, Alan, and Ted Grant

1995 *Reason in Revolt.* Wellred Publications, London.

Wurst, LouAnn

1999 Internalizing Class in Historical Archaeology. In *Confronting Class,* ed. L. Wurst and R. K. Fitts. Special issue of *Historical Archaeology* 33(1):7–21.

2006 A Class All Its Own: Explorations of Class Formation and Conflict. In *Historical Archaeology,* edited by M. Hall and S. W. Silliman, pp. 190–208. Blackwell Publishing, Oxford, U.K.

Wurst, LouAnn, and Randall H. McGuire

1999 Immaculate Consumption: A Critique of the "Shop Till You Drop" School of Human Behavior. *International Journal of Historical Archaeology* 3(3):191–199.

Wylie, Alison

1991 Gender Theory and the Archaeological Record: Why Is There No Archaeology of Gender? In *Engendering Archaeology,* edited by J. Gero and M. Conkey, pp. 31–56. Blackwell Publishers, Oxford, U.K.

1994 Introduction. In *Equity Issues for Women in Archaeology,* edited by M. C. Nelson, S. M. Nelson, and A. Wylie, pp. 1–4. Archaeological Papers of the American Anthropological Association 5. American Anthropological Association, Washington D.C.

1999 Why Should Historical Archaeologists Study Capitalism? In *Historical Archaeologies of Capitalism,* edited by M. P. Leone and P. B. Potter Jr., 23–50. Plenum, New York.

2002 *Thinking from Things: Essays in the Philosophy of Archaeology.* University of California Press, Berkeley.

Yadin, Yigael

1966 *Masada: Herod's Fortress and the Zealots' Last Stand.* Random House, New York.

Yamin, Rebecca

1997 Museum in the Making: The Morven Project. In *Presenting Archaeology to the Public: Digging for Truths,* edited by J. Jameson, pp. 205–221. AltaMira Press, Walnut Creek, Calif.

Yarwood, John

1999 *Rebuilding Mostar: Reconstruction in a War Zone.* Liverpool University Press, Liverpool.

Yates, Michael

2000 Us versus Them: Laboring in the Academic Factory. *Monthly Review* 51(8):40–49.

Yorke, Rowan, and Uzi Baram (editors)

2004 *Marketing Heritage: Archaeology and the Consumption of the Past.* AltaMira Press, Walnut Creek, Calif.

Zavarzadeh, Donald

1995 Post-ality: The (Dis)Simulations of Cybercapitalism. In *Post-ality: Marxism and Postmodernism,* edited by M. U. Zavarzadeh, T. L. Ebert, and D. Morton, pp. 1–75. Transformations, Vol. 1. Maisonneuve Press, Washington, D.C.

Zeder, Melinda A.

1997 *The American Archaeologist.* AltaMira Press, Walnut Creek, Calif.

Zimmerman, Larry J.

1989 Made Radical by My Own: An Archaeologist Learns to Accept Reburial. In *Conflicts in the Archaeology of Living Traditions,* edited by R. Layton, pp. 60–67. Routledge, London.

1992 Archaeology, Reburial, and the Tactics of a Discipline's Self-Delusion. *American Indian Culture and Research Journal* 16(2):37–56.

2005 First, Be Humble: Working with Indigenous Peoples and Other Descendent Communities. In *Indigenous Archaeologies: Decolonizing Theory and Practice,* edited by C. Smith and H. M. Wobst, pp. 301–314. Routledge, London.

Žižek, Slavoj

1994 The Spectre of Ideology. In *Mapping Ideology,* edited by S. Žižek, pp. 1–33. Verso, London.

Index

9/11, 121–22
2000 U.S. presidential election, 186n7

Aboriginal Australians, 78–79, 80
academy, the, 9, 48; apprenticeship in,
116, 119–22, 126, 133, 134, 135;
archaeology in, 99–100, 101, 109–11,
115, 120, 121, 122, 126, 137; bill of
rights, 135–36; and bourgeois class,
105, 116; community colleges, 118;
and cultural resource management,
115–16, 122–23, 124–25, 126, 127,
137; deskilling, 135; fast capitalism's
impacts on, 9, 99–100, 111, 112, 115–
22, 135, 136, 225; hierarchy of, 118,
122; Indian people and, 79, 116; Latin
American autonomous universities, 66;
and middle class, 101, 103, 104; Spanish, 66, 67; star system in, 114, 118,
122; and women, 76, 77, 121
Active Museum of Fascism and
Resistance, 34
adjunct faculty. See workers, adjunct
faculty
AFL-CIO, 99, 100, 115, 129, 133, 188,
192, 220n1, 234; Union Summer
Program, 218
Africa, 17, 29, 77
African Americans, 24, 72, 73, 111, 114,
116, 146, 194, 196, 198
Africans, 66, 152, 186n3
age, 47, 75, 87
age grades, 8
agency, 2–4, 38–39, 43, 44, 62, 63, 84,

202; to change fast capitalism, 134,
138, 224; collective, 39, 42–46, 62, 87,
90, 138, 192, 193–94, 203–4, 212,
223, 228–29, 235
Agger, Ben, 21, 28, 84–85, 134
Ajo (Arizona), 165
Ajodhya, India, 26, 144, 222, 232
Ak Chin Indian Community, 181, 183
Akimel O'odham. See Tohono O'odham
(Papago): Akimel O'odham (Pima)
alienation, 4–5, 14, 22, 32, 54, 73, 87–
88, 92–93, 128, 203, 210, 216, 232;
and archaeology, 6, 7, 42, 109, 224.
See also emancipation, human
Allende, Salvadore, 172
Allen Mine, 214
Altar (Sonora), 170. See also Río Altar
alternative archaeologies, 3, 6, 52; praxis
in, 63–64
Althusser, Louis, 71, 72
Alverez, Ana María, 172, 173
amateur archaeologists, 100, 108
American Anthropological Association, 76
American Association of University Pro-
fessors, 136
American Bar Association, 138
American Cultural Resource Association
(ACRA), 100, 126, 127, 129–31
American Egg Board, 130
American Federation of Teachers, 220n1
American Indian Movement, 78, 154–55
American Medical Association, 138
American Museum of Natural History
(New York), 154

CALIFORNIA SERIES IN PUBLIC ANTHROPOLOGY

The California Series in Public Anthropology emphasizes the anthropologist's role as an engaged intellectual. It continues anthropology's commitment to being an ethnographic witness, to describing, in human terms, how life is lived beyond the borders of many readers' experiences. But it also adds a commitment, through ethnography, to reframing the terms of public debate—transforming received, accepted understandings of social issues with new insights, new framings.

Series Editor: Robert Borofsky (Hawaii Pacific University)

Contributing Editors: Philippe Bourgois (University of Pennsylvania), Paul Farmer (Partners in Health), Alex Hinton (Rutgers University), Carolyn Nordstrom (University of Notre Dame), and Nancy Scheper-Hughes (UC Berkeley)

University of California Press Editor: Naomi Schneider

1. *Twice Dead: Organ Transplants and the Reinvention of Death,* by Margaret Lock

2. *Birthing the Nation: Strategies of Palestinian Women in Israel,* by Rhoda Ann Kanaaneh (with a foreword by Hanan Ashrawi)

3. *Annihilating Difference: The Anthropology of Genocide,* edited by Alexander Laban Hinton (with a foreword by Kenneth Roth)

4. *Pathologies of Power: Health, Human Rights, and the New War on the Poor,* by Paul Farmer (with a foreword by Amartya Sen)

5. *Buddha Is Hiding: Refugees, Citizenship, the New America,* by Aihwa Ong

6. *Chechnya: Life in a War-Torn Society,* by Valery Tishkov (with a foreword by Mikhail S. Gorbachev)

7. *Total Confinement: Madness and Reason in the Maximum Security Prison,* by Lorna A. Rhodes

8. *Paradise in Ashes: A Guatemalan Journey of Courage, Terror, and Hope,* by Beatriz Manz (with a foreword by Aryeh Neier)

9. *Laughter Out of Place: Race, Class, Violence, and Sexuality in a Rio Shantytown,* by Donna M. Goldstein

10. *Shadows of War: Violence, Power, and International Profiteering in the Twenty-First Century,* by Carolyn Nordstrom

11. *Why Did They Kill? Cambodia in the Shadow of Genocide,* by Alexander Laban Hinton (with a foreword by Robert Jay Lifton)

12. *Yanomami: The Fierce Controversy and What We Can Learn from It,* by Robert Borofsky

13. *Why America's Top Pundits Are Wrong: Anthropologists Talk Back,* edited by Catherine Besteman and Hugh Gusterson

14. *Prisoners of Freedom: Human Rights and the African Poor,* by Harri Englund

15. *When Bodies Remember: Experiences and Politics of AIDS in South Africa,* by Didier Fassin

Text: 10/13 Sabon
Display: Sabon
Compositor: BookMatters, Berkeley
Printer and binder: Maple-Vail Book Manufacturing Group

Lightning Source UK Ltd.
Milton Keynes UK
UKHW012016220819
348429UK00002B/217/P